THE CAMBRIDGE COMPANION TO
TWENTIETH-CENTURY ENGLISH POETRY

The last century was characterised by an extraordinary flowering of the art of poetry in Britain. These specially commissioned essays by some of the most highly regarded poetry critics offer an up-to-date, stimulating and reliable overview of English poetry of the twentieth century. The opening section on contexts will both orientate readers relatively new to the field and provide provocative syntheses for those already familiar with it. Following the terms introduced by this section, individual chapters cover many ways of looking at the 'modern', the 'modernist' and the 'postmodern'. The core of the volume is made up of extensive discussions of individual poets, from W. B. Yeats and W. H. Auden to contemporary poets such as Simon Armitage and Carol Ann Duffy. In its coverage of the development, themes and contexts of modern poetry, this Companion is the most useful guide available for students, lecturers and readers.

NEIL CORCORAN is King Alfred Professor of English Literature at the University of Liverpool.

THE CAMBRIDGE
COMPANION TO

TWENTIETH-CENTURY ENGLISH POETRY

THE CAMBRIDGE
COMPANION TO
TWENTIETH-CENTURY ENGLISH POETRY

EDITED BY
NEIL CORCORAN

CAMBRIDGE
UNIVERSITY PRESS

CAMBRIDGE UNIVERSITY PRESS
Cambridge, New York, Melbourne, Madrid, Cape Town, Singapore, São Paulo

Cambridge University Press
The Edinburgh Building, Cambridge CB2 8RU, UK

Published in the United States of America by Cambridge University Press, New York

www.cambridge.org
Information on this title: www.cambridge.org/9780521691321

© Cambridge University Press 2007

First published 2007

Printed in the United Kingdom at the University Press, Cambridge

A catalogue record for this publication is available from the British Library

ISBN 978-0-521-87081-8 hardback
ISBN 978-0-521-69132-1 paperback

CONTENTS

CONTENTS

CONTRIBUTORS

DANIEL ALBRIGHT, Harvard University

LINDA ANDERSON, Newcastle University

NEIL CORCORAN, University of Liverpool

SANDRA M. GILBERT, University of California at Davis

KEVIN HART, University of Notre Dame

PETER HOWARTH, Queen Mary, University of London

EDWARD LARRISSY, Queen's University of Belfast

MICHAEL O'NEILL, University of Durham

REDELL OLSEN, Royal Holloway College, University of London

ADAM PIETTE, Sheffield University

JAHAN RAMAZANI, University of Virginia

JOHN REDMOND, University of Liverpool

STEPHEN REGAN, University of Durham

NEIL ROBERTS, Sheffield University

FIONA STAFFORD, Oxford University

M. WYNN THOMAS, Swansea University

TIMOTHY WEBB, University of Bristol

CHRONOLOGY

1901   Death of Victoria

1902   Coronation of Edward VII

1903   Emmeline Pankhurst founds the Women's Social and Political Union

1907   W. H. Auden born

1908   Ford Madox Ford founds the *English Review*

1909   Ezra Pound, *Personae*

1910   W. B. Yeats, *The Green Helmet, and Other Poems*
        Death of Edward VII, accession of George V

1912   The first *Georgian Poetry* anthology includes work by Rupert Brooke,
        D. H. Lawrence, Walter de la Mare and John Masefield

1913   Marcel Proust, *Du côté de chez Swann*

1914   W. B. Yeats, *Responsibilities*
        Outbreak of First World War

1915   Rupert Brooke dies on his way to the battle at Gallipoli

1916   Charlotte Mew, *The Farmer's Bride*

1917   T. S. Eliot, *Prufrock and Other Observations*
        Ivor Gurney, *Severn and Somme*
        Edward Thomas killed in action at Arras
        The Balfour Declaration lends British support for the creation of a
        Jewish national home in Palestine
        Revolutions in Russia

1918   *Poems of Gerard Manley Hopkins*
        Siegfried Sassoon, *Counter-Attack, and Other Poems*

Edward Thomas, *Last Poems*
Wilfred Owen killed during the crossing of the Sombre-Oise Canal
Isaac Rosenberg killed on the Somme
End of First World War
Representation of the People Act gives the vote to women (over thirty)
for the first time

1919   Treaty of Versailles

1920   T. S. Eliot, *The Sacred Wood: Essays on Poetry and Criticism*
Wilfred Owen, *Poems*
Ezra Pound, *Hugh Selwyn Mauberley*
Government of Ireland Act and the creation of Northern Ireland

1921   Ludwig Wittgenstein, *Logisch-Philosophische Abhandlung*

1922   T. S. Eliot's *The Waste Land* published in *The Criterion*
Thomas Hardy, *Late Lyrics and Earlier: with Many Other Verses*
A. E. Housman, *Last Poems*
James Joyce, *Ulysses*
W. B. Yeats, *Later Poems*
Ivor Gurney's family have him declared insane
Founding of the BBC

1923   D. H. Lawrence, *Birds, Beasts and Flowers*

1924   André Breton, *Manifeste du surréalisme*
Ramsay MacDonald becomes the first Labour Prime Minister

1926   Hugh MacDiarmid, *A Drunk Man Looks at the Thistle*
The General Strike is unsuccessful in forcing the government to act to
prevent wage reduction and worsening conditions for coalminers

1927   Martin Heidegger, *Sein und Zeit*
Marcel Proust, *Le Temps retrouvé*

1928   W. B. Yeats, *The Tower*
Thomas Hardy dies
Charlotte Mew commits suicide

1929   Collapse of the New York stock market

1930   W. H. Auden, *Poems*
T. S. Eliot, *Ash-Wednesday*
William Empson, *Seven Types of Ambiguity*
John Masefield appointed Poet Laureate
The Great Depression hits Great Britain

1932   F. R. Leavis, *New Bearings in English Poetry*

1933   W. B. Yeats, *The Winding Stair, and Other Poems*

1936   London International Surrealist Exhibition
Death of George V. Following the abdication of his successor Edward VIII, George VI ascends to the throne
Start of Spanish Civil War

1937   David Jones, *In Parenthesis*
Stevie Smith, *A Good Time Was Had By All*

1939   W. B. Yeats dies
Beginning of Second World War

1940   Dunkirk evacuation
The London Blitz

1941   James Joyce dies
America enters the war after the Japanese bombing of Pearl Harbour

1943   Jean-Paul Sartre, *L'Être et le Néant*

1944   T. S. Eliot, *Four Quartets*
D-Day landings in Normandy
Keith Douglas killed in the days after the D-Day invasion

1945   German unconditional surrender
Surrender of Japan after atomic bombs dropped on Hiroshima and Nagasaki
Labour win a landslide election victory

1946   Dylan Thomas, *Deaths and Entrances*
R. S. Thomas, *The Stones of the Fields*
Ezra Pound is found insane and committed to St Elizabeth's Hospital, Washington, DC

1947   Edith Sitwell, *The Shadow of Cain*
India gains independence from British rule, initiating the post-war break-up of the British Empire
The Partition of Palestine

1948   Robert Graves, *The White Goddess: A historical grammar of poetic myth*
Ezra Pound, *The Pisan Cantos*
Founding of the NHS
The *Empire Windrush* lands 492 Jamaicans at Tilbury, carrying the first large group of West Indian immigrants to the UK. The 'open door'

policy continues during the 1950s to address the post-war shortage of labour

1949   W. S. Graham, *The White Threshold*

1952   David Jones, *The Anathemata*
Lynette Roberts, *Gods with Stainless Ears*
George VI dies, accession of Elizabeth II

1953   Dylan Thomas dies

1954   Dylan Thomas, *Under Milk Wood*

1955   W. H. Auden, *The Shield of Achilles*
Philip Larkin, *The Less Deceived*

1956   British invasion of, and withdrawal from, Suez
Hungarian revolt suppressed by the Soviets

1957   Thom Gunn, *The Sense of Movement*
Ted Hughes, *The Hawk in the Rain*

1958   Beginning of the Campaign for Nuclear Disarmament

1959   Geoffrey Hill, *For the Unfallen*

1960   Penguin Books acquitted of obscenity for publishing *Lady Chatterley's Lover*, resulting in far greater freedom to circulate explicit material

1961   Major expansion of British universities

1962   Benjamin Britten, *War Requiem* (which includes settings of poems by Wilfred Owen)
The Cymdeithas yr Iaith Gymraeg (the Welsh Language Society) is founded to campaign for the future of the Welsh language: in 1967 the First Welsh Language Act is passed
Second Vatican Council

1963   Sylvia Plath commits suicide
The Beatles release their first LP, *Please Please Me*

1964   Philip Larkin, *The Whitsun Weddings*
House of Commons vote to end the death penalty

1965   T. S. Eliot dies
Sylvia Plath, *Ariel*
First big Arts Council *Poetry International* festival in London; Ted Hughes one of the organisers

Students in Czechoslovakia elect Allen Ginsberg King of the May
First US combat troops arrive in Vietnam; the last leave in 1973

1966   Basil Bunting, *Briggflatts*
Seamus Heaney, *Death of a Naturalist*
'Swinging London' is hailed in *Time* magazine
Bob Dylan tours the UK with an electric backing band

1967   Abortion legalised
Homosexual acts between consenting adults legalised

1968   J. H. Prynne, *Kitchen Poems*
Enoch Powell makes a controversial speech attacking immigration policies
The Prague Spring

1970   Ted Hughes, *Crow*

1971   Geoffrey Hill, *Mercian Hymns*

1972   R. S. Thomas, *H'm*
John Betjeman appointed Poet Laureate

1973   Paul Muldoon, *New Weather*
W. H. Auden dies
The United Kingdom joins the European Economic Community

1974   Philip Larkin, *High Windows*
David Jones dies

1975   Seamus Heaney, *North*
Linton Kwesi-Johnson, *Dread, Beat an' Blood*
Ezra Pound dies

1977   Rise of punk rock

1978   Geoffrey Hill, *Tenebrae*
Hugh MacDiarmid dies

1979   Ted Hughes, *Moortown*
Craig Raine, *A Martian Sends a Postcard Home*
Christopher Reid, *Arcadia*
Margaret Thatcher begins a premiership (lasting until 1990) that will be characterised by support for freedom of economic competition and privatization, and opposition to the trade unions

1981   Creation of the Social Democratic Party

1982   James Fenton, *The Memory of War: Poems 1968–1982*

1983   James Fenton, *The Memory of War and Children in Exile: Poems 1968–1983*
Paul Muldoon, *Quoof*

1984   John Betjeman dies
Philip Larkin declines the post of Poet Laureate; Ted Hughes is appointed instead

1985   Tony Harrison, *V*
Benjamin Zephaniah, *The Dread Affair*
Philip Larkin dies
Coalminers' strike; violence on Yorkshire coalfields

1989   Simon Armitage, *Zoom!*
Fall of the Berlin Wall

1990   Derek Walcott, *Omeros*

1991   Collapse of the USSR
The Gulf War

1993   The second Welsh Language Act places Welsh on an equal footing with English in Wales

1994   End of apartheid in South Africa

1995   Seamus Heaney awarded the Nobel Prize for Literature

1997   Don Paterson, *God's Gift to Women*
Tony Blair's New Labour government is elected.

1998   Ted Hughes dies. Publication of *Birthday Letters*
Re-establishment of the Scottish Parliament and creation of the National Assembly for Wales

1999   Edwin Morgan appointed as Glasgow's first poet laureate
Launch of the European single currency: Britain declines membership

Introduction

Now that the succeeding century is well advanced into its first decade, it seems a good time to take a purchase and a perspective on the poetry of the twentieth century. This Companion offers an availably intelligible and stimulating account of the current state of its critical reception, of the issues and challenges to which it gives rise in our own cultural and social climate, and of the various engagements between poetic form and history which it offers as both problems and examples to succeeding poets and readers.

The poetry treated here is 'English' in the sense that it's written in the English language, or versions of it, by poets who are, or were, of English, Scottish or Welsh origin, or have an origin or family attachment overseas but have been resident in Britain or taken British nationality. The place of nation in the construction of personal and poetic identity is itself an issue in some of this work; and the fact that the latter part of the century witnessed a form of the devolution of political power to Scotland and Wales has found effects and emphases in some of the poetry discussed here, and not only poetry from Scotland and Wales.

The Irish story, which of course intersects with these stories at numerous points, is not told here, mainly on the practical grounds that, a separate story too, it is already the subject of Cambridge Companions: one on W. B. Yeats edited by Marjorie Howes, and one entitled *Contemporary Irish Poetry* edited by Matthew Campbell. Even so, Yeats, although he has no essay to himself in this book, is a towering presence within it. Discussions of his place include the elaborately artful self-revisions of his lengthy career, notably those encouraged by Ezra Pound (whose more general place in this story is outlined in several essays in this volume too); his formidable technical expertise and refusal of modernist experimentation; his establishing of the poetic sequence as a highly influential modern form; and the enduring challenge of W. H. Auden's response to him, particularly in his elegy 'In Memory of W. B. Yeats', published in 1939, which is cited and discussed several times. The impact of the poetry of Northern Ireland since the mid-1960s, and particularly of the work of Seamus Heaney and Paul Muldoon, with its transformations of lyric possibility, is made clear in several essays too, as is the significance of the work of Patrick Kavanagh and Austin Clarke as an enabling resource in the evolution of the poetic of the Welsh poet R. S. Thomas. If the Irish story is not told here, then, the ways in which the story that is being told crosses with it are frequently to the fore.

Although T. S. Eliot does not figure individually in this Companion, his varieties of Modernism are, as much as Yeats's influence, crucial to an understanding of the poetry of this period, and the impact of his poetry, his criticism and, indeed, of his person (in his role as an influential publisher of poetry, for instance) are extensively treated in what follows. Aspects of this include his paradoxical similarity to Yeats in his views of poetic tradition and traditional form; his modulation of personae in *Four Quartets* as one of the crucial contributions made by Modernism to the art of poetry; his ambivalent attitude to D. H. Lawrence, which is rich with implication for the entire history of the poetry of the period; and the desire he shares with Lawrence for a newly naked or bare-boned poetry, however differently they actually expressed this desire and wrote out of it. One essayist in this book suggests that English poetry in this period has never 'got over' Auden, and this may well be so. But the evidence punctiliously adduced and construed here suggests, perhaps surprisingly, that it is Eliot who casts the larger shadow across the poetic century.

But Auden's impact is also wide-ranging, sometimes in contradistinction to Eliot's: from his commandeering position in relation to other writing of the 1930s and 1940s, including William Empson's, and his early turning of a newly Modernist poetic towards sociopolitical concerns, through his overwhelming effect on the young Philip Larkin, to his absorption by James Fenton and others in poetry from the 1980s on. It will come as no news, of course, that Yeats, Eliot and Auden have such standing in this story; but it is still compelling to see this manifested in the various ways that it is in these essays.

A Companion such as this, which offers a view of an extensive chronological period and a great variety of published work, must of necessity be selective. But individual essays do consistently pick up and re-examine the terms offered as 'contexts' in the opening section. The volume makes a persistent inquiry – on what is sometimes still virtually a field of battle – into the applicability of the terms 'modern', 'Modernist', and 'postmodern' as ways of understanding the poetry of the twentieth century and its implicit or explicit politics; and also into the comparative merits and value of the work being so defined.

This inquiry has some salient features to which I think it is worth alerting the prospective reader at the outset. One is the characteristic refusal of contemporary critics to take the Victorians at the modernists' estimate of them, and the consequences of this for more recent writing. To read Victorian poetry as formally innovative and radical is to look more sceptically at the self-justificatory and self-advertising claims of experimental Modernism, and to become more alert to the oedipality of its struggles, while still crediting the remarkable experiments and effects actually demonstrable in Modernist work. In the narrative of inheritance, with its strategies of evasion as well as gratitude, the poetic achievement of the Victorian Gerard Manley Hopkins, and his posthumous publication, reputation and absorption by others, is an especially complicating factor that undermines some clichés of formal radicalism and technical experimentation. Other such factors include the often occluded persistence of influences from both Algernon Charles Swinburne and Walt Whitman.

A further feature of this inquiry is the examination of some ways in which form may be both traditional and radically modern in poets who reject – or just ignore – the radicalism of modernist forms. In some poets of the period – Yeats, for instance, Hardy, Edward Thomas and Charlotte Mew – traditional form may be so originally wrought as to become something quite different from itself and, thereby, a means for the articulation or realisation of things which Modernism itself could not articulate or realise. Proposals such as this – and several of the kind are made in this book – tend to collapse what are coming to seem increasingly jaded or wearyingly *parti pris* hostilities between critical camps of the 'modern' and the 'Modernist'; and that collapse is, invitingly, more of a breakthrough than a breakdown.

And the final feature of inquiry which I will mention here is the one undertaken into what may and may not be allowed to constitute the 'postmodern' in poetry. The essay on the term in the 'Contexts' section of this book holds it sceptically, or 'uneasily', between inverted commas, worries at its elasticity, and offers, as alternatives actually used by poets and critics, the terms 'neo-Modernist' and 'late modernist'. That essay also takes the Movement poets of the 1950s to task for their hostility to Modernism and suggests, rebukingly, that in them we have 'the "postmodernism" we deserve'. Yet the individual essay on Philip Larkin, who is sometimes read as the quintessential 'Movement' poet, on the contrary makes much of his early absorption of Eliot and other Modernists, and also of his assimilations of both Auden and Louis MacNeice. The essay proposes, as a consequence, that Larkin is a much more complex 'late modern' or even 'postmodern' figure, philosophically as well as aesthetically, than he has often appeared, even – perhaps especially – in his own prose statements. There are involving arguments about subjectivity, authenticity and the survival of the lyric 'voice' in all of this, as there are elsewhere in this book too; and such contradictory readings have, I think, a stimulatingly provocative relationship with one another. They contribute to a sense of the permanently uncompleted business that literary criticism – indeed, that reading itself – is, at its best.

Some concluding thoughts. It is notable how frequently in these essays the word 'contradiction' occurs. It is accompanied by many cognates or near-synonyms: 'division', 'fission', 'dissonance', 'ambiguity', 'conceit', 'self-questioning', 'multi-perspectivism', 'difference', 'discrepancy', 'destabilisation', 'hybridity', 'translocation'. And these are joined by a related set of apparently opposed or mutually undermining binaries: 'constraint' and 'liberation'; 'dualism' and 'dialogism'; 'oral' and 'literary'; 'identification' and 'distance'; 'critique' and 'longing'; 'the real self' and 'acting out'. Individual essays also describe articulate anxieties about 'belatedness', 'community' and 'audience', and some define the various kinds of mobility which poets make available to themselves by engaging in translation, version and pastiche – the self-disguise or self-modification of ventriloquism, for instance, and the opportunity for extensions of, or challenges to, cultural or national consciousness. (Christopher Reid's *Katerina Brac*, published in 1985, which is discussed in the essay on 'lyric adaptations', is, among other things, an exquisite set of variations on these themes.)

Literary critics like contradiction, of course, since it feeds the opportunity for exposition and argument on which critical essays tend to depend: criticism needs crisis. Yet I think that the critics gathered here do offer ample evidence that poems of modernity, whether they fall, or may be allowed to fall, under the rubrics of 'modern', 'Modernist' or 'postmodern', characteristically appear to speak against themselves, to engage in sometimes fraught dialogues of the self with the self, or of the poem with its own origins, traditions and generic characteristics. Poems become the scenes of anxieties, tensions, distresses, uncertainties, contentions and mobilities, in relation to what may loosely be labelled as both the private and the public life or sphere. Or, rather, the poem is that place where, in language and form, the private and the public converge or coinhere, where matters of the deepest moment – of sexual, class, national and racial identity, in particular, and occasionally, still, of religious or quasi-religious identity and belief, or of scepticism about or antagonism to it – are approached, acknowledged and articulated at their most subtle and most complicated levels. The poem is not necessarily the place where such contradictions will be resolved or analysed into harmony: indeed, 'resolution' is a word which virtually never figures in these essays, and being painfully on both sides or having it anxiously both ways is something the modern poem also characteristically does. The twentieth-century English poem is the place where urgencies of desire, and responsibilities of acknowledgement, indebtedness, moral choice and witness are brought into focus or relief, brought into play, and brought to book.

And in many modern poems this happens self-consciously: a further continuous thread of critical narrative in what follows has to do with what the poetry, metacritically, has to say about itself, about its own modes and procedures, and about its potential consequences and effects. Eliot in the *Quartets* is there at the Modernist origin of this impulse when, in 'East Coker', he modulates persona as he moves away from traditional form at a point of self-critique: 'That was a way of putting it – not very satisfactory / A periphrastic study in a worn-out poetical fashion.' Auden is crucially there in the Yeats elegy, with its hauntingly ambivalent assertion – if it is an assertion, exactly – that 'poetry makes nothing happen', which has proved a magnet – as a puzzle, a support or a scandal – for subsequent poets and critics. And we find it too, variously, in such places as W. S. Graham's late meditations on the role of language in consciousness; in Philip Larkin's sceptical view of the gap between word and world; in R. S. Thomas's late linguistic self-reflexivity, with its sense of the provisionality of a poetry attempting to chart ultimately elusive realities; in Geoffrey Hill's sceptical placing of the allure of poetry in relation to the allure of theology and religious belief; and in Tony Harrison's insider–outsider status as the combative occupier of canonically exclusionary iambics. Modern poetry, it seems, is nowhere more characteristic of itself than when anxiously but scrupulously doubting itself.

PART ONE

Contexts

I

TIMOTHY WEBB

Victorian to modern

I

In 1886 William Butler Yeats was introduced to Gerard Manley Hopkins in Dublin. Both were to play a significant part in the history of English verse, yet they constitute an ill-matched pair. Hopkins was a Jesuit priest but also an English patriot who felt painfully out of place in Catholic Ireland, whereas the young Yeats was far from orthodox in his religious beliefs, although descended from a Church of Ireland clergyman. When confronted with Hopkins he seems to have experienced a reaction which was pre-dictably Irish and recognisably Protestant: his impression was the usual Irish one that Hopkins was 'a detested aesthete' and that he had brought a 'faint theatrical Catholicism to Ireland'; the Irish, Yeats told Humphry House, apropos of Hopkins, had 'no sympathy with English Aesthetic Catholicism'.[1] Many years later, Yeats wrote about Hopkins as someone 'whom I knew', vacillated about which poems should be included in *The Oxford Book of Modern Verse* and mis-remembered, or misrepresented, the occasion: 'a boy of seventeen, with Walt Whitman in his pocket, had little interest in a querulous, sensitive scholar.'[2]

Yeats may have had a copy of Whitman in his pocket, a detail intended to suggest a wide gulf of taste, but the example of the American poet seems to have left little trace on his own verse. On the other hand, Hopkins once said that, even if he had only read 'half a dozen pieces at most', 'I always knew in my heart Walt Whitman's mind to be more like my own than any other man's living.'[3] This suggests an undeclared and significant affinity with the poet recognised by D. H. Lawrence in *Studies in Classic American Literature* (1923) as 'greatest of the Americans'. Nor was Yeats only seventeen at the time, since he had been born in 1865; yet the instinct to exaggerate his own youthfulness is understandable because, for all his own apparent youth, Hopkins was twice the age of Yeats and destined to die only three years later, whereas Yeats survived till 1939. At the time of the meeting, Yeats had published 'The Two Titans' ('a strained and unworkable allegory', opined Hopkins, though not to Yeats's face) and the verse-play *Mosada*; Hopkins was known to be a sensitive figure with pronounced aesthetic predilections yet, at this point, he had published very little; his standing was largely based on his appointment as Professor of Classics at University College Dublin, and he was scarcely known as a poet.

Like so many encounters in literary history, this meeting seems anti-climactic. The case of Hopkins undermines the neat patterns to which literary history sometimes aspires: few of his poems reached print during his own lifetime, though several were included in anthologies, especially by Robert Bridges, who published sixteen of his poems between 1889 and the appearance of his own edition of the *Poems* in 1918 (a second, enlarged edition by Charles Williams appeared in 1930). Publication did not mean immediate acceptance: the first edition sold only 750 copies over the course of ten years.

For some time, Hopkins has been classified as a recognisable product of the Victorian age: in his hearty patriotism; in his aesthetics; in his scientific approach to the 'aspects of things' which, as Patricia Ball has shown,[4] links him both with his Romantic predecessor Coleridge and with his older contemporary Ruskin; in his highly developed interest in language and especially dialect; in his profound interest in religion; in his innocent but powerful sexuality; in his fondness for adjectival affirmation, which sometimes seems to counter the more startling verbal acrobatics of his poetry; in his strong though inquisitively directed preference for the natural world; and in his avoidance of urban realities, even though he lived in Glasgow, Liverpool and Dublin.

Such corrective insistence is justified and salutary; yet it is also worth remembering that, in its linguistic innovations, *Poems* has much in common with the experimental writing of the Modernists and especially with that of James Joyce. For example, Hopkins wrote: 'where, where was a, where was a place?' ('The Wreck of the Deutschland'), and 'his riding / Of the rolling level underneath him steady air' ('The Windhover'), and 'how the boys / With dare and with downdolfinry and bellbright bodies huddling out, / Are earthworld, airworld, waterworld thorough hurled' ('Epithalamion'). Since he died in 1889, and since these quotations date from the 1870s or the 1880s, Hopkins could not have qualified as a Modernist, but his verbal innovations indicate that, even within the confines of Victorian literature, some contributions were strikingly experimental. The case of Hopkins might even lead to a reconsideration of the attributes of what is properly 'Victorian' and of Yeats's famous claim in his introduction to *The Oxford Book of Modern Verse* that 'Victorianism had been defeated'.

Several influential modern writers acknowledged its significance. Even if Hopkins was largely dismissed by Ezra Pound (who, like Yeats, had embarrassingly featured in *The Oxford Book of Victorian Verse*) and, less predictably, T.S. Eliot, he was celebrated by I.A. Richards, William Empson, Robert Graves and W.H. Auden, most of whom were practising poets as well as critics. Auden, in particular, identified Hopkins as a strong but dangerous influence; he once claimed that 'Hopkins ought to be kept on a special shelf like a dirty book.'[5] Although Hopkins had usually worked within the compass of traditional verse form, he was widely associated with innovative poetry, particularly because of his linguistic courage. When F. R. Leavis produced *New Bearings in English Poetry* in 1932, Hopkins was the single focus of its final chapter, largely because of his capacity to admit and enact the realities of struggle. As late as 1936 when Michael Roberts compiled the influential *Faber Book of Modern Verse*, Hopkins was installed as founding father, represented by thirteen poems. (Yeats, who was placed directly after Hopkins, only got eight.)[6] So, through the vagaries of religious restriction and the curious patterns of publication and literary influence, Hopkins was, to some extent, lifted out of his period and connected, positively, with the 'new' and the 'modern'. The Victorian poet became an inspirational model, if not always a direct or immediate poetic influence, on English poetry after the First World War.

The gradual evolution of the poetic standing of Hopkins is an exceptionally good example of the delayed manner in which certain literary reputations are established, long after the death of the poet. The case of Hopkins demonstrates how our sense of a 'Victorian' writer has evolved and achieved greater complexity with the passage of time. With a poetic reputation beyond his own control, he had much in common with Wilfred Owen and Isaac Rosenberg, poets who had not survived the First World War, but who were accorded the stabilising notice of book publication in the early years of peacetime (Owen in 1920, and Rosenberg in 1922).

In contrast, the route followed by Yeats was strikingly different. Very much not dead, he played a significant part both in keeping his own work before a reading public and in transforming his poetic self over a number of years. Since Yeats has now been dead for more than sixty years, it is easy to fail to notice the significance of this process of change and the centrality of Yeats himself to this extraordinary choreography. Yet the patterns were sometimes surprising and apparently controlled, or at least permitted, by Yeats himself. Take, for instance, these facts assembled by George Bornstein:

> The importance of *Poems* (1895) and its successors to Yeats's public image cannot be overstated. This was the volume by which Yeats was best known to readers for nearly four decades, until the publication of *Collected Poems* in

1933. Its first edition of 750 copies ... sold well, as did the American edition. Revised editions appeared in 1899, 1901, 1904, 1908, 1912, 1913 (with further slightly revised impressions in 1919, 1920, 1922 [twice], 1923, and 1924), 1927, and 1929.[7]

With whatever revisions, therefore, this relatively early volume continued to sell well even during the years of the First World War, the Troubles, the Irish Civil War and the first, difficult, years of the Irish Free State, while Yeats was giving expression to an exceptional poetic maturity with the publication of *Responsibilities* (1916), *The Wild Swans At Coole* (1919), *Michael Robartes and the Dancer* (1921) and *The Tower* (1928). Yeats was prepared to sanction publication, or re-publication, of poems such as 'Down by the Salley Gardens' (first published, 1889), 'The Lake Isle of Innisfree' (first published, 1890), 'The Sorrow of Love' (first published, 1892) and 'Who Goes with Fergus?' (first published, 1892), at the time when he was also writing and publishing such unsparingly modern texts as 'The Second Coming' (first published, 1920; in book form, 1921), 'Sailing to Byzantium' (first published, 1927; in book form, 1928), 'Meditations in Time of Civil War' (first published, 1923; in book form, 1924) and 'Leda and the Swan' (first published, 1924; in book form, 1924).

Such apparent clashes and contradictions suggest that Yeats possessed an unusually canny instinct for commercial possibilities though he also may have recognised not so much a blunt disconnection as a process of continuity. Privately, he admitted: 'This book [*Poems* (1895)] for about thirty years brought me ... twenty or thirty times as much as all my other books put together.'[8] He might have wished it otherwise; but there is no evidence that he curtailed or tried to prevent these revealing ambiguities of publication. The record clearly shows that we need to re-examine received notions of the poet putting the past behind him as he rejects the encumbering coat of old mythologies, appearing to move on without a backward glance from a discarded style to the new.

2

The evidence of the early volumes also shows that Yeats was much exercised by the opportunities of ordering the poems in his volumes. This directive input, often radical, revealed much about Yeats and usually carried enduring consequences. As George Bornstein puts it, in examining one notable instance: 'The arrangement of the early lyrics in *Poems* established a paradigm still present even in posthumous arrangements of Yeats's verse.'[9] Perhaps the most famous example of the construction of a volume is exemplified by the carefully planned volume *The Tower* (1928), which was assembled from a variety of sources, including poems published as early as 1919 and as recently as 1927. Such attentiveness may have reached a rich climax in *The Tower* but the revisionary procedure left its impress on much earlier stages of his work.

If Yeats was much concerned with such organisational matters, he also paid particular attention to style. This gradual process of rewriting and revision helped to transform his poetry from a state of expression which was passively beautiful, if often merely Victorian or late-Victorian, to a form which was more acutely responsive to the troubling and often ugly facts of a modern world. Unlike Hopkins, who partly rejected the restrictions and inadequacies of Victorian diction, and unlike Owen who responded to the pressures of trench warfare by moving from a language which was lushly adjectival and 'Keatsian' to a sparer articulation more suited to his shocking subject matter, Yeats followed a slower trajectory but also gradually replaced an inappropriate poetic diction with something more starkly functional.

A particularly rich example is provided by the history of what was first published in 1890 as 'The Old Pensioner', which later evolved into 'The Lamentation of the Old Pensioner'. Although the title was altered as early as *The Countess Kathleen* (1892), the text remained unchanged till the 1925 version of *Early Poems and Stories*. The original version, which was based on an anecdote told by George Russell, was in effect a transposition of that experience and ran to only two stanzas. A third stanza (the second in standard editions) was not introduced till 1925, at which point the whole poem changed its status, becoming less anecdotal and giving voice to a completely new ferocity both of vision and poetic diction. A diction largely sentimental and sometimes old-fashioned ('Ah, wherefore murmur ye') has been replaced by an utterance which is more simple ('I spit into the face of Time'), more fiercely direct and more brutally physical. In the revised version there is no effort to capture the voice or mode of speaking of the old pensioner; the outspokenness of the Yeatsian persona expresses the proud indignation of old age rather than the depression of any reduced individual and looks forward to the unrestrained utterances of Crazy Jane, which combine metaphysical insights with an understanding which is almost shockingly physical.[10]

The shocking detail of spitting, and the revised version of the text which includes it, did not appear till 1925, when Yeats was sixty; and, at that point, the rewritten text was published in a book called *Early Poems and Stories*, with the result that, whatever the author's intentions, the true path of Yeats's poetic progress was largely concealed or occluded. Ironically, he later attacked Hopkins in a passage which unfairly suggests that he had forgotten the long course of this progress and that the two poets were separated by a simple divergence of practice. Hopkins, claims Yeats, is 'typical of his generation where most opposed to mine'. His meaning is 'like some faint sound that strains the ear ... his manner a last development of poetical diction.' Whereas Yeats himself, he says, belongs to another set of writers which pursues very different objectives: 'My generation began that search for hard positive subject-matter, still a predominant purpose.'[11]

Quite apart from the fact that Yeats was not prepared to admit the linguistic courage and the experimental audacity of his predecessor, he has also significantly misrepresented the curve of his own development. One of the most interesting elements in Yeats's work is the slow way in which it retreats from a stylistic manner and a subject matter which are distinctively Victorian to versions which are more in accord with a modern world and with 'hard positive matter'; from tapestries, gold cloth, dreams and 'dim' landscapes to 'violence of horses', 'A sort of battered kettle at the heel' and 'the foul rag and bone shop of the heart'. This difficult and hard-earned transformation owes a great deal to the ways in which the decoratively adjectival has been changed to the brutally physical: from wishing for the cloths of heaven or remembering forgotten beauty to 'A shudder in the loins' or a 'rough beast' which 'Slouches towards Bethlehem to be born'.

3

With scarcely any exceptions, the Victorian poets operated within a conception of verse form which was essentially traditional. Hopkins may have been a great innovator but, with whatever difficulties and prevarications, he worked inside the boundaries of traditional verse form (perhaps this combination of obedience to a discipline with personal innovations and adventures paralleled his dilemma as a Jesuit and sharpened the edge of his creativity). Many of his most daring poems are cast in the form of a sonnet, a form which in his original versions runs from just over ten lines (in 'Pied Beauty'), to twenty-four (in 'That Nature is a Heraclitean Fire'). Tennyson's *Maud* is a long dramatic monologue centred on a consciousness which at best is seriously destabilised, and at worst is mad; but although its verse form is varied and fluctuating, the poem never expresses extreme states of mind through extreme and uncharted poetic forms. Likewise, *In Memoriam* may be divided into one hundred and thirty-three sections, but it is held together both by its troubled and ruminative central consciousness and the repeated formality of its quatrains; while, in spite of its apparently intrusive patterns of colloquial speech, Clough's *Amours de Voyage* is a sustained attempt to import the classical hexameter creatively into the received modes of English verse.

This devotion to form continued to leave its impress on poetic composition, even though subject matter necessarily changed, and even though this period includes the decadent experiments of the *fin de siècle*; the Boer War; the exciting though troubled years leading up to the First World War; the unimaginable and protracted experience of the war itself; the Easter Rising in Dublin and the Bolshevik Rising in Moscow; the strengthening claims of feminism; post-war elation, turmoil and redefinition; the Irish Troubles followed by the creation of the Irish Free State and the Irish Civil War.

Though T. S. Eliot (an American living in London) had allowed himself the challenges of free verse in 'Portrait of a Lady' (whose title celebrated another Harvard graduate living in England) and 'The Love Song of J. Alfred Prufrock', he could not entirely abandon the urbanity and apparent security of rhymed verse (as in 'The Hippopotamus', 'Whispers of Immortality' and 'Mr Eliot's Sunday Morning Service'): seven out of the eight English-language poems in his *Poems* (1920) were written in quatrains, though usually with only one pair of rhymes to each four-line unit. Ezra Pound (another American living in London, before he moved to Paris), the energetic author of *The Cantos* (which had begun to appear as early as 1917) and the controversial 'translator' of Propertius, was also responsible for 'Hugh Selwyn Mauberley' (1920), which balances its passages of free verse with sections both in rhyme and in tightly controlled metre which, like the quatrains of Eliot, owe a direct debt to French examples.

While even Eliot and Pound showed themselves susceptible to the attractions of traditional verse form, the aesthetic securities were even more alluring to poets who were unquestionably English. The poets of the Nineties (many of whom Yeats knew personally and memorialised in *The Tragic Generation*) were usually conventional in verse form and poetic diction, even if they were occasionally shocking in their choice of subject matter and outrageous in their private lives. Even Arthur Symons (who shared a flat in London with Yeats) wrote a timid, rhyming verse, an odd form of expression for the friend of Rimbaud and Verlaine and the importer of French Symbolism. The poets collected in the five volumes of *Georgian Poetry* between 1913 and 1922 (including the pioneering but ill-fated Rupert Brooke) were apparently content to speak for values which were representatively English in a verse strangely separated, in content, language and form, from the pressures of a changing world. Its verse forms were stanzaic and strongly traditional: only two of the poems it published were in free verse (one of these was D. H. Lawrence's 'Snake').

There is much evidence that this concentration on pastoral virtues and traditional verse forms was a patriotic act of defiance aimed at those disturbing changes which might be identified as continental or even 'German'.[12] There were also the notable cases of Rudyard Kipling (1865–1936) and Thomas Hardy (1840–1928), who pursued a long poetic career which extended from the 1860s till his death and who concentrated on writing poetry during the last thirty years of his life. In the first part of the twentieth century Hardy was extremely active poetically. He produced several volumes which showed a keen poetic ear and an attentiveness to the metrical lessons of folk-song and hymn but he confined its strong experimental tendency to executing variations on traditional verse form rather than attempting something entirely original. Free verse he regarded as 'a jumble of notes' and, in his view, Whitman 'wrote as he did, formlessly, because he could do no better'.[13] Dennis Taylor, the expert on Hardy's sophisticated versification, has described his last works as 'most unusual metrical experiments, poems written in unique, complex stanzas' and introduced comparisons with William Carlos Williams as well as Herbert; yet, just as Hardy planned, the strength of these poems derives from the fact that they operate, with whatever audacity, inside a recognised tradition.[14]

The polarities were forcefully articulated by Yeats in a late essay called 'A General Introduction for My Work' intended for a complete edition of his writing which, in the event, did not appear in his lifetime. Yeats makes it clear that he is seriously at odds with many of the poets who would claim to be 'modern'. According to his philosophy, a successful poet must tune in not only to the voices of the present but the powerful, or even ghostly, voices of the poetic past. He admits that he had discovered 'some twenty years ago that I must seek, not as Wordsworth thought, words in common use, but a powerful and passionate syntax, and a complete coincidence between period and stanza'. The direct consequence was a return to poetic traditions: 'Because I need a passionate syntax for passionate subject-matter I compel myself to accept those traditional metres that have developed with the language.' Or again, he asserts: 'I must choose a traditional stanza, even what I alter must seem traditional.' In a characteristically Yeatsian passage, he develops this point in a flurry of images and an unambiguous declaration: 'Talk to me of originality and I will turn on you with rage. I am a crowd, I am a lonely man, I am nothing. Ancient salt is best packing.' A little later, he describes his troubled excitement on reciting the opening line of Milton's *Paradise Lost*, where he can detect that 'the folk song is still there, but a ghostly voice, an unvariable possibility, an unconscious norm.

What moves me and my hearer is a vivid speech that has no laws except that it must not exorcise the ghostly voice.'[15]

By a strange chance (or perhaps it is no coincidence), Yeats's declaration bears a curious resemblance to Eliot's defence of *vers libre* which had been published in 1917. There, Eliot had claimed (no doubt, in defence of his own practice): 'the ghost of some simple metre should lurk behind the arras in even the "freest" verse; to advance menacingly as we doze, and withdraw as we rouse. Or, freedom is only truly freedom when it appears against the background of an artificial limitation.'[16] There is more in common between Yeats and Eliot than one might imagine from their practice; and their respective invocations of 'the ghostly voice' and 'the ghost ... behind the arras' suggest that, with whatever difference, both were sensitively attuned to the relations between the forms of traditional verse and those modes of fashionable expression which might seem to have succeeded and superseded them.

The complexity of the case is well illustrated by Yeats's 'The Second Coming', first published in November 1920. For many years this visionary poem has been acknowledged as an iconic intimation of the collapse of civilisation, and formulations such as 'Things fall apart; the centre cannot hold' are still widely quoted. The poem has much in common with the later poems 'Nineteen Hundred and Nineteen' and 'Meditations in Time of Civil War', which hold within patterns of harmonious versification, and the stabilising and protective presence of rhyme, the harsh evidence of a country which acknowledges no such restraints. But 'The Second Coming' expresses its terrifying vision of collapse not as a counterpoint to such intricate patterns but through the medium of verse which is apparently blank.

As a glance through any volume of Yeats will quickly show, this verse form was used elsewhere, but it does not seem to have been one of his regular poetic choices. In 'A General Introduction' he celebrates its force but seems to suggest some difficulty in combining past and present: 'When I speak blank verse and analyse my feelings, I stand at a moment of history when instinct, its traditional songs and dances, its general agreement, is of the past. I have been cast up out of the whale's belly though ... I smell of the fish of the sea.'[17] In its turn, 'The Second Coming' makes conscious use of the possibilities of blank verse but, although it never entirely forgets its powerfully primitive origins, it enriches our reading experience by reminding us of other forms which are never far away. In this case, at least one of those ghostly voices is the tradition of verse in Irish which Yeats cannot have known intimately but which provides a strongly directive presence for a poem which seems to dispense with the traditional formalities of rhyme. Ancient salt proves to be an inestimable resource.

Yeats begins by drawing our attention to the possibilities of end-rhyme, which the poem is soon to abandon:

> Turning and turning in the widening gyre
> The falcon cannot hear the falconer;
> Things fall apart; the centre cannot hold;
> Mere anarchy is loosed upon the world.

The falconer might seem to be linked to the gyre in the sort of half-rhyme or pararhyme which Wilfred Owen had evolved out of the intense but unharmonious experiences of war, or which Yeats himself increasingly employed to blunt any simplistic response (for example, 'faces' and 'houses', 'gibe' and 'club', 'comedy' and 'utterly', 'verse' and 'Pearse', in 'Easter 1916'). Even the move from 'hold' to 'world' might hint at a rhyming connection while miming that breakdown of order and relation which it so resonantly articulates. In this poem, though, the possibilities of traditional end-rhyme are soon withdrawn, emphatically denied by the marked repetition of 'is loosed' in lines 4–5. This strangely different kind of discourse reaches climax in the stunned progression of lines 9–11: 'Surely some revelation is at hand; / Surely the Second Coming is at hand! / The Second Coming!'. The intensity of the poem's vision and its distance from received patterns is indicated by these mesmerised repetitions. Although there is a brief flicker of end-rhyme in the conjunction of 'man' and 'sun' at the end of lines 14 and 15, the poem generally avoids such apparently easy patterns of connection.

Paradoxically, though, Yeats's poem is not a free expression of disconnection but a carefully contrived piece of poetic art. Like 'Nineteen Hundred and Nineteen', though with greater concentration, it revists and rewrites Yeats's earlier poetry in the light of an experienced understanding more obviously in accord with the precepts of the 'modern' and the disillusionment of a post-war world. While the reference to 'Herodias' daughters' in that poem looks back to 'The Hosting of the Sidhe', 'the blood-dimmed tide' shockingly redeploys the adjective 'dim' which features in so many early poems and achieves an ugly precision in its compound adjective which is later matched by the arrogant physicality of 'Slouches'. Not only does 'The Second Coming' rewrite the adjectival tradition of the earlier poems; it is also a strongly alliterative poem which carries some patterns of assonance or internal rhyme.

In such ways, it has something in common with the practice of Hopkins who occasionally employed Anglo-Saxon alliteration and the intricate patterns of Welsh *cynghanedd* to add extra determination to the form of the sonnet or the rhyming stanza. Of course, Yeats does not require the double securities of Hopkins; nor, on the other hand, does he allow himself the calculated collapse into fragmentation which marks the end of *The Waste Land*. Like Eliot's five-part vision, 'The Second Coming' is driven by intimations of collapse and exploits terms of reference which invoke Christian explanation but, unlike Eliot, Yeats does not simulate collapse by imitating its effects. As he once told Pound, '*vers libre* is prose', and Yeats prefers not to capitulate by admitting the prosaic.[18] As I have written elsewhere: 'Eliot, the self-declared classicist, employs a technique which is expressionist and mimetic, which to some extent participates in the fragmentation which it laments. On the other hand, Yeats, the self-declared Romantic, approaches the subject of impending anarchy with a formal control which might be described as classical.'[19]

Even though 'The Second Coming' is expressed in the form of blank verse, it insists on a tightness of structure and recurrent evidence of intelligible control which defy those forces of destruction which it so frighteningly but resolutely envisages. 'The Second Coming' is unflinchingly modern; but it deliberately rejects any temptation to be Modernist.

The poem's strength is also increased by its gradual evacuation of political particularities. The drafts show that Yeats was thinking of other examples of social breakdown – the French Revolution and the Bolshevik Rising – but 'The Second Coming' achieves a superior generality precisely because it eliminates any reference which is historically specific, cunningly avoiding any mention of William Pitt, Edmund Burke, Marie Antoinette, the Germans and Russia. This unified concentration is intensified by the final choice of one unparagraphed piece of verse: in the last typescript version, Yeats had divided the poem into three distinct sections but now all divisions are omitted, with the effect of increasing the inevitability of the social decline which begins with the escape of the falcon from his handler's control.[20]

4

Yeats's progress exhibits another significant shift which seems to represent a move from 'Victorian' to 'modern'. That is, the clear but gradual transition from a poetry which had strong connections with narrative to a form of expression avoiding 'story' or 'plot' and finding utterance through modes appearing more characteristically and exclusively 'poetic'. To many writers who considered themselves 'modern', the apparent simplicities of narrative seemed increasingly inadequate to a world of growing complexity. As Eliot put it in 1921: 'it appears likely that poets in our civilization, as it exists at present, must be *difficult*.²¹ For some time, even novelists had been showing their impatience with the seemingly imperative requirements of plot: so, in their different ways, James, Conrad, Joyce and Woolf all found ways to minimise or redistribute the traditional structures of narrative continuity. In the work of most of these writers, the English novel also extended its range to include a linguistic sensitivity and a symbolic suggestiveness which traditionally had been attributed to poets rather than novelists.

Naturally, there were also some continuities. The young Yeats had been much impressed by William Morris, who was particularly well known for his narratives in verse, including *Sigurd the Volsung* (1876), which Yeats invokes with apparently nostalgic innocence at the end of his broadcast/ essay on 'Modern Poetry'. Much closer to the chronology of Yeats's own life was that of Rudyard Kipling, who published many ballads and who combined verse and prose in a number of his books. There was the example of John Masefield, who published widely before and after the War and throughout his life continued a practice of telling stories in verse. His war letters reveal a rawness of experience which cannot be guessed from his verse. This incapacity to integrate his war experience creatively suggests a flaw both in his temperament and in his attitude to poetry (or 'verse-making', as he revealingly calls it).

There was the Scottish poet John Davidson, best known as the creator of 'Thirty Bob a Week', but also the author of an ambitious if depressing narrative of Edwardian London, *The Testament of a Prime Minister* (1904), set in disappointingly turgid blank verse. Here again, the poem seems to be fettered by the decision to cast it in the shape of a traditional narrative and the equally conventional choices of poetic diction and verse form. Yet another, and different, case is that of the whimsical and inventive Walter De la Mare, who published copiously in prose and wrote a great deal of poetry, some of which (like the much-anthologised 'The Traveller') is uncanny or eerie and relates in suggestive ways to his more 'prosaic' inventions.

This powerful and continuing strand should not be ignored; yet there was also an undeniable and intentional departure from the gratifications of narrative. Nowhere is this exemplified more clearly than in Thomas Hardy who had published fourteen novels and over forty short stories when *Wessex Poems* appeared in 1898. From that point till his death nearly thirty years later, Hardy abandoned the writing of fiction ('the novels seem immature to me') but published another seven individual books of poetry. For all his unfashionable awkwardness, his rejection of literary experiment and his homage to Tennyson rather than T. S. Eliot or the precepts of Modernism,

Hardy finally evolved into one of the most distinctive poetic voices of the twentieth century. Admittedly, some of his volumes, notably *Time's Laughingstocks* (1909) and *Satires of Circumstance* (1914), are still informed by an active narrative consciousness, and this can be sensed (if more obliquely) even in later poems such as 'During Wind and Rain' or 'Voices from Things Growing in a Churchyard'. Yet Hardy's distinctive vision transcends the limitations of narrative and expresses itself with a lyrical force and intensity and a truly creative strangeness which is unique.

For all Hardy's achievement, or that of the much younger Robert Graves, who graduated from the *Georgian Anthology* and the educating realities of war to a theory of poetry which was concentrated on the brief and the lyrical, assumptions about the structure of narrative and the organization of poetry certainly died hard. Clear evidence of this can be found in the attempts of critics to deduce a biographical narrative from poems such as Eliot's 'A Cooking Egg'. Even Virginia Woolf was puzzled by the structure of *The Waste Land* when she heard Eliot read it: 'He sang it & chanted it [&] rhythmed it. It has great beauty & force of phrase: symmetry; & tensity. What connects it together, I'm not so sure.'[22] This is a striking example of residual beliefs about the nature of poetry since it was Woolf who, with her husband Leonard, would first publish Eliot's poem in book form in 1923 and since, as a novelist, she had publicly rebelled against the traditional formalities of plot, in books such as *Jacob's Room* (1922) and polemical essays such as 'Modern Novels' (which she revised as 'Modern Fiction').

Even Eliot himself seems to have succumbed to these imperatives since some of the notes to his poem imply a traditional coherence which the text itself escapes through the alternative patterning of its imaginative logic. Just as striking is the layout of Yeats's *Collected Poems* which was published as late as 1950. This large and supposedly definitive volume enacts an important generic segregation. At the end, it places a separate section which is entitled 'Narrative and Dramatic'. This is made up of 'The Wanderings of Oisin' (1889), 'The Old Age of Queen Maeve' (1903), 'Baile and Ailinn' (1903), *The Shadowy Waters* (1906), 'The Two Kings' (1914) and 'The Gift of Harun Al-Rashid' (1923). Like other poems in this collection, these six works are presented in their final form so, for example, the many stages of revision which led to *The Shadowy Waters* and Yeats's creative struggles with 'The Wanderings of Oisin' [or 'Usheen'] are totally ignored.

Of the works classified as 'Narrative and Dramatic', only *The Shadowy Waters* can be counted as 'dramatic', though this is not a play for staging but a verse-play in the traditions of nineteenth-century poetry. The final poem, which dates from relatively late in Yeats's career, constitutes his most obvious debt to Browning and shows that, in his case as in those of Pound and Eliot, modern poetry owed a particular debt to Browning's example in the dramatic monologue. It is also a sign of a changed emphasis that 'The Wanderings of Oisin', which Yeats had chosen to open most of his selected or collected volumes, is now significantly displaced. By 1950 the uses of narrative poetry would seem to have been limited or regarded as part of a previous age; yet, by relegating these poems to the end of the book and by setting them apart so obviously, Yeats's editor (or editors) has illuminated the strength of Yeats's debt to the nineteenth century and the formative part played by narrative verse in helping him to become the 'modern' poet we immediately recognise as W. B. Yeats.

NOTES

1 Cited in Norman White, *Hopkins in Ireland* (Dublin: University College Dublin Press, 2002), p. 207; cited in Norman White, *Hopkins: A Literary Biography* (Oxford: Clarendon Press, 1992), p. 435.
2 *The Oxford Book of Modern Verse 1892–1935*, ed. W. B. Yeats (Oxford: Clarendon Press, 1936), p. v.
3 *The Letters of Gerard Manley Hopkins to Robert Bridges*, ed. Claude Colleer Abbott, 2nd (revised) impression (London, New York and Toronto: Oxford University Press, 1935), pp. 154–5.
4 Patricia M. Ball, *The Science of Aspects: The Changing Role of Fact in the Work of Coleridge, Ruskin and Hopkins* (London: Athlone Press, 1971).
5 Cited in Humphrey Carpenter, *W. H. Auden: A Biography* (London, Boston and Sydney: George Allen and Unwin, 1981), p. 59.
6 See Michael Roberts, *The Faber Book of Modern Verse*, 2nd impression (London: Faber and Faber, 1936), p. 4: 'he [Hopkins] moulded a style which expressed the tension and disorder that he found inside himself'.
7 *The Early Poetry, Vol. II: "The Wanderings of Oisin" and Other Early Poems to 1895 / Manuscript Materials by W. B. Yeats*, ed. George Bornstein (Ithaca and London: Cornell University Press, 1994), p. 16.
8 Holograph on flyleaf, cited in *The Early Poetry: Volume II*, ed. George Bornstein, p. 17.
9 *The Early Poetry*, Vol. II, ed. George Bornstein, p. 16.
10 For full details, see W. B. Yeats, *Selected Poems*, ed. Timothy Webb, revised edn ([1991]; London: Penguin Books, 2000), pp. 35–6 and Introduction, for an account of Yeats's revisionary practice.
11 *The Oxford Book of Modern Verse*, p. xxxix.
12 Samuel Hynes, *A War Imagined: The First World War and English Culture* (London: Pimlico, 1992), especially Chapter 1.
13 Cited in Dennis Taylor, *Hardy's Metres and Victorian Prosody* (Oxford: Clarendon Press, 1988), p. 193.
14 Taylor, *Hardy's Metres and Victorian Prosody*, p. 6.
15 *Essays and Introductions* (London: Macmillan, 1961), pp. 521–24.

16 *Selected Prose of T. S. Eliot*, ed. Frank Kermode (London: Faber and Faber, 1975), pp. 34–5.
17 *Essays and Introductions*, p. 524.
18 Cited in James Longenbach, *Stone Cottage: Pound, Yeats, and Modernism* (New York and Oxford: Oxford University Press, 1988), p. 213.
19 Yeats, *Selected Poems*, p. xxvi.
20 For Yeats's draft and a transcription, see *Michael Robartes and the Dancer: Manuscript Materials by W. B. Yeats*, ed. Thomas Parkinson with Anne Bannen (Ithaca and London: Cornell University Press, 1994), pp. 146–65.
21 *Selected Prose of T. S. Eliot*, p. 65.
22 *The Diary of Virginia Woolf*, Vol. II: *1920–1924*, ed. Anne Olivier Bell (London: Hogarth Press, 1978), p. 178.

Further reading

Beckson, Karl, *London in the 1890s: A Cultural History*, New York: Norton, 1992
Kenner, Hugh, *The Pound Era*, London: Faber, 1972
Kermode, Frank, *Romantic Image*, London: Routledge and Kegan Paul, 1957
Millard, Kenneth, *Edwardian Poetry*, Oxford: Clarendon Press, 1991
North, Michael, *Reading 1922: A Return to the Scene of the Modern*, Oxford: Oxford University Press, 1991
Parkinson, Thomas, *W. B. Yeats, Self-Critic: A Study of his Early Verse and The Later Poetry*, Berkeley and London: University of California Press, 1971
Rainey, Lawrence, *Institutions of Modernism: Literary Elites and Public Culture*, New Haven, Conn.: Yale University Press, 1998
Rosenthal, M. L., and Sally M. Gall, *The Modern Poetic Sequence: The Genius of Modern Poetry*, New York and Oxford: Oxford University Press, 1983
Ross, Robert H., *The Georgian Revolt: Rise and Fall of a Poetic Ideal, 1910–22*, London: Faber, 1967
Stead, C. K., *Pound, Yeats, Eliot and the Modernist Movement*, London: Macmillan, 1986
  The New Poetic: Yeats to Eliot, revised edition [1964]; London: Athlone Press, 1998

2

DANIEL ALBRIGHT

Modernist poetic form

If Modernism implies experimentation with the limits of art, shocks and thrills beyond all previous bounds, then, in the matter of poetic form, the Victorians were more Modernist than the Modernists themselves. As inventors of new stanza forms, transgressors of prosodic boundaries and explorers of new sonorities of verse, the Victorians were unsurpassable – the Modernist poets began their careers in a world in which the Victorians had already broken all the rules and developed strange and idiosyncratic new rules. It might be good to start this review of Modernist poetic form with a catalogue of some of the formal innovations of the nineteenth century, and their relation to the aesthetics of Modernism.

Scrutiny of rhyme

Rhyme has always been a somewhat dubious attribute of English poetry, partly because classical Greek and Latin poetry did not use it. Around 1603 Samuel Daniel felt he had to publish *A Defence of Ryme*, because Campion and others had attacked it; and Milton began *Paradise Lost* (1674) with a note defending the rhymelessness of his epic: he called rhyme 'to all judicious ears, triveal, and of no true musical delight'. By the nineteenth century the propriety of rhyming was no longer an issue – the canon of rhymed poetry was obviously too magnificent to be dispensed with – but poets kept experimenting with aspects of rhyme. There is a moment in the second part of Goethe's *Faust* (1832) when Helen of Troy, in the gothic North, hears rhymed poetry for the first time:

> *Lynceus.* Already see the army tame,
> all their swords are blunt and lame,
> before that noble splendid form
> the sun itself seems dull, unwarm,
> and from that face a glory falls
> that makes all empty, and all null ...

Helena. Many wonders I see, and many hear.
Amazement strikes, questions come to mind.
But first I wish instruction, why this man's speech
rings so strange, amiable and yet so strange.
One sound, it seems, conforms itself to others,
and if a word is conjoined to the ear,
another comes, sweetly to fondle the first.

The nineteenth-century poets sometimes wanted their contemporaries to hear rhyme with some of this same novelty, this uncanny sweetness – to hear rhyme as if no one had ever heard rhyme before. Robert Browning had a gift for making rhyme feel fresh, obtrusive:

> Nor brighter was his eye, nor moister
> Than a too-long-opened oyster ...

This is from a children's poem, 'The Pied Piper of Hamelin' (1842), but conspicuous rhymes usually sound childlike or comical; the Victorian age is the great age of nursery rhymes, limericks and operettas:

> About binomial theorem I'm teeming with a lot o' news –
> With many cheerful facts about the square of the hypotenuse.
> (W. S. Gilbert, *The Pirates of Penzance*, 1879)

In general poets have avoided too ingenious rhymes for fear of embarrassment; where technique calls attention to itself the possibility of doggerel is always strong.

Browning, a boisterous introvert, had no qualms about his moister oysters, but he also experimented with the opposite sort of virtuoso performance: extremely inconspicuous rhymes. Anyone who teaches 'My Last Duchess' can discover Browning's success by asking the students about the poem's metre: almost everyone remembers it as blank verse, when in fact it is rhymed couplets, enjambed with such nonchalance that you hear the poem without rhymes. Tennyson played the opposite trick, by writing lyrics in blank verse, such as 'Tears, idle tears', that linger in the memory with the fragrance of rhyme, even though the unrhymed stanzas are bound together by repetition, assonance and refrain.

The most searching and influential work with rhyme, however, was that of the American poet Emily Dickinson:

> I heard a Fly buzz – when I died –
> The Stillness in the Room
> Was like the Stillness in the Air –
> Between the Heaves of Storm –   (*c.* 1862)

Dickinson's slant rhyme derives its effect from the hymn-like strictness of metre: where the metre is simple, strong and familiar, the false rhyme of room/storm makes itself heard emphatically. An early editor in fact rewrote the second line to read 'The stillness round my form' to 'improve' the poem. But the very discord of the rhyme creates a kind of shiver, appropriate to the poem's macabre theme: Dickinson's taste for dissonance became part of the general taste of Modernism.

Is there a Modernist style of rhyming? The Modernist preoccupation with self-conscious technique, artifice exposing its own artificiality, sometimes turns into a kind of preciosity:

> Should I, after tea and cakes and ices,
> Have the strength to force the moment to its crisis?
> (T. S. Eliot, 'The Love Song of J. Alfred Prufrock', 1911)

Both Eliot and Ezra Pound inherited a strain of brittle rhyme, often using arcane or scientific vocabulary, from French *fin-de-siècle* ironists such as Jules Laforgue:

> He had passed, inconscient, full gaze,
> The wide-banded irides
> And botticellian sprays implied
> In their diastasis ...   (Pound, 'Mauberley (1920)')

> Non, je resterai seul, ici-bas,
> Tout à la chère morte phtisique,
> Berçant mon cœur trop hypertrophique
> Aux éternelles fugues de Bach.

> (No, I huddle in my solitude,
> Devoted to the phthisic dead
> While my heart hypertrophied
> Cradled in Bach's eternal fugues.)
> (Laforgue, 'Complainte de l'organiste de Notre-Dame de Nice')

These poems all concern ineffectual personages, permanently at a loss; and the fussy diction, the finical rhyming, suggest their incapacity to deal with twentieth-century asperities. Rhyming is read as a retreat, a cowering before modern life. In some sense both Prufrock and Mauberley are personifications of rhyme itself, of passé modes of writing poems.

And yet, there is a great deal of rhyming poetry in Modernism; rhyme is part of the Tradition that the Individual Talent embraces, but at arm's length. The half-rhyme often seems a satisfying way of respecting the tension between the Old Dispensation and the New. For example, look at the opening lines of Yeats's ' The Second Coming' (1919):

> Turning and turning in the widening gyre
> The falcon cannot hear the falconer;
> Things fall apart; the centre cannot hold;
> Mere anarchy is loosed upon the world ...

This poem is composed in blank verse, and yet these opening lines almost fall into couplets – and in fact when Yeats began writing this he envisaged a poem in rhyme. There is a ghost of order; but the poem is falling into rhymelessness, just as the falconer is losing control of the falcon. Lapsing rhymes suggest disorder more strongly than no rhymes at all.

Another form of dissonant Modernist rhyme, invented by the war poet Wilfred Owen and developed by Auden, consists of repeating whole syllables while altering the vowel:

> It seemed that out of battle I escaped
> Down some profound dull tunnel, long since scooped
> Through granites which Titanic wars had groined.
> Yet also there encumbered sleepers groaned ...
>> (Owen, 'Strange Meeting', 1918)

> Acquire that flick of wrist and after strain
> Relax in your darling's arms like a stone,
> Remembering everything you can confess,
> Making the most of firelight, of hours of fuss ...
>> (Auden, 'Venus Will Now Say a Few Words', 1929)

Such poems gain momentum from the continual discolouration of vowel-sounds; Owen's poem is about imagining one's own death, and Auden's concerns blind evolutionary process – in both cases the phonic distortion becomes an image of unpleasant mutation. Auden was a master of rhyme as a form of dissonance:

> I cannot grow;
> I have no shadow ...
> I cannot err;
> There is no creature ...
>> ('Anthem for St Cecilia's Day', 1940)

The technical term for this sort of rhyme is anisobaric – the rhyming of a stressed syllable with an unstressed. It has usually been considered a comic device or a technical fault; but Modernist poets found exotic sonorities in the land of error.

Scrutiny of metre

'To break the pentameter, that was the first heave', Pound tells us in Canto 81, but, from the beginning of Modern English, the pentameter is continually being broken and re-formed.

In every age there have been poets with a strong taste for prosody remote from the da-DUM iambics that come so naturally to a language in which most sentences begin with an unstressed article or pronoun followed by a word accented on the first syllable. Here is a passage from John Donne's Satyre IV (?1590s):

> He knowes who'hath sold his land, and now doth beg
> A licence, old iron, bootes, shooes, and egge-
>   shels to transport ...
> He with home-meats tries me; I belch, spue, spit,
> Looke pale, and sickly, like a Patient; Yet ...

Donne more or less observes the ten-syllable rule for heroic verse, but deliberately makes the movement of the verse jarring, appropriate for the mangled ethics of the courtier in question. The iambic pulse is strongly disrupted by clots of stressed syllables: 'I belch, spue, spit, / Looke pale'; 'bootes, shooes, and egge- / shels' – note how he splits the word *eggshells* in half, so thick and broken is the verbal texture. In the eighteenth century Alexander Pope felt impelled to rewrite this in decent heroic couplets, ironing out all the knots of rhythm:

> As one of Woodward's patients, sick, and sore,
> I puke, I nauseate – yet he thrusts in more ...

Pope pukes and nauseates in even iambs; he doesn't vomit out undigested syllables.

But again the great experimentalists in prosody are the Victorians, despite their reputation for genteel conservatism. Matthew Arnold was a school inspector and an advocate for educational reform; he was also sporadically engaged in the reform of the metres of English poetry:

> When the white dawn first
> Through the rough fir-planks
> Of my hut, by the chestnuts,
> Up at the valley-head,
> Came breaking, Goddess!
> I sprang up, I threw round me
> My dappled fawn-skin ...
>
> ('The Strayed Reveller', 1849)

This is recognisable as verse not because it can be broken down into a regular sequence of metrical feet, but because short, often prepositional, phrases function as pseudo-feet, creating a chant-like sound. In most verse there is a tension between syntax and metre: the syntax spills over the cuts between one foot and the next, between one line and the next; but Arnold manages to make syntax itself do the work of metre, by parcelling out the long sentence into choppy exclamatory units. On the one hand this gives the poem an antique feel, as if it were a literal translation of some non-existent Greek original; on the other, the poem seems advanced in its organicism, its perfect identity of metre and syntax, form and content.

Organicism, specifically the organicist desire to make sound conform to sense, explains much of the history of prosodic experiment. There has always been a certain desire to bend the rules of metre in order to accommodate the kinesthesis of the poem's subject – Pope gives some handy advice on this theme:

> When Ajax strives some rock's vast weight to throw,
> The line too labours, and the words move slow:
> Not so when swift Camilla scours the plain,
> Flies o'er th' unbending corn, and skims along the main ...
>
> (*Essay on Criticism*, 1711)

Not only does Pope expand the last line to a hexameter, but he contracts four syllables (*over the un-*) to two in order to suggest how Camilla's gossamer foot barely grazes the ground.

But Pope's slow Ajax and swift Camilla are both moderates compared to some of the experiments in poetic dynamism in the nineteenth century. In America Walt Whitman watched two eagles whirling together, and responded with a whirl-shaped poem:

> Skirting the river road, (my forenoon walk, my rest,)
> Skyward in air a sudden muffled sound, the dalliance of the eagles,
> The rushing amorous contact high in space together,
> The clinching interlocking claws, a living, fierce, gyrating wheel,
> Four beating wings, two beaks, a swirling mass tight grappling,
> In tumbling turning clustering loops, straight downward falling ...
>
> ('The Dalliance of the Eagles', 1880)

Here strings of present participles and participial phrases act as pseudo-feet, do the work of metre by organising the rhythm around forms of energy. Especially noteworthy is the phrase *swirling mass tight grappling*, a sort of involved participial loop, a single huge foot so emphatic that the only unstressed syllables are the -*ing* endings. Everywhere the syntax wheels around without terminating in a clear subject-verb-object pattern: in the entire poem there isn't a single finite verb – in the participles, noun and verb are all balled up together, just as the eagles are. The speech unit is the syntax unit; there is no metre that can be abstracted from the sonorities of the specific words. There is recurrence, but unpredictable recurrence; the metre of the poem is more weather than dance.

Whitman's eagles may be compared with an equally radical bird, Gerard Manley Hopkins's falcon – here are the first eight lines as Hopkins scanned them:

> I: cáught this |mórning |mórning's | mínion, | kíng-
>   dom of | dáylight's | dáu(phin), dapple- | dáwn-drawn | Fál(con),
>   in his | ríding
>
> Of the | ró(lling) level | únder | néath (him) steady | áir, and | stríding |
>
> Hígh   there, how he | rúng upon the | réin of a | wímpling | wíng
>
> In his | écstasy! Then | óff, | óff | fórth on | swíng,
>
> As a | skáte's (heel) sweeps | smóoth on a | bów-bend: the | húrl
>   and | glíding
>
> Re | búffed the | bíg | wínd. My | héart in | híding |
>
> Stírred for a | bírd, – the a | chíeve of, the | mástery of the | thíng! |
> ('The   Windhover', 1876)

The texture of 'The Windhover' is a hovering, not an explicit stating: nouns are bent into adjective compounds (*dapple-dawn-drawn*), present participles usurp the place of nouns for many of the rhyme-words, for in a poem such as this, more like an electromagnetic field than a piece of parsable grammar, the subject is energy – what Hopkins called instress, the flashing-forth of God's creative force from the falcon.

The reticent Jesuit Hopkins was influenced by the pantheist pansexual Whitman – Hopkins once wrote, 'I always knew in my heart Walt Whitman's mind to be more like my own than any other man's living' (18 Oct. 1882, to Robert Bridges). But Hopkins went further than Whitman in trying to notate his poems as a sort of musical score. The sonnet form is twisted and pulled by the rhythm – what Hopkins called Sprung Rhythm (every foot begins with a stressed syllable, and the unstressed syllables, of variable number, are crowded together so that each foot takes exactly the same amount of time to pronounce): the isochronous line introduces accelerations and hesitations, emphases, cuts, turns – the very form of the bird's flight, its careening around enjambements, is incarnate in the word flow. Compared to Whitman's savage eagles, the falcon seems to have little ornithological existence: it is a pretext for impressing onto the syllables a feeling for a certain sort of motion through air.

Hopkins's poetry was almost unknown until 1918, long after his death, when his friend Robert Bridges published an edition of his work. Though Hopkins lived as a Victorian, his fame was that of a Modernist, since his poems, coming to light at the end of the First World War, seemed to have something of the jazz and pizzazz, the linguistic torsion, of Edith Sitwell and other experimentalists. His notion of rethinking metre according to musical form also found congenial ears: the three tenets of Imagism, the movement founded in 1912 by Pound, Richard Aldington and Hilda Doolittle ('H.D.') were:

1. Direct treatment of the 'thing' whether subjective or objective.
2. To use absolutely no word that does not contribute to the presentation.
3. As regarding rhythm: to compose in the sequence of the musical phrase, not in sequence of a metronome.[1]

Pound's dislike of iambs was strong. In his maturity, he only rarely tried to write regular English verse, and when he did he usually stiffened the texture with spondaic substitutions, as in the parody of the *Rubáiyát* stanza at the end of Canto LXXX (1946):

> Tudor indeed is gone and every rose,
> Blood-red, blanch-white that in the sunset glows
> Cries: 'Blood, Blood, Blood!' against the gothic stone
> Of England, as the Howard or Boleyn knows.

But often the Modernists overtly rejected traditional English metres, looking elsewhere for their rhythms. The main sources for alternative rhythmic schemes were: (1) Old English; (2) Greek and Latin; (3) Japanese and Chinese; and (4) none of the above – pure intuition.

Alternative metres (1): Old English

There is a strong Modernist tendency to seek for authenticity in the archaic – to try to ground language in some primal linguistic act, such as the Sanskrit thunder-word *DA* in Eliot's *The Waste Land*. So it is not surprising that Modernists might tend to reform metre by looking at the earliest extant poetry in English, the poetry written in Anglo-Saxon from the eighth to the eleventh century, before the Norman Conquest of 1066 broke the Germanic spine of the language by imposing French vocabulary and syntax.

The corpus of Old English poetry was recovered slowly. A fascination with Germanic and Celtic archaism can be seen in eighteenth-century verse, but among the Victorians the scholarly study of the ancient language started to influence poetry in many ways. Some Victorians felt that English had been weakened by its adoption of French words, French diction; Old English seemed hard, swift, concrete. As Hopkins wrote Bridges:

> Rev. Wm. Barnes ... has published a 'Speech craft of English Speech' = English Grammar, written in an unknown tongue, a sort of modern Anglosaxon ... He does not see the utter hopelessness of the thing. It makes one weep to think what English might have been; for in spite of all that Shakspere and Milton have done with the compound I cannot doubt that no beauty in a language can make up for want of purity. In fact I am learning Anglosaxon and it is a vastly superior thing to what we have now. But the madness of an almost unknown man trying to do what the three estates of the realm together could never accomplish!
>
> (To Robert Bridges, 26 Nov. 1882)

Hopkins thought Barnes had gone too far, but nonetheless pined for an unfallen English, with its old purity and precision somehow restored.

So did other poets, who became fascinated with the metre of Old English – a pattern of paired half-lines of two stressed syllables each (and a varying number of unstressed syllables), bound together by alliteration. Tennyson's son, a scholar of Old English, published a prose version of *The Battle of Brunanburh* (AD 937) that his father consulted in his verse translation:

> Bow'd the spoiler,
> Bent the Scotsman,
> Fell the ship-crews
> Doom'd to the death.
> All the field with blood of the fighters
> Flow'd, from when the first the great
> Sun-star of morning-tide
> Lamp of the Lord God Lord everlasting,
> Glode over earth till the glorious creature
> Sank to his setting.

Tennyson does not obey the strict rules of alliteration, but he provides a good deal of it – sometimes rather too much. He imitates the gnarly quality of the syntax with his inversions (Bow'd the spoiler, / Bent the Scotman); and by using *glode* as the past tense of *glide* he delves into the prehistory of the modern word. The rough-hewn texture of Old English verse is suggested, though Tennyson tends to default to a dactyl + trochee metre (*Lámp of the|Lórd God*; *Lórd ever- |lásting*; *Sánk to his |sétting*).

Ezra Pound knew Robert Bridges and inherited something of Bridges' love of extending English vocabulary through archaic words and metres.

Bridges delighted in some of the strange words in Pound's early poetry, as Pound remembered in Canto LXXX:

> 'forloyn' said Mr Bridges (Robert)
> 'we'll get 'em all back'
> meaning archaic words

And in 1911 Pound published the most influential of all translations of Old English poetry, 'The Seafarer':

> Bitter breast-cares have I abided,
> Known on my keel many a care's hold,
> And dire sea-surge, and there I oft spent
> Narrow nightwatch nigh the ship's head
> While she tossed close to cliffs. Coldly afflicted ...

Here is a compelling combination of immediacy and artifice – language that cuts near the bone, and literal imitation of the compound epithets, called kennings, that mark Old English verse. The poem provides a shiver both with its icy subject matter and with its clash of stressed syllables abutting.

This use of Old English to strip poetry of decorative elements, to simplify into strangeness, was explored throughout the twentieth century – from Auden's 'The Wanderer' through Seamus Heaney's distinguished translation of *Beowulf*.

Alternative metres (2): Greek and Latin

Poets and critics have had difficulty in trying to establish a clear relation between the Germanic elements of English prosody, based on stress, and the classical elements, based on quantity. Greek and Latin words had stresses, but the metre was determined not by how loudly you pronounced a syllable, but by how much time you took to do so. So a classical line is conceived as an array of half-notes and quarter-notes, whereas a Germanic line is conceived as an array of strong and weak accents.

It is possible, of course, to transpose the classical feet – iambs, trochees, anapests – from a quantitative to an accentual system, and English poetry has thrived by adopting that procedure. But it works well only with classical metres that don't contain too many long or short syllables in a row: we hear little in English poetry of such feet as the molossus (– – –) or the bacchius (◡ – –) or the tribrach (◡◡◡) because the rhythms of the language resist them. A sequence of consecutive strong syllables will tend to be read with certain weakenings in the middle, and vice versa. When the Countess of Winchilsea wrote, 'Faintly the inimitable rose', she came about as close as any poet could to writing a line with a strong stress at each end and seven unstressed syllables in the middle; and yet stresses keep popping up in regular alternation, whether bidden or not.

But from the beginnings of Modern English, poets have contrived ways of forcing English feet into classical shoes that do not easily fit. In 1602 Thomas Campion offered this sample of the 'English *Sapphick*'–'The first three verses therefore in our English *Sapphick* are merely those *Trochaicks* ... excepting only that the first foote of either of them must ever of necessity be a *Spondee*, to make the number more grave':

Fáiths púre | shíeld, the | Chrístian | Diána,
Énglánds | glóry | crównd with | áll de-| vínenesse,
Líve lóng | wíth tri- | úmphs to | blésse thy | péople
Át thy | síght tri-|úmphing.[2]

It isn't easy to read the third verse according to Campion's desired scansion.

Milton made similar experiments with classical metres, and later Tennyson. In almost all of these cases, the reader notes the abundance of spondees and dactyls – feet that begin with a stomp, feet that have a heavy but uncertain tread, because normal expectations of kinesis are violated. In Modernist imitations of classical metres, this provisionality of footing sometimes itself becomes a theme:

See, they return; ah, see the tentative
Movements, and the slow feet,
The trouble in the pace and the uncertain
Wavering!

See, they return, one, and by one,
With fear, as half-awakened;
As if the snow should hesitate
And murmur in the wind,
            and half turn back;
These were the 'Wing'd-with-Awe',
Inviolable.

This is Pound's 'The Return' (1912), concerning the return of the Greek gods, and of the Greek metres too: just as the gods struggle to realise themselves in an uncongenial world, so the metres struggle towards clarity of rhythm without quite attaining it. Yeats considered this one of the few successful poems written in free verse but also felt that 'he has not got all the wine into the bowl, that he is a brilliant improvisator'.[3] But perhaps the poem is *about* not getting all the wine into the bowl, *about* the ways in which English words keep squirming out of Greek metrical patterns. The poem is full of third epitrites (-- ⌣ -), but the footing is slippery, treacherous.

Classical prosody and Germanic alliterative verse have little in common. Yet, in the canon of Modernist experiments, they sometimes have a similar sonority. The trochee, the spondee and the dactyl are the natural alternatives to the iambic and anapestic rhythms of normal English verse. The snow shower of Greek gods in 'The Return' is somewhat different from the 'hail-scur' that troubles the hero of 'The Seafarer'; but rhythms that deviate strongly from iambic pentameter tend to follow similar paths of deviation, if they are to remain rhythms at all.

Alternative metres (3): Chinese and Japanese

A tendency toward the gnomic and fragmentary can be found in late nineteenth-century poetry, particularly in America:

> You tell me this is God?
> I tell you this is a printed list,
> A burning candle, and an ass.　(Stephen Crane, *War Is Kind*)

> To make a prairie it takes a clover and one bee,
> One clover, and a bee,
> And revery.
> The revery alone will do,
> If bees are few.　(Emily Dickinson, #1755)

This tendency toward the severely reductive started to be understood as a sort of Orientalism as the poetry of Japan, especially the seventeen-syllable haiku form, became known in the West. Crane takes God and keeps subtracting, until nothing is left but list, candle and ass; Dickinson performs a subtraction in two stages, until nothing is left but reverie.

The Imagists and Vorticists in Pound's circle adopted a self-consciously Asiatic aesthetic, working toward metres that might be called metres of deletion. In his September 1914 Vorticism article, Pound quotes the 'substance' of a Japanese haiku:

> The fallen blossom falls back to its branch:
> A butterfly.[4]

Then he tells a story about how he made a long poem about seeing beautiful faces on a subway platform, but kept paring down this work 'of second intensity' until he had the following '*hokku*-like sentence':

> The apparition　　of these faces　　in the crowd　:
> Petals　　　　on a wet, black　　bough　.

Only in its first two printings did the poem appear without punctuation and with gaps in the lines. In this original form, the six elements of the poem look like erratic feet, or like phrase units compressed into something like ideograms.

Chinese poetry does not typically have the stark brevity of Japanese, but Chinese also influenced the rhythms of Modernist poetry. Pound went to trouble to publish Ernest Fenollosa's essay *The Chinese Written Character as a Medium for Poetry*:

> A true noun, an isolated thing, does not exist in nature. Things are only the terminal points, or rather the meeting points, of actions, cross-sections cut through action, snap-shots. Neither can a pure verb, an abstract motion, exist in nature. The eye sees noun and verb as one: things in motion, motion in things, and so the Chinese conception tends to represent them ...

> The Chinese have one word, *ming* or *mei*. Its ideograph is the sign of the sun together with the sign of the moon. It serves as verb, noun, adjective. Thus you write literally 'the sun and moon of the cup' for 'the cup's brightness'. Placed as a verb, you write 'the cup sun-and-moons,' ... i.e. shines.[5]

This doctrine tended to turn Whitman into a Chinese poet in spite of himself: his way, in 'The Dalliance of the Eagles', of smearing nouns and verbs into a sort of participial soup is, by Fenollosa's definition, ideogrammic. Pound's Vorticist poetry often shows a Whitmanesque fondness for present participles, as in 'Dogmatic Statement on the Game and Play of Chess: Theme for a Series of Pictures':

> Red knights, brown bishops, bright queens
> Striking the board, falling in strong 'L's' of colour,
> Reaching and striking in angles,
>
> > Holding lines of one colour ...
> > Their moves break and reform the pattern:
> Luminous greens from the rooks,
> Clashing with 'x's' of queens ...

The participles again create a dynamic that spills out of normal sentence patterns; and the 'L's' and the 'x's' are alphabet letters made to do the work of ideograms, as if Pound were trying to make letter-shapes embody the vectors of the chess pieces.

Alternative metres (4): free verse

The prose poem was invented in the nineteenth century, by Baudelaire, Mallarmé and other French poets; and no verse could be freer than

Whitman's. This left the Modernists in the retrograde position of having to defend a poetic manner less radical than their predecessors'. Eliot published a single prose poem, 'Hysteria', and Auden considered that his prose text 'Caliban to the Audience' was the best thing he ever wrote; but for the most part the Modernists tried to defend a middle position, somewhere between the scannable and the unscannable. Robert Frost compared free verse to playing tennis without a net; and in his earliest reprinted essay, Eliot claimed that:

> *Vers libre* does not exist ... the most interesting verse ... has been done either by taking a very simple form ... and constantly withdrawing from it, or taking no form at all, and constantly approximating to a very simple one. It is this contrast between fixity and flux, this unperceived evasion of monotony, which is the very life of verse.[6]

We can take this as a typical Modernist position on free verse. In 1917 Pound approved Eliot's 'No *vers* is *libre* for the man who wants to do a good job', adding, 'I do not think one can use to any advantage rhythms much more tenuous and imperceptible than some I have used.'[7] Even William Carlos Williams, so often hostile to Eliot, agreed in this disparagement of free verse:

> free verse since Whitman's time has led us astray ... Relativity gives us the cue ... We have today to do with the poetic, as always, but a *relatively* stable foot, not a rigid one ... Without measure we are lost.[8]

Williams's notion of a poetic unit consisting of an intuitive and variable foot seems to rest on something difficult to understand: unstable measurement. To cite the authority of Einstein does not solve the difficulty. On the other hand, some of Williams's best poems, such as 'The Dance' (1944), are fairly easy to understand as approximations to or evasions of traditional metres. The idea of a dance liberated from strict beats governs many of the wildest passages of Modernist poetry. Edith Sitwell, inspired by Stravinsky's *Petrushka* (1911) and Liszt's études, wrote poetry in which the metre frisks and syncopates beyond any Shakespearean rag or Tennysonian cakewalk:

> Watched the courses of the breakers' rocking horses and with Glaucis,
> Lady Venus on the settee of the horsehair sea!
> Where Lord Tennyson in laurels wrote a gloria free,
> In a borealic iceberg came Victoria; she
> Knew Prince Albert's tall memorial took the colors of the floreal
> And the borealic iceberg; floating on they see ...
>
> ('Hornpipe', from *Façade*, 1922)

Sitwell claimed that 'The poems in *Façade* are *abstract* poems – that is, they are patterns in sound. They are ... virtuoso exercises in technique of extreme difficulty.'[9] The notion of pure rhythm, liberated from every burden of meaning, is one of many Modernist dreams of the artistic absolute.

Scrutiny of the stanza

The idea that a poem should shape itself around the thing it represents is old – George Herbert's wing-shaped 'Easter Wings' (1633) is a famous example – but in the nineteenth century this notion of poem-icon was taken to stunning lengths. In Victor Hugo's 'Les Djinns' (1829) the first stanza consists of lines of two syllables each, the second three syllables, until a nine-syllable stanza is reached, at which point the stanzas start to contract: the djinns come in a whirlwind, and in a poem shaped like a whirlwind. Among the Modernists, the notion of a stanza embodying the dynamic form of its subject matter is strong: there is no exact English equivalent of Apollinaire's *Calligrammes*, in which the lines twist and curl, spin themselves into recognisable shapes, but Pound's Canto XC (1955) has a passage shaped like a vortex:

> thick smoke, purple, rising
> bright flame now on the altar
>   the crystal funnel of air
> out of Erebus, the delivered,
>   Tyro, Alcmene, free now, ascending
> e i cavalieri
>   ascending,
> no shades more,
>   lights among them, enkindled ...

And Eliot's favorite passage from his *Waste Land* (1922) was a song about drops of water consisting of audible drips:

> If there were rock
> And also water
> And water
> A spring
> A pool among the rock
> If there were the sound of water only ...
> Drip drop drip drop drop drop drop
> But there is no water

The poem strives to configure itself into the shape, the sound, of the water, the absent water.

But there is another side to Modernist poetics, one that questions every possibility of creating an identity between form and content. Some poets allege that there is *no* relation between form and content. Auden resisted Paul Valéry's theory that all poetic form is arbitrary:

> If [formal restrictions] really were purely arbitrary, then ... the experience which every poet has had, of being unable to get on with a poem because he was trying to use the 'wrong' form ... would be unknown.[10]

But he was evidently determined to try every poetic form known to the human race, for the sheer exhilaration of technical challenge. Here is his attempt to imitate the Old Norse form, the *drottkvaett*, one so muscle-bound that a poet, in English, finds it almost impossible to say anything at all:

> Hushed is the lake of hawks,
> Bright with our excitement,
> And all the sky of skulls
> Glows with scarlet roses ...[11]

Like Sitwell's experiments with abstract rhythms, this English *drottkvaett* seems an experiment with an abstract stanza form, an object for pure play. So – Modernism vacillates between incarnational and disengaged ideals of poetic form.

Sometimes it even seems as if poets have outgrown traditional forms and their strong music, and need to cast them aside:

> Comets weep and Leonids fly
> Hunt the heavens and the plains
> Whirled in a vortex that shall bring
> The world to that destructive fire
> Which burns before the ice-cap reigns
>
> That was a way of putting it – not very satisfactory:
> A periphrastic study in a worn-out poetical fashion ...
>
> (Eliot, 'East Coker', 1940)

But Eliot prints the stanza, even in the act of repudiating it.

Here Eliot adjusts his persona in the very act of adjusting poetic form: a critical, captious, weary voice speaks in long prosaic lines, undoing the confident prophet who spoke in rhymed tetrameter. A poem that mixes disparate poetic forms becomes a tracing of the various modalities of a single sensibility – its continual modulation from one persona to the next. This sort of mixture is one of the contributions of Modernism to the art of poetry.

The original title of *The Waste Land* was *He Do the Police in Different Voices*, and Eliot's more ambitious poems are acts of vocal impersonation, in which different voices adopt different sorts of poetic stanzas. In his

PhD dissertation, Eliot wrote that the human self is essentially incoherent and multiple:

> the life of the soul does not consist in the contemplation of one consistent world but in the painful task of unifying (to a greater or less extent) jarring and incompatible ones, and passing, when possible, from two or more discordant viewpoints to a higher which shall somehow include and transcend them.[12]

The Modernist sense of plurality of the self finds its natural expression in the rapid passage from one stanza form to another. Even Yeats wrote that, as he considered the complete array of human personalities, it was like staring 'at my own form ... in a room full of mirrors'; and in the poem 'Vacillation' he changes stanza form as he changes mood, changes self.[13] When Yeats writes a sonnet, he adopts the persona of a sonnet writer, such as John Donne:

> A sudden blow: the great wings beating still
> Above the staggering girl, her thighs caressed ...
>
> ('Leda and the Swan')

> Batter my heart, three-person'd God, for you
> As yet but knock, breathe, shine, and seek to mend ...
>
> (Donne, 'Holy Sonnets' XIV)

Modernist poetic form generally poises itself between extreme systemlessness and radical resystematisation. The poet manipulates forms, but noncommitally – the form is at best a provisional resting-place amid a constant shifting. In 'The Auroras of Autumn' (1947), Wallace Stevens wrote of 'form gulping after formlessness' – and a Modernist stanza is often less like a perfected design than the outline of an animal in the python's belly, slowly losing its contour. Or, as Robert Frost put it, 'Like a piece of ice on a hot stove the poem must ride on its own melting.'[14]

NOTES

1 Ezra Pound, *Literary Essays* (New York: New Directions, 1968), p. 3.
2 *The Works of Thomas Campion*, ed. Walter R. Davis (London: Faber and Faber, 1969), p. 309.
3 *The Oxford Book of Modern Verse*, ed. W. B. Yeats (London: Oxford University Press, 1966), p. xxvi.
4 *Ezra Pound and the Visual Arts*, ed. Harriet Zinnes (New York: New Directions, 1980), p. 205.
5 Ernest Fenollosa, *The Chinese Written Character as a Medium for Poetry* (San Francisco: City Lights Books, 1969), pp. 10, 18.

6 T.S. Eliot, *To Criticize the Critic* (New York: Farrar, Straus, 1965), pp. 183, 185.
7 Pound, *Literary Essays*, pp. 12–13.
8 William Carlos Willimas, *Selected Essays* (New York: New Directions, 1969), pp. 339–40.
9 Edith Sitwell, *The Canticle of the Rose: Poems 1917–1949* (New York: Vanguard Press, 1949), p. xii.
10 W.H. Auden, *Forewords and Afterwords* (New York: Random House, 1973), p. 364.
11 W.H. Auden, *Secondary Worlds* (New York: Random House, 1968), p. 68.
12 T.S. Eliot, *Knowledge and Experience in the Philosophy of F.H. Bradley* (New York: Farrar, Straus, 1964), pp. 147–8.
13 W.B. Yeats, *A Vision* (New York: Macmillan, 1961), p. 214.
14 Robert Frost, *Complete Poems* (New York: Holt, Rinehart, 1958), p. viii.

Further reading

Attridge, Derek, *Poetic Rhythm: An Introduction*, Cambridge: Cambridge University Press, 1995

3

REDELL OLSEN

Postmodern poetry in Britain

If the era of 'postmodernity' is increasingly seen as 'a socio-economic mode that has intensified and surpassed modernity itself' then poetry produced under this new 'socio-economic mode' might rightly be dismissed as another form of 'postmodern' candyfloss neatly packaged for our quick or therapeutic consumption.[1] On the other hand perhaps poets, often relatively uninvested in the capital of a culture industry, which is currently terming itself in its latest guise as 'postmodern', are one of the few cultural producers left who can afford to be sceptical of the current era and of the claims of culture itself. Paradoxically, this means that poetry has the potential to be the most 'postmodern' and the most '*anti*-postmodern' of the arts. Anthologies of the period reflect the unease with which contemporary poets and critics have embraced and subsequently distanced themselves from such an elastic term. Although there is some overlap between poets represented in anthologies of British poetry since 1980, what is most striking is the divergence between them that marks an important and decisive split in post-war poetry in Britain. Poets from both groupings have been termed 'postmodern'.

There are clearly a number of definitions of the 'postmodern' in operation here. The first is linked to the branding, dilution (under the guise of accessibility) and commodification of intellectual and creative activity which have become key features of the 'postmodern' era. The second relates to the formal and conceptual features of 'postmodernism' as it has developed in relation to other disciplines such as architecture and the visual arts. The editors of *The New Poetry* (1993) describe their selection as emphasising 'accessibillity, democracy and responsiveness, humour and seriousness'.[2] These are all features which appear to relate to the eclecticism of 'postmodernism', as it has been described by critics such as Charles Jencks and Hal Foster, but they are also consistent with the commodification of art in the 'postmodern socio-economic mode' identified by Nigel Wheale. In their introduction to the *Penguin Book of Contemporary British*

Poetry (1981), Blake Morrison and Andrew Motion suggest that the poets included in their anthology 'do represent a departure, one which may be said to exhibit something of the spirit of postmodernism'.[3] It is not clear which features of the poetry Morrison and Motion are referring to, but Ian Gregson has called this an 'unhelpful and at worst simply wrong' use of the term applied as it is here to poets such as Seamus Heaney, Tony Harrison and Douglas Dunn, whose lyric sensibilities and commitment to normative syntax do not allow for the kind of radical questioning of the limits of representation itself which are key features of the postmodern artwork.[4] By contrast some, though certainly not all, of the contemporary poets included in *A Various Art* (1987), *The New British Poetry* (1988), *Conductors of Chaos* (1996) and the *Oxford Anthology of Twentieth-Century British and Irish Poetry* (2001) do have characteristics in common with the conceptual, formal and political possibilities of postmodernism as they have been emerging in other disciplines. This does not make them exempt from the all-pervasive effects of cultural marketeering and the attendant culpability associated with the postmodern. As Robert Hampson points out in relation to Ezra Pound's famous dictum, ' "Make It New" has to confront the fact that "the new" is also used to sell the latest car or weapons system.'[5]

Another distinction between contemporary poetries can be made between their different strategies of production and distribution: 'Unlike the *Penguin Anthology*, both *A Various Art* and *The New British Poetry* draw on a wealth of poetic production that was enabled in the 1960s and 1970s by cheapish mimeo and offset litho.'[6] Hampson's comment draws attention to the way in which some contemporary poets have continued to operate through networks of production and distribution which have different priorities than those of the dominant market forces. The possibilities of a particular type of postmodern poem in Britain can be seen to have resisted definition by the current 'socio-economic mode' at the same time as they have utilised its emerging technologies, i.e., cheaper and more widely available office reproduction equipment such as mimeo and photocopying machines, to make chapbooks and magazines. Craig Saper has coined the term 'intimate bureacracy' to describe such artist-led operations which 'appropriate the trappings of systems now common in big business' and 'perform processes, rituals and trappings of bureaucracies, but as alternatives to mass-media distribution networks'.[7] Despite this performative appropriation (which often occurs both in the making and writing of the work itself and in its modes of publication and distribution), many of these poets are keen to avoid the use of the term 'postmodernism', allied as it is with delusions of cultural capital and a culture industry which is intent on commodifying intellectual labour. In recent years the decision to call oneself 'neo-modernist', 'late modernist' as opposed to 'postmodernist' is a determined gesture on the part of some poets and critics to avoid the latest dominant cultural whim of the fashion market in ideas. Those poets whose work has most in common with postmodernism's conceptual and formal possibilities in other disciplines are least likely to want to apply the term 'postmodernism' to their work. As Peter Middleton argues, 'Maybe the difficulty that the term "postmodernism" raises is due to its readiness to supplant those other capacious names for our condition: imperialism, capitalism, and particularly consumerism.'[8]

Nevertheless, some of the aspects of postmodernism worth pursuing in relation to poetry include those conceptual and formal possibilities for the postmodern artwork outlined by Francois Lyotard in *The Postmodern Condition* (1979). A consideration of representation and its apparently inevitable 'impossibility' is fundamental to Lyotard's description of the tendencies of the postmodern artwork. In the work of many contemporary poets this translates into a particular approach to language itself; language is utilised not as an apparently transparent conduit for the emotions of the poet. Language has been shaped by and is shaping the social and political forces throughout our culture and this is the necessary subject of the postmodern poet who does not approach representation in language as pure and unmediated material: instead language becomes foregrounded as both the medium and the potential subject of poetry. As Richard Kerridge writes of the work of J. H. Prynne, 'Language is exposed as system, not inhabited as utterance.'[9] This is analogous with the postmodern move in the visual arts to produce work which acts like 'a dye in the bloodstream [...] to delineate the circulation system of art'.[10] For the poet, the actual language of the poem is the 'dye in the bloodstream' that highlights and diverts the routes of the everyday 'bloodstream' of communication and representation. This is similar to Charles Jencks's description of 'Post-Modernism' in architecture as 'double coding: the combination of Modern techniques with something else'.[11] In poetry this 'double coding' is at work in writers who draw attention to forms and genres and who recast them in contemporary settings; a more complex and endlessly refracting 'double-coding' occurs when poets foreground the coded nature of language itself and its saturated ideologies. This is the case in Drew Milne's *Go Figure* (2003):

> This imperium's eagle spreads ancient wings
> as the saying goes ahem friends Romans
> and globalists most dextrous ego-surfers
> of the remotest control say go figure
> let slip the bristling clusters and gas

from each harsh Doric column stabbed long
and hard into a ruin of sea and dimpled air
most cleaving indifference over physical
features that depict no political borders
lost upon spicy chicken wings as claws
do special resolutions in pink cartoons
nails down tankers the chalk on board thing
and the gas is all for oil, galley slave
of this grade class fellow-guzzling petrol[12]

The poem is more than 'double-coded' with a variety of registers:
Shakespeare (Mark Antony's speech on Caesar's death), the language of
the Internet and digital communications, the vocabulary of war and of
specific bombs and weapons used in Afghanistan and Iraq, classical architecture, globalism, fast-food, advertising, education, slavery, oil, flight and
quantification. In Milne's poem none of these codings is allowed to remain
fully intact and impermeable, each is bent and refracted to meet another
'double-coding' which proliferates at each intersection into further
contextual overlays before it can become fixed in anything as simple as
parody or quotation. The reader proceeds through recognition and continual readjustment of expectation as 'countrymen' become 'globalists',
'channel surfers' become 'ego-surfers' and political borders are lost. The
poem is at once a Disney-like cartoon of existence and also a diagrammatic-
cartoon; 'the chalk on board thing' of a landscape or a world-view from the
fractured perspective of a 'galley slave' or airline passenger, whose class
identity is determined by the 'grade' on his ticket rather than his social
background.

Lyotard describes the postmodern era as being characterised by a dis-
persal of 'clouds of narrative language elements' and within each cloud 'are
pragmatic valencies specific to its kind' and 'each of us lives at the intersection of many of these'.[13] This description is useful as a way to think
about reading elements of Drew Milne's *Go Figure* which sometimes
appear to be made up of 'clouds of narrative language elements' which have
been dispersed across a series of tightly controlled structures. The poem
offers us a 'pragmatics of language particles' which are to be negotiated as
the reader makes her way through its 'intersections'. For Lyotard it is
essential that the postmodern artwork occupy the space at the 'intersection
of the clouds' as an alternative to the usual structures of power and control:

> The decision makers, however, attempt to manage these clouds of sociality
> according to the input/output matrices, following a logic which implies that
> their elements are commensurable and that the whole is determinable.[14]

Go Figure is in direct conflict with the attempt to manage these 'clouds' with numbers. The logics of management are not commensurable with the linguistic project of the poem which is to resist the tyranny of statistics that seek to replace *figures* with 'figures'.

One of the defining features of the so-called postmodern era has been the academic rehabilitation of many of the different strands of Modernism which were initially passed over or actively lost from the official histories of the first part of the twentieth century. At the same time some recent accounts of postmodernity have been just as sceptical of the inclusion of poetry as poets have been of being termed postmodern. If postmodernism is 'a principled reaction to modernism', then the problem of situating British poetry in relation to the contexts of postmodernism has to confront the vexed question of the relationships contemporary poetry in Britain can be said to have to the formal innovations, politics and new subjectivities that Modernism produced.[15]

There are a number of positions which seem tenable. At first glance the *apparently* single and certainly dominant grand narrative account of post-war verse history sketched through successive anthologies such as *The Penguin Book of Contemporary Poetry* (1982) and *The Penguin Book of Poetry from Britain and Ireland Since 1945* (1998) might imply that con-temporary British poetry is in fact both *ante*-modern and *anti*-modernist. That is to say that, for the most part, the contemporary poets featured in these anthologies bypass the radical trajectory of possibilities offered by writers such as Hope Mirrlees, Ezra Pound, Mina Loy, David Jones, Hugh MacDiarmid and W. S. Graham, in favour of an extension of the dispiriting conservatism of the Movement poets whose roots lie in the poetry of Thomas Hardy and early W. B. Yeats.

The reaction of the Movement poets to the modernisms of the earlier century can certainly be read as a 'principled reaction to modernism' in that they wrote as if Modernism had never happened. Chronologically speaking the Movement poets of the 1950s *are* the postmodernists of twentieth-century poetry and perhaps in them we have the postmodernism we deserve. Edward Lucie-Smith writes somewhat regretfully in 1985, in the revised introduction to his anthology *British Poetry Since 1945*, that:

> In general ... it must be said that the full reconciliation between the mod-
> ernist spirit and British poetry which I looked forward to in 1970 has yet to
> take place. The most discussed new poets, often brilliantly accomplished
> within the fairly strict limits they have chosen for themselves, are often not
> only conservatives, but ones bold enough to flaunt their own conservatism.
> Indeed, they seem to look upon a declared hostility to modernism as being in

itself a form of innovation – which perhaps, taken in the broader context, it actually is.[16]

Rather than innovations of form, the 1950s produced innovative hostilities to Modernism which have been maintained in official verse culture to the present, and this necessarily has implications for how it becomes possible to draw a map of a possible postmodern poetics.

In contrast to the Movement, increasingly it has become the task of the contemporary poet and critic to approach Anglo-American Modernism as the 'cultural construction around selective aesthetic and ideological values, and not as a thing in itself'.[17] The reinterpretation of this 'cultural construction' opens new paths of conceptualisation between the early twentieth century and the twenty-first century. Similarly, the relationship between both what Brooker calls 'hegemonic modernism' and the twentieth-century's avant-garde is essential to consider if the postmodern poem is to be read as more than a by-product of capitalism, or what Drew Milne calls 'the hot air balloon debates of postmodernism', in which 'Madonna and Public Enemy fight it out for critical attention'.[18] This suturing of a previous century's avant-garde onto the consideration of contemporary writing clearly throws up problems of terminology for Lyotard in the naming of the postmodern art work:

> I do not like the term avant-garde, with its military connotations, any more than anyone else. But I do observe that the true process of avant-gardism was in reality a kind of work, a long obstinate and highly responsible work concerned with investigating the assumptions implicit in modernity.[19]

Lyotard's description connects the ethical responsibilities of the avant-garde with that of the postmodern poet and it aligns the potential of the postmodern poem with a practice of writing bent on 'investigating the assumptions implicit in modernity' which does not situate itself beyond the possibility that it will be complicit with the very fabric of the cultural ideologies which it seeks to unfix.

To emphasise the continuities with Modernism, Rod Mengham (*Vanishing* xvii) and Drew Milne use the terms 'late Modernist' and 'Neomodernist Avant-Garde' respectively to describe poetry which, because of its formal characteristics, might in other discussions of contemporary art forms be termed 'postmodern'. This alternative terminology, employed to uphold the links between contemporary British poetry and radical or avant-garde modernist writings, forcibly rejects a connection to the Movement poets and their successors whose verse can be characterised as 'a closed, monolineal utterance, demanding little of the reader but passive consumption'.[20] By contrast many of the formal strategies of the 'late modernist' and 'Neo-Modernist avant-garde' poem – lack of closure, narrative redistribution, use of procedural methodologies of writing, fragmentation and proliferation of the lyric subject, use of found material, a demand for the active engagement of the reader and so on – are clearly to be found in the work of British Modernists such as Hope Mirrlees, Basil Bunting, David Jones, Mina Loy and W. S. Graham. Nevertheless, the danger of such strategies of extended recuperation is that they might be seen as merely a 'carrying-on, in somewhat diluted form, of the avant-garde project that had been at the very heart of early modernism' rather than presenting new directions for contemporary work which breaks with previous traditions.[21] This recuperation is more than this as it offers a new space for the contextualisation of contemporary work which highlights the innovative and the experimental use of form and procedure as central to the history of poetry and poetics in the twentieth and twenty-first century.

Ironically, this history is itself a series of what Lyotard would term 'postmodern micronarratives' which are partial and fractured and emerge from many different *modernisms*. These micronarratives are themselves in flux and are constantly being reshaped according to the constant critical reshaping of modernism. According to Lyotard, 'the "post-" of "postmodern" does not signify a movement of *comeback, flashback* or *feedback*, that is, not a movement of repetition but a procedure in "ana-": a procedure of analysis, anamnesis, anagogy and anamorphosis which elaborates an "initial forgetting"'.[22]

Modernism is certainly not the only context for considering a 'postmodern' poetry. Eric Mottram termed the period between 1960 and 1975 'The British Poetry Revival' because so many magazines, presses and publications flourished in Britain at this time. Wendy Mulford, poet and publisher, whose work emerged from a generation of writers who came to prominence in the UK in the late 1970s and early 1980s, describes the direction of influence on her and her contemporaries as involving a 'search [which] took them to the theoretical considerations about language welling up in Europe, and back to the USA'.[23] One of the important contexts for the development of postmodern poetry was the rediscovery of European Modernism as mediated by the US Modernist tradition. Donald Allen's ground-breaking anthology *The New Poetry, 1945–1960* (1960) introduced new American and British readers to the late Modernist poetry of the Black Mountain, New York and San Francisco schools. Later UK magazines such as *Reality Studios, Spectacular Diseases, Archeus* and *fragmente* were crucial in facilitating the ongoing 'transatlantic shuffle' in late Modernist poetry.[24] Fulcrum Press published work by Modernist writers such as Basil Bunting and George Oppen and introduced a British audience to poets such as Ed Dorn and Robert Duncan. It also published British poets such as Tom Raworth and Lee Harwood so as to emphasise a parity of concerns between poetry in the United States and Britain. The readers of such magazines also absorbed the influences of Black Mountain, the Beats, the New York School and the ideas and techniques of writers associated with the magazine $L = A = N = G = U = A = G = E$ (1978–1982).

There is certainly an eclecticism of influence in British postmodern poetries that shows a merging of high and low culture, of previous and contemporary styles from 'open field, projective verse, sound text, concrete poetry, surrealist and dada developments, pop lyrics, and various conceptual forms'.[25] Contemporary poets such as Denise Riley are involved in a play of identification and subversion of many of the forms and traditions of poetry. Riley offers a reworking and reconsideration, rather than an absolute rejection, of poetic conventions such as the lyric subject. This is seen in 'Wherever You Are, Be Somewhere Else', which presents an intertextual fabric of echoes and allusions embedded at various depths within the poem, recycling lines from Scottish ballads and *The Peach Blossom Fan* by K'ung Shang-jen. The poem juxtaposes the conventional idea of the function of poetry as a form of lyric transport out of the everyday with the potential escapism of a computer game; both are inhabited by the poet and found to be wanting. There is no hierarchical distinction made between the solace of the lyric poem and that of the computer game, and the boundaries between each mode of escapism are blurred by the interchangable role of the computer as a games console and an instrument for writing lyric poetry. The technologised mediation of subjectivity is foregrounded in both poem and game. In keeping with this the poem simultaneously describes both its own construction and that of its lyric subject in the first verse as:

> A body shot through, perforated, a tin sheet
> beaten out then peppered with thin holes,
> silvery, leaf-curled at their edges; light flies
>
> right through this tracery, voices leap, slip side-
> long, all faces split to angled facets: whichever
> piece is glimpsed, that bit is what I am, held
>
> in a look until dropped like an egg on the floor
> let slop, crashed to slide and run, yolk yellow
> for the live, the dead who worked through me.[26]

This is an uneasy affirmation of the lyric voice foregrounded alongside the fact of its own constructed nature which is as 'artificially made' as the poem itself: 'a tin sheet / beaten out then peppered with thin holes' and a 'tracery' through which 'voices leap'. The hybridity of this lyric voice is emphasised by the title of the poem which echoes a Nintendo *Game Boy* slogan. The artificial is not simply confined to the allusions to technology, it also relates to the language registers of the poem itself. Lines 10–27 outline a nightmare vision of eggs cracking open to reveal snakes, a near-suicidal leap over a glacier and a blinded and gagged lyric speaker who is terrified of 'being left' alone. This, it seems, is just an illusion, akin to the unfolding narrative on a *Game Boy* that has been worked up by the poet:

> I can try on these gothic riffs, they do make
> a black twitchy cloak to both ham up and so
> perversely dignify my usual fear of ends

Riley is trying on various guises offered to the lyric subject, hamming it up without identifying with any single subject position or discourse: 'a million surfaces without a tongue and I never have wanted / "a voice" anyway, nor got it. Alright'. As Lyotard points out, the postmodern writer positions herself outside the possibility of an identification with one 'Voice'; instead she writes to undo any such certainty: 'One writes against language but not necessarily with it. To say what it already knows how to say is not writing.'[27] Riley expresses a desire for the self-expression of the lyric 'I' at the same time as she recognises that this is a nostalgic reaching after a simulacra of authenticity which she knows to be illusory: 'so I go to the wordprocessor longing for line cables / to loop out of the machine straight to my head'. Language does not loop out of her head in natural waves; there is no binary split between a 'natural' voice of poetry and an 'unnatural' medium of technology. Both seem to offer modes of speaking or writing but each represents its own barrier or interface, however negotiable, between subject and the world that cannot be taken for granted. This is very different from a poem which 'assumes' that it 'is the record of an "I" speaking its loves and losses' directly and transparently to the reader, which, as Peter Middleton says, is 'a self untouched by postmodernism'.[28]

Another strand of poetic production in Britain, characterised by the very different work of Allen Fisher, Bob Cobbing and cris cheek is one which foregrounds process and procedure in the making of the work. This emphasis has some similarities to the pataphysical writings of the French Oulipo group but the work of these British poets is less explicit rule-based and is more likely to derive its dynamic from the repetition, translation and transformation of various sonic, semantic or visual characteristics of an initial text.

Fisher's main works include two poem sequences that have been published serially as chapbooks and pamphlets since the 1970s and recently collected as *Place* (2005) and *Gravity* (2005). *Place* moves through London on various experiential and textual levels. In his introduction Fisher describes his mode of composition as both 'process and process-showing', an approach which he has developed out of a methodological synthesis of the 'open field' poetics of Charles Olson with the process-showing systematic procedures of Jackson Mac Low. Mac Low often prefaces his poem sequences with an account of the steps he has taken to make a poem. Fisher does not include such details but often the actions that have been performed on the text become apparent through patterns of sonic or visual repetition in the reading of the poem. Like Mac Low, Fisher includes a list of the source materials that he has consulted and used within each poem. These are not so much a reading list that has to be followed to understand the poem but more like a demarcation of the textual field.

Like Olson, Fisher uses the page visually, incorporates found materials and uses a process-based poetics that has similarities to Olson's 'FIELD COMPOSITION' poetics as outlined in 'Projective Verse'. In this well-known manifesto Olson calls for a move away from a poetry based on the individual ego of the poet, what he calls 'the private-soul-at-any-public-wall' which produces a 'closed verse'. He sees the poem as 'a high energy-construct' and 'at all points, an energy discharge' which is mediated between poet and reader.[29] Similarly, Fisher's poems demonstrate an interest in the physics of conducted energy between different substances. This also becomes an analogy for reading and writing. In 'SECOND RELEASE Homage to Charles Olson', Fisher writes:

> Your place is this moving field of resources
> around a war of the intellect
> that is exuberant and not aggressive
> a dance preceding mechanics knowing rest in kinesis
> 'how to act fiercely but, with dignity'
> not centred but craving to continue, speaking
> getting at matters that way learning
> how to alert hearing in intense extempores
> that continually reshape the going moves.[30]

Fisher's own practice has much in common with what he identifies in Olson here as being a strategy of writing which balances out apparently opposing impulses towards a fixing and an unfixing of meaning in 'a war of the intellect', or between the 'preceding mechanics' of poetic form and the 'dance' or energy of the poem which manifests itself in a process of writing which generates its own logics of continuation and proliferation. Similarly the 'hearing' and attention of the poet is directed through writing even as it remains open to all possibilities, 'in intense extempores', of risk and chance encounter which might deflect the poem from its apparent subject. Important for both Fisher and Olson is the way in which the writing and reading process can keep in play 'this moving field of resources' that is 'continually' reshaping itself through the negotiation of this dynamic.

This stress on motility and fluidity in both Olson and Fisher might usefully be considered in relation to the distinction that Roland Barthes makes between 'work' and 'text'; Barthes differentiates between the tangible and physical quality of 'the work' as it appears as 'a fragment of substance' in books and libraries and the text which is experienced as 'a methodological field', 'a process of demonstration' or through 'an activity of production'.[31] Fisher's *Place* would seem to be studded with fragments of works (local history, science, literature, philosophy and music) that have been activated in a methodological field of encounter which blurs the distinction between the activities of reading and writing. *Place* can be approached as a 'text-between' of many others which must be *set going* by the reader rather than consumed.

Place was being planned and written at the same time as Fisher was involved in the development of *Fluxus* in Britain during the 1970s; Fisher's poetics are allied to the redefinition of visual arts practice which 'dematerialised' the art object. Art objects were replaced with language, diagrams, ephemeral propositions, performance. In *The Topological Shovel* Fisher describes how 'art as objects and poetry as poems' have 'gradually lost credibility', to be replaced by 'many attentions of activity' that are 'process' and 'idea-oriented'.[32] This redistribution of 'attentions of activity' is central to any consideration of the political possibilities of a contemporary poetry. It also clearly stands at odds with a poetry which marks accessible vocabulary and easily assimilable thematic content as necessarily democratic and inclusive to the exclusion of all other forms of writing. The reaching after these 'attentions of activity' might have the effect of transforming the poem utterly away from known poetic conventions; from 'poetry as poems'.

Lyotard characterises a postmodern artist or writer as one who produces a text that cannot be judged by 'the application of given categories'. Like Allen Fisher, who has also made work in performance and the visual arts as well as poetry, a growing number of practitioners are producing work at the interstices of disciplinary boundaries, often between the visual arts and writing in bookarts, installation, digital poetics, live-art and performance. These practitioners are engaged in what Lyotard terms the investigation into 'rules and categories' of the contexts and sites of their textual practice and often their work moves in various manifestations between the gallery and the page. Practitioners in this mode include Susan Johanknecht, Brian Catling, Caroline Bergvall, John Cayley and cris cheek.

Susan Johanknecht's *Modern (Laundry) Production* (2001) is a striking example of a bookart that also functions as a sculptural installation. In bookarts the physical form and the linguistic content of the book are often read simultaneously. Johanknecht's book is a double-sided concertina-folded sheet of paper that comes in a slip case. The poem utilises found images and text from 1940s manuals and accounts of laundry production in combination with Donna Haraway's 'A Manifesto for Cyborgs: Science, Technology, and Socialist Feminism for the 1980s' (1985). When it is unfolded horizontally it is long enough to be held between the fully out-stretched arms of the reader, but in order to read the text of the bookwork the reader must feed it vertically through her hands, an action which, as the reading progresses, begins to echo the actions of a laundry worker feeding sheets through an industrial press. The book has also been shown as part of gallery installations: in this context it hangs from the ceiling and is situated alongside a video monitor showing slides of cropped images of the laundresses at work. Through the reader's physical interaction with *Modern (Laundry) Production* a wry comparison is invited between the performance of reading and the performance of the role of the laundress in an increasingly industrialised and dehumanising environment.

We are now, according to Alan Gilbert, in the 'twilight' of a postmodern era, in which grand narratives such as 'economic realm market fundamentalism' reassert themselves.[33] Some poets, eager for assimilation, have been co-opted into service by the cultural-*lite* demands of the postmodern high street, while others prefer to maintain a foothold in alternative modes of production and networks of distribution which have been recently facilitated by the Internet and by the development of new technologies of printing and production. Although it seems inevitable that poetry cannot possibly stand in isolation from the emerging new economies of labour, leisure and consumption of which it too is a part, it does appear necessary to distinguish between a postmodern poetics which actively resists the commodification of culture, and a poetry that is being branded with terms such as 'postmodernism' for ease of marketability, a term which is often in the 'postmodern era' wrongly made synonymous with accessibility. The work of Milne, Riley, Fisher and Johanknecht reaches out of the autonomous niche afforded to poetry by closely guarded disciplinary and nationally constituted boundaries. Each writer foregrounds practices and methodologies of writing which demonstrate an awareness of and a refusal to capitulate to the commodification of the cultural, conceptual and formal possibilities of the 'postmodern'. Their work makes links back to a previous century's avant-garde while it remains radically engaged with the possibilities and inevitable contradictions inherent in the negotiation and formulation of a poetry and poetics of the present.

NOTES

1 Nigel Wheale (ed.), *The Postmodern Arts: An Introductory Reader* (London and New York: Routledge, 2005), p. 14.
2 Michael Hulse, David Kennedy and David Morley (eds.), *The New Poetry* (Newcastle upon Tyne: Bloodaxe, 1993), p. 16.
3 Blake Morrison and Andrew Motion (eds.), *The Penguin Book of Contemporary British Poetry* (Harmondsworth: Penguin, 1982), p. 20.
4 Ian Gregson, *Contemporary Poetry and Postmodernism: Dialogue and Estrangement* (London: Macmillan, 1996), p. 209.
5 Robert Hampson and Peter Barry (eds.) *New British Poetries: The Scope of the Possible* (Manchester: Manchester University Press, 1993), p. 134.
6 Hampson and Barry (eds.), *New British Poetries*, p. 5.
7 Craig Saper, *Networked Art* (Minneapolis: University of Minnesota Press, 2001), p. 16.
8 Peter Middleton, *Distant Reading: Performance, Readership and Consumption in Contemporary Poetry* (Tuscaloosa: University of Alabama Press, 2005), p. 201.
9 Richard Kerridge and N. H. Reeve, *Nearly Too Much: The Poetry of J. H. Prynne* (Liverpool: Liverpool University Press, 1995), p. 109.
10 Hal Foster, 'Subversive Signs', in Lawrence E. Cahoone (ed.), *From Modernism to Postmodernism* (Oxford: Blackwell, 2003), p. 313.
11 Charles Jencks, *What is Post-Modernism?* (New York: St Martin's Press, 1987), p. 14.
12 Drew Milne, *Go Figure* (Cambridge: Salt, 2003), p. 4.
13 Jean-Francois Lyotard, *The Postmodern Condition: A Report on Knowledge* (Manchester: Manchester University Press, 1984), p. xxiv.
14 *Ibid.*
15 Stuart Sim (ed.), *The Routledge Companion to Postmodernism* (London and New York: Routledge, 2005), p. x.
16 Edward Lucie-Smith (ed.), *British Poetry Since 1945* (Harmondsworth: Penguin, 1985), pp. 24–5.
17 Peter Brooker, 'Postmodern Postpoetry: Tom Raworth's "Tottering State"', in Anthony Easthope and John O. Thompson (eds.), *Contemporary Poetry Meets Modern Theory* (London: Harvester Wheatsheaf, 1991), p. 154.
18 Drew Milne, 'Agoraphobia, and the Embarrassment of Manifestos: Notes towards a Community of Risk', *Parataxis: Modernism and Modern Writing*, 3 (Spring 1993), 28.
19 Lyotard, *The Postmodern Condition*, p. 93.
20 Richard Caddel and Peter Quatermain (eds.), *Other: British and Irish Poetry Since 1970* (Middletown, Conn.: Wesleyan University Press, 1999), p. xv.
21 Marjorie Perloff, *21st-Century Modernism: The 'New Poetics'* (Oxford: Blackwell, 2002), p. 3.

22 Jean-Francois Lyotard, *The Postmodern Explained to Children: Correspondence 1982–1985* (Sydney: Power Publications, 1992), p. 93.
23 Wendy Mulford, 'Curved, Odd ... Irregular': A Vision of Contemporary Poetry by Women', *Women: A Cultural Review*, 1, 3 (Winter 1990), 263.
24 Geoff Ward, *Statutes of Liberty: The New York School of Poets* (Basingstoke: Palgrave, 2001), p. 186.
25 Hampson and Barry (eds.), *New British Poetries*, p. 16.
26 Denise Riley, *Selected Poems* (London: Reality Street, 2000), p. 47.
27 Lyotard, *The Postmodern Explained*, p. 105.
28 Peter Middleton, 'Who Am I to Speak? The Politics of Subjectivity in Recent British Poetry', in Hampson and Barry (eds.), *New British Poetries*, p. 119.
29 Quotations from Charles Olson, *Selected Writings*, ed. Robert Creeley (New York: New Directions, 1966).
30 Allen Fisher, *Place* (Hastings: Reality Street, 2005), p. 398.
31 Roland Barthes, *Image, Music, Text*, ed. Stephen Heath (London: Fontana, 1982), pp. 157, 163.
32 Allen Fisher, *The Topological Shovel* (Ontario: The Gig, 1999), p. 6.
33 Sim (ed.), *The Routledge Companion to Postmodernism*, p. xi.

Further reading

Caddel, R., and P. Quatermain (eds.), *Other: British and Irish Poetry Since 1970*, Middletown, Conn.: Wesleyan University Press, 1999
Hampson, R., and P. Barry (eds.) *New British Poetries: The Scope of the Possible*, Manchester: Manchester University Press, 1993
Mengham, R., and J. Kinsella (eds.), *Vanishing Points: New Modernist Poems*, Cambridge: Salt, 2004
Middleton, P., *Distant Reading: Performance, Readership, and Consumption in Contemporary Poetry*, Tuscaloosa: University of Alabama Press, 2005
Tuma, Keith (ed.), *Anthology of Twentieth-Century British and Irish Poetry*, New York: Oxford University Press, 2001
Wheale, N. (ed.), *The Postmodern Arts: An Introductory Reader*, London: Routledge, 1995

PART TWO

Moderns

4

PETER HOWARTH

Fateful forms: A. E. Housman, Charlotte Mew, Thomas Hardy and Edward Thomas

In their formally patterned styles and rural sympathies, the poets in this chapter are usually understood as a more traditional alternative to the metropolitan Modernism of Eliot and Pound. But rather than judge poetry on a scale of progression, it is perhaps more illuminating to ask what those styles enabled each poet to say which could not be said in the Modernists' freer or more fragmented forms. Each poet deals with division and constraint, in some way, whether it is the sense of despairing Fate for Hardy and Housman, or the mind's own differences from itself in Mew and Thomas. Each, too, ironises conventions of rural idyll to express their sense of being haplessly at odds with the social world. As such, they have been as powerful an influence on post-1950 British poetry as the Modernists, who for their part generally respected this distinctive poetry when they knew it. If Pound could name Hardy one of his greatest influences, then it should be possible to explore why this poetry, too, has its meaning and moment in the upheavals and uncertainties of the twentieth century.[1]

Fastidious, venomously critical and glacially silent to all but a few, A. E. Housman (1859–1936) was no one's idea of a hedonist. But this is what he called himself late in life, when he seems to have thawed enough to think it worthwhile patiently correcting for posterity a young American correspondent, Houston Martin, who had called his verse the work of a Stoic pessimist:

> In philosophy I am a Cyrenaic or egoistic hedonist, and regard the pleasure of the moment as the only possible motive of action. As for pessimism, I think it almost as silly, though not as wicked, as optimism. George Eliot said she was a meliorist; I am a pejorist, and also yours sincerely A. E. HOUSMAN.[2]

Despite Housman's tone of mild outrage, it is not hard to see why Martin was misled. In Housman's world of moonlit prisons, unlucky lads and soldiers in foreign graves, life is unhappy and unamendable, with only the comfortless consolation that present pain will end in death sooner or later. The frightened soldier of *A Shropshire Lad* (hereafter *ASL*) LVI is advised 'take the bullet in your brain' now, rather than be shot for cowardice in the future, and the troubled speaker of 'On Wenlock Edge' knows he and his problems will be 'ashes under Uricon' with his Roman forebear by tomorrow (*ASL* XXXI). As some guessed during his lifetime, one of the chief sources for this astringent disappointment was Housman's thwarted sexuality, both his hopeless, single-minded passion for his undergraduate friend Moses Jackson, and his wider feeling, as his brother put it, that the 'inhibition imposed by society on his fellow-victims' was 'both cruel and unjust ... having not more power of choice in the matter than a man has about the colour of his hair'.[3] Housman translated his sense of the world's pitiless injustice into a Shropshire where the same fateful end awaits both criminal and victim, faithful and faithless lover, and in whose graves all men will lie with other men sooner or later (*ASL* XII). Its unchanging rural landscape is the sign not of pastoral solace but a place where choices make little difference, and Housman's beautifully engineered formal technique guarantees the inevitability of the poem's unhappiness.

Housman was nothing if not precise, though, and his donnish insistence on 'Cyrenaic' needs to be taken seriously to appreciate the ironies of his position. The diverse ethical doctrines of the Cyrenaics drew on a common epistemology where the only things we really know are subjective sensations. Since these are unique to the individual, the logical goal should be to seek as much momentary pleasure as is consistent with perfect self-mastery, rather than practice Stoic virtues of endurance, public reason and compassion. The Cyrenaics sought the individual pleasure of the moment as the only knowable good, though some with more delayed gratification than others; one, Theodorus, was banned from Athens for deploring the gods and preaching situational ethics; another, Hegesias, was accused of encouraging his audience to commit suicide, since he argued that suffering was endemic to body and soul and the only goal was to live without pain.[4] All of these are attitudes with which Housman's poems sympathise, whether he is hating 'whatever brute and blackguard made the world' and its rules (*Last Poems* (hereafter *LP*) IX), sternly imploring someone to live for the present ('Think no more, lad; laugh, be jolly: / Why should men make haste to die?') (*ASL* XLIX) or equally sincerely, to forget it all:

> 'Lie down, lie down, young yeoman;
> The sun moves always west;
> The road one treads to labour

Will lead one home to rest,
And that will be the best.'   (*ASL* VII)

The contradiction between poems which urge you to 'be drunk for ever /
With liquor, love, or fights' (*LP* X) and the poems which long for the peace of
death makes Housman appear philosophically incoherent. But what
underlies both types of poem is his passionate desire for a state without any
anxious self-division, and like the Cyrenaics, Housman got into trouble for
railing against the external interferences which prevented such integrity. In
poetry, he deplored the 'foreign laws of God and man' (*LP* XII) which
imposed tyranically on his privacy. In his literary criticism, he castigated
eighteenth- or nineteenth-century verse which imposed its mechanical,
intellectualised or moralised forms on its material, making its poets 'captives
singing hymns in the prison chapel'. Poetry, like people, was ideally 'pure and
self-existent'.[5]

When Housman came to summarise these ideas in 'The Name and Nature
of Poetry' in 1933, his conclusion that true poetry was therefore simple,
'unaccountable', and not of the intellect was welcomed as the plain truth by
the self-appointed Georgian ruralist, J. C. Squire, and deplored as dangerously naive by his Eliot-supporting enemies, Richards and Leavis.[6] But in the
controversy, the ironies of Housman's hedonistic, homoerotic subtext went
unnoticed. Housman's litmus tests for poetry are private and bodily; it
comes from somewhere uncultivated, 'obscure and latent', it makes his body
tremble, prickle and shiver, and he feels a sensation which, as Keats says of
Fanny Brawne, ' "goes through me like a spear" '.[7] The effect is to align
poetry's name and nature with anarchic sexual desire rather than the processes of thought or reflection. Such a definition of poetry is not only a
sophisticated echo of Cyrenaic doctrine, but, closer to home, a literalisation
of Walter Pater's definition of art as purely individual sensation in his
infamous 'Conclusion' to *The Renaissance*, a text of huge importance to
Wilde and the homophilic decadent movement. To be sure, Housman's
idiom is very different from theirs, and his star rose with the Edwardian-
Georgian enthusiasm for the simple life and fell with the Orwell generation's
dislike of its false simplicity. Yet both Pater and Housman were interested in
defining art not by what it represents, but in terms of one's immediate
experience of it. Both consequently make the aesthetic a subjective, non-
discursive sensation, so intense one will 'hardly have time to make theories'
(Pater) since it 'leaves no room in me for anything besides' (Housman).[8] And
both were attempting to claim the aesthetic was 'unaccountable' to public
standards of truth or morality in order to make art a space where homoerotic sensuality would be as permissible as any other sort.

But the problem with privatising poetry like this is that while Housman preserves a pleasure free from public censorship, he also trivialises his most deeply felt emotions. Housman reserved public morality for his textual scholarship, launching relentless salvos at rivals who failed to 'repress self-will' and amended texts on the basis of 'the literary mind', with its 'facile emotions and its incapacity for self-examination'.[9] By implication, poetry is self-indulgent play or mere style, 'a tone of the voice, a particular way of saying things'.[10] Yet if so, what it talks about is of no matter, whether it is the deepest sexual desire or the suffering that results from its disappointment. As Housman once wrote to Gilbert Murray, with disarming equanimity:

> When man gets rid of a great trouble he is easier for a little while, but not for long: Nature instantly sets to work to weaken his power of sustaining trouble, and very soon seven pounds is as heavy as fourteen pounds used to be ... it looks to me as if the state of mankind always had been and always would be a state of just tolerable discomfort.[11]

If subjective misery is unrelated to objective circumstances, then Housman's deepest unhappiness, too, may be equally self-sustaining and objectively trivial. And Housman knew this: the insight of Auden's line that Housman 'kept tears like dirty postcards in a drawer', lies in insinuating not just that he kept his sadness hidden, but that he drew it out to indulge lovingly in private.[12] Housman was as much a connoisseur of misery as Pater was of sensation, and this gives his poetry its peculiar mixture of intense personal sadness, a self-conscious sense of its unimportance and a certain satisfaction in knowing so. *ASL* LX, for instance, counsels the lonely soldier not to fear by saying that 'in all the endless road you tread / There's nothing but the night', which resolutely compresses a peaceful acceptance of death and savage despair into one another. A confession of love may be too devastating to contemplate, or it may be just mutual narcissism:

> Look not in my eyes, for fear
> They mirror true the sight I see,
> And there you find your face too clear
> And love it and be lost like me.   (*ASL* XV)

It is not only that the beloved might see how dangerously important he is to the speaker by seeing himself reflected in the latter's gaze; 'the sight I see' might equally be the speaker's own face reflected in the beloved's eyes, gazing lovingly on himself. The same blend of satisfaction and self-scorn is evident in Housman's blasphemous attacks on Christianity, too, since the more successful they are in demonstrating the wickedness of God, the more ruthlessly they ironise his own self-aggrandising melancholy in using divine epithets for himself, as when a lover describes his misery as 'world without end' (*ASL* XIV) or sneers at the sexually untroubled 'men whose thoughts are not as mine' (LI).

It is not difficult to de-code Housman's interest in faithless ploughboys, criminals and soldiers, the emblems of all-male comradeship and breakers of heterosexual relationships, powerless to escape their own death and therefore free for encounters without consequence. Like his poetry, Housman's sexuality is a 'secretion', in the sense of a secret which cannot help working its way out everywhere.[13] But sex was not the only source of his unhappiness; the great crisis of 1894–5 which produced so many poems was not only prompted by the shock of Jackson's marriage or Oscar Wilde's trial, but of his father's death and the failure of fourteen years of scholarly work on Propertius. Housman compresses a feeling of being cruelly bereft into the general rules for his emotional Shropshire, so that the only sense of companionship possible is between the dead, or with anonymous unlucky lads whose trouble he cannot know, as they cannot know his (*LP* II). The cadet who shoots himself to save others from homosexual 'disgrace' is crowned with a wreath, as if he were a war hero (*ASL* XLIV). Housman's bitterest irony is that in a hostile world, isolation is the only possible kind of faithfulness.

The work of Housman's less famous contemporary, Charlotte Mew (1869–1928), also stands on its own, since no one has ever found a satisfactory literary label for her. Angela Leighton introduced her as the last Victorian poet, struggling to break free of social and sexual propriety, while others have insisted that her characters' fractured monologues and her appearance in *The Egoist* mean she must be a type of Modernist.[14] Her prose work was first published with the *Yellow Book*, associated with 1890s decadence and the sexual independence of the New Woman; her first and most important poetry collection, *The Farmer's Bride*, however, came out twenty-six years later with Harold Monro's Georgian-friendly Poetry Bookshop. Neither can she be classified according to her admirers, poets as diverse as Thomas Hardy, Ezra Pound, Walter de la Mare and Marianne Moore, or her most characteristic verse form. Metrical passages give way to free-verse lines of enormously varying lengths which come in fits and starts with the outbursts of her speaker's emotion, but are rhymed so insistently that they give the effect of simultaneous self-containment, as if the poem were talking to itself in stifled paranoia:

> Red is the strangest pain to bear;
> In Spring the leaves on the budding trees;
> In Summer the roses are worse than these,

> More terrible than they are sweet:
> A rose can stab you across the street
>   Deeper than any knife:
> And the crimson haunts you everywhere –
> Thin shafts of sunlight, like the ghosts of reddened swords have
>   struck our stair
> As if, coming down, you had spilt your life.

('The Quiet House')

Sensuality and mortification are often linked in Mew's poems, probably because her own desires, like Housman's, were publically inadmissible. Although the primary evidence for her lesbianism is skimpy, turning mostly on second-hand stories of a failed proposition to May Sinclair and rumours of belated recognition by her friends, it would fit with what we know of her penchant for cross-gendered clothing and her extreme biographical reticence.[15] Unlike the celebratory 'Sapphism' of her wealthy contemporaries H. D. or Natalie Barney, Mew's poems are often about the fear of self-revelation, so that in 'Saturday Market' and 'The Forest Road', the metaphor of 'giving your heart' to someone is gruesomely literalised as a bloody disembowelment. Those poems which do imagine love or sex tend to see it in a wistful afterlife or in a nightmarish death; her obsession with loose hair, in particular, draws simulaneously on the Victorian codes of hair as a symbol of sex (the uncovered bride or the prostitute), and of living death, that part of us which survives as our body rots.

This sense of fear, however, does not make Mew's poetry any less queer, both in the older sense of strange or disturbing, and in the newer of working to unsettle identificatory sexual categories. Her most powerful pieces are disturbing *cris de coeur* from figures at the borders of normality: fairy changelings or prostitutes, the hysterical, haunted and insane. But rather than coding a secret identity in these excluded figures, the poems' interest lies more in imaginatively dissolving the borders which keep them excluded.[16] In her most famous poem, 'The Farmer's Bride', for instance, the sympathy appears to be all with the young, captive bride who shrinks from her husband for three years, preferring the company of children and animals. But in the last stanza, he suddenly bursts out:

> She sleeps up in the attic there
>   Alone, poor maid. 'Tis but a stair
> Betwixt us. Oh! my God! the down,
> The soft young down of her, the brown,
> The brown of her – her eyes, her hair, her hair!

Veering between expressing the farmer's desire for his marital rights and fearful pity for the bride as a timid, rabbit-like creature, the poem empathises both with women who shrink from men, and with those who passionately desire women, and fear being repulsed. Like 'The Changeling', whose speaker is half fairy, half child, 'The Asylum Road' is a poem about being on both sides. It describes an encounter with a sad group of asylum inmates who cannot respond to the jokes and smiles of the townspeople who see them. Despite being let out of their hospital of 'darkly stained or coloured glass', their mental windows still allow little outside light in. Yet in their noisy human cheerfulness, the sane are shown to be similarly locked into their own world, drowning out the natural life around them, and by the end of the poem, it is not clear who 'we' or 'they' are, any longer:

> The gayest crowd that they will ever pass
> Are we to brother-shadows in the lane:
> Our windows, too, are clouded glass
> To them, yes, every pane!

Insanity was a deeply personal topic for Mew, whose brother and sister were confined to an asylum, and she had the agreement of the family not to marry in case hereditary taint was passed on, as the eugenicists were teaching it would be. This may have suited her in one way, of course, but in another it only confirmed her sense of being on both sides of the sane/insane division; as Jessica Walsh remarks, 'lesbianism in Mew's time was considered by most medical professionals to be a mental illness, not a subversive lifestyle'.[17] In 'Ken', the speaker is guilt-stricken for allowing the harmless, childlike Ken, who went to church to 'see the lights', to be incarcerated for having immobile fits and shrieking 'take it away' at the crucifix:

> So, when they took
> Ken to that place, I did not look
> After he called and turned on me
> His eyes. These I shall see –

The poem breaks off, as if the speaker is choked, silenced and staring like Ken, who has also been taken away and rendered immobile by a world which claims to worship the figure pinned on the crucifix. The sane, it is implied, are simply re-enacting what Ken did in his madness. In 'Le Sacré-Coeur', too, the boundaries between sin and redemption are confused, as the speaker looks down from the basilica at the blazing lights of Paris and thinks of the city as a prostitute. But the waiting Christ in the church above is described as 'the Man who bought you first', as if repentance, marriage and prostitution were ultimately part of the same economy.

In person, Mew lived a restricted domestic life looking after her mother and sweet-natured sister, her masculine suits and incessant smoking two of the few small signs of a life not entirely sacrificed to feminine propriety. But if Marjorie Garber is right that cross-dressing is always a cultural signal of a 'category crisis elsewhere', then Mew's poems and her wardrobe were both part of an imaginative life in which the socially defined oppositions that split her own life – between women and men, sane and mad, spirituality and sex – are continually undermined.[18]

Thomas Hardy (1840–1928) so admired one of Mew's later poems, 'Fin de Fête' that he copied it out long-hand, where it was found amongst his closest possessions after his death. It describes the Babes in the Wood sleeping under the leaves the birds have laid for them:

> So you and I should have slept, – But now,
> Oh, what a lonely head!
> With just the shadow of a waving bough
> In the moonlight over your bed.

Mew's first biographer thought this evidence of a coded affair, but it is much more likely that in its regretful ambiguity of address – is the 'you' simply sleeping alone, or dead? – Hardy saw a poem he might have written about his first wife Emma. Hardy had been writing his unique poems for as long as he had been writing novels, but by general consent, his finest work came from the delayed shock of Emma's death in 1912, after their early passion had soured into years of hostility, resentment, sleeping apart and not speaking. Only after she died could Hardy voice his feelings to her, and the poems resonate with the tones of an on-going domestic argument as much as anguished regret.[19] 'The Going' opens with a plaintive, resentful question:

> Why did you give no hint that night
> That quickly after the morrow's dawn,
> And calmly, as if indifferent quite,
> You would close your term here, up and be gone?

'Indifferent' implies that Emma vanished because she didn't care enough to tell him, and the poem closes on the same note:

> I seem but a dead man held on end
> To sink down soon ... O you could not know
> That such swift fleeing
> No soul foreseeing –
> Not even I – would undo me so!

At the same time as the last sentence seems to acknowledge it might not have been her fault, the phrase 'not even I' spikes into antagonism. Emma had always disliked Hardy's haunted poetry, and in her last, mentally unwell months, had delusions that he was plotting her death like Dr Crippen.[20] But here, Hardy insists, 'not even I', your death-obsessed husband, could have foreseen your death's impact. Many of the poems of 1912–13 play on the ambiguity of Emma's deathly indifference to him, trying to come to terms with bald fact and being unable to feel it except as some kind of haughty riposte. 'I shall not know . . . I shall not care', Emma is made to say in 'Your Last Drive', to which Hardy replies:

> You are past love, praise, indifference, blame.

At the same time as it resigns itself to stop ventriloquising her, the line's metrical ambiguity between stressing 'past' or 'love' makes it flicker with the angry tones of a break-up, where Emma is indeed a 'past love'.

Yet although his first wife's death came as a shock, in another sense it only intensified the themes of Hardy's earlier poems; the voice of the dead ironising the living, and the conspicuous absence of a kindly Providence. Freed from the demands of prose realism after his turn to poetry full-time in 1897, Hardy could distil his plots into hundreds of poems about a world where love never stays, and to understand life is to be too late to mend it. 'Experience *un*teaches – (what at first one thinks to be the rule in events)' he noted in middle age, and his poems are haunted by endless ghostly figures who return to the scene of their mistakes, aware of what went wrong but powerless to alter it.[21] Later poems attribute such helplessness to the designs of the 'Immanent Will', the blind evolutionary life force which patterns human lives on the grandest scale, without being consciously aware of the effects of what it does. However implausible this philosophy seems, it makes some sense of one of the abiding mysteries of Hardy's poetry, its mechanical, clunky awkwardness. His prolific stanza forms always seem to hammer their content into shape through misplaced stresses, syntax-bending hyphenations and forced rhymes. Some of his contemporaries ascribed it to Hardy's rural clumsiness; others thought it unconsciously expressive.[22] But in his vast, unstageable poetic drama *The Dynasts*, Hardy once compared the Immanent Will to a certain kind of poetic genius:

> It works unconsciously, as heretofore,
> Eternal artistries in Circumstance,
> Whose patterns, wrought by rapt aesthetic rote,
> Seem in themselves Its single listless aim
> And not their consequence.[23]

Hardy's own method, too, was to work out his poetic forms in 'verse skeletons', patterns made for their unity's sake rather than the results for the material within them.[24] Unlike the Immanent Will, though, he was never unconscious of the result. Two of Hardy's philosophical sources for the idea of an unconscious life-force, Schopenhauer and von Hartmann, saw the supreme example of its activity in the successfully integrated, organic work of art. For von Hartman, the Unconscious works like an artist, embracing 'all means and ends in one'; for Schopenhauer, the poet inspired by the Will will produce an 'easy and unforced' rhyme, 'as if the idea expressed in it already lay predestined'.[25] But Hardy's verse sounds predestined because it is unhappily rhymed; the form's stylistic detachment registers the hurtful indifference with which the forms woven by Fate structure their hapless content. 'The Convergence of the Twain', for example, describes with some relish the twin destinies of the iceberg forming over aeons in the Arctic, and the Titanic which was destined to hit her:

> Alien they seemed to be:
> No mortal eye could see
> The intimate welding of their later history

'Welding' emphasises the unnatural force of the join, and as if to point out the strain, the third beat of the line falls on the unstressed syllable 'of', making the rhythm dominate its material, just as the *aaa* rhymes lean heavily on unstressed syllables to fit:

> Over the mirrors meant
> To glass the opulent
> The sea-worm crawls – grotesque, slimed, dumb, indifferent.

The double rhythmic stress on 'indifferent' emphasises both its meanings – that the sea-worm doesn't care who it feeds on, and that such indifference cannot but be felt as cruelty. As has often been noticed, Hardy also describes the moment of collision as a 'consummation', as if his own marriage were also a predestined disaster. Yet it is Hardy who patiently makes the forms which tell it so, as if he writes as both vehicle and victim of the Will.

In the sense that Hardy's complaints against the Will are also anxieties about artistic responsibility, then his awkward poetic forms are already rehearsing what will be the emotional cruxes of 1912–13. 'The emotions have no place in a world of defect, and it is a cruel injustice that they should have developed in it', he once wrote.[26] But just as 'cruel' implies intentional ill will at the same time as Hardy is saying the Law (or the Will) has no designs, so thirty years later, his poems about his failed marriage would imply contrivance and thoughtlessness in both parties. In this ambivalence between unconscious Will and loaded meaning, Hardy's poems are both private workings-out of grief, and a counterpart to other, more avant-garde explorations of artistic chance and responsibility in a directionless modern world.

Edward Thomas (1878–1917) was a great admirer of Hardy's – 'the master of living poets', as his widow Helen Thomas put it – but he was always uncomfortable with what he felt was Hardy's manipulation of his material.[27] 'Seldom does anything creep in,' Thomas complained, 'to give his work a something not to be accounted for in what he actually says'; later he called Hardy 'tyrannous' in allowing no 'richness and diversity of interpretation'.[28] If this comment seems unduly harsh, it is perhaps because Thomas's own deepest ambition was to free his own writing from over-control, in particular the self-conscious stylistic preciousness of his own former idol, Walter Pater. As a young man at Oxford at the turn of the century, Thomas had been drawn to Pater's ideal of an intense, jewelled style to represent his own passionate feeling for the natural world. But as he grew older, he came to feel that Pater's aesthetic had strangled his own chances of artistic expression, for although it promised to eliminate everything formal and habitual, it actually led to nothing but the exquisite self-consciousness that had tormented the depressed poet for years. In his 1913 biography, Thomas emphasised how Pater's doctrine of artistic autonomy tried to eliminate all but the writer's chosen meaning, whereas actually 'no man can decree the value of one word, unless it is his own invention' and the result of trying to do so is a would-be autonomous work which actually speaks of nothing but its author's self-assertion.[29]

For the same reasons, Thomas grew equally dissatisfied with his contemporaries, scorning the self-conscious individualism of the Imagists and the self-conscious ordinariness of the Georgians alike.[30] Thomas wanted instead a more unassuming poetry, written in a common language which could never be its author's private possession. As he put it in his own poem about writing poetry, 'Words':

> Out of us all
> That make rhymes,
> Will you choose
> Sometimes –
> As the winds use
> A crack in the wall
> Or a drain,
> Their joy or their pain
> To whistle through –
> Choose me,
> You English words.

The happy uncertainty of that 'sometimes' is present in the poem's subtle blend of free-verse rhythm and unpredictably spaced rhymes, some fifteen lines apart, as if the poem were making its own connections across time casually, in passing, and beyond the speaker's or reader's conscious awareness.

Much of Thomas's poetry is about such unanticipated moments, being caught off-guard by the surprise of his own poems, by birdsongs or silences, or by his own black and squally depressions. As this entwining of self-expression with self-dispossession might suggest, though, it is also poetry whose happiest moments of unself-consciousness are reminders of Thomas's suicidal depressions, and foretastes of his own coming death. These intimations shadow his most well-loved poem, 'Adlestrop', which opens with an interjection – 'Yes: I remember Adlestrop' – and goes on to remember a surprised interruption to a train journey:

> The steam hissed. Someone cleared his throat.
> No one left and no one came
> On the bare platform. What I saw
> Was Adlestrop – only the name
>
> And willows, willow-herb, and grass,
> And meadowsweet, and haycocks dry,
> No whit less still and lonely fair
> Than the high cloudlets in the sky.

The heavy full stops mark the moment's uncertain silence, interrupting the routine; then, as Thomas's speaker gets carried away into the fields and sky, the hypotactic 'ands' seem to let the impressions flow in naturally and unforcedly. But as the hints of Wordsworth's 'Daffodils' in those high, lonely clouds indicate, this is actually a poem about remembering the moment, and it points subtly to the present, different circumstances in which such ecstasy is being recalled. Thomas had been on his way to see his friend the poet Robert Frost when the train stopped unwontedly at Adlestrop in the hot, beautiful August 1914, a month before the First World War began, and soon after this visit Thomas finally let himself be tempted by Frost's encouragement and began to try poetry himself. By early 1915, when this poem was written, the trickle was turning into a flood, but Thomas also knew that his poetry didn't pay, and that he could only afford to continue if he gave up the literary journalism he so hated, and enlisted in the Army. 'Adlestrop', then, recalls a moment of peace before the war, but both memory and the poem can only exist because of the war, and Adlestrop's bright, unpeopled landscape stands out because it seems to prefigure Thomas's own present and future absence from it.

More generally, Thomas's rural England is distinguished less by its pastoral contentedness than by its emptiness. What catches his eye are ruined or broken things left behind by those long dead (the pipe in 'Digging', dead weasels caught by a gamekeeper, bits of china plate), or flowers unpicked and fallen trees unmoved by newly dead farmhands ('As the Team's Head-Brass'). Of those who remain, there are few farmers and many more tramps, beggars and wayfarers picking their way across this depopulated landscape. In Thomas's travel prose, these vagrants occur like free spirits of nature, but in the poems their homelessness echoes the soldier-author's too, writing his verses on bumpy trains between his home at Steep and army camp, looking forward to sleeping outdoors like the ploughman 'dead in battle', alone in the night and the cold like the 'soldiers and poor, unable to rejoice' of 'The Owl', passing 'for good' into the twilight like the tramp in "Twill take some getting'.

Thomas did not manage to stop being self-conscious about his own self-consciousness, of course, and the poems are often thickets of ifs, yets and buts as the poet restlessly turns his own feelings over. But in the end, all the choices seem to baffle one another, and the poems settle into a state of suspension between 'both tears and mirth' ('Liberty'), Winter and Spring, wondering endlessly 'where he shall journey, O where?' ('The Signpost'). Such melancholy, contented indecision is less an abject failure of will than the counterpart to Thomas's increasing sense that as France grew nearer, his own choices were ceasing to make much difference. In June 1915, Frost had sent him the first draft of 'The Road Less Traveled', partly to tease him about hesitation between the two diverging roads of prose and poetry. But Thomas's reply in 'Roads', written six months later, was that neither his poetry nor his life were matters of choice any longer:

> Now all roads lead to France
> And heavy is the tread
> Of the living; but the dead
> Returning lightly dance.

'I love roads', the poem begins, simply, and on this perpetual road Thomas walks 'in remote time' with the Roman soldiers into Wales, in 1916 with the dead back from France, and also with Wordsworth, who loved a public road and met the discharged soldier on it. 'The road ... is always going: it has never gone right away, and no man is too late', and its endless going makes Thomas's certainty that everything in his life is passing away into a kind of suspended continuity:[31]

> Roads go on
> While we forget, and are

Forgotten like a star
That shoots and is gone.

Thomas's favourite enjambed, unstressed rhyme slides 'are' into 'forgotten', like the trace of his own poetic star, seen always as it is vanishing. His poetry was made on the road to France as it was ended by it, and on the journey, the fearful and joyful senses of losing his own life become the same thing. But Thomas was wrong in thinking that while the road went on, he would be forgotten.

NOTES

1 Ezra Pound, *Confucius to Cummings*, ed. Ezra Pound and Marcella Spann (New York: New Directions, 1971), p. 40.
2 Reproduced in *A. E. Housman: Collected Poems and Selected Prose*, ed. Christopher Ricks (Harmondsworth: Penguin, 1988), p. 471.
3 Lawrence Housman, 'A. E. Housman's "De Amicitia"', annotated by John Sparrow, *Encounter*, 39, 4 (1967), 36–7.
4 See A. A. Long, 'The Socratic Legacy', in Keimpe Algra (ed.), *The Cambridge History of Hellenistic Philosophy* (Cambridge: Cambridge University Press, 1999), pp. 632–39.
5 Ricks (ed.), *Housman*, p. 360.
6 *Ibid.*, p. 370. J. C. Squire, in *A. E. Housman: The Critical Heritage*, ed. Philip Gardner (London and New York: Routledge, 1992), p. 279.
7 Ricks (ed.), *Housman*, p. 370.
8 Walter Pater, *The Renaissance*, ed. Adam Phillips (Oxford: World's Classics, 1986), p. 152. Housman, in Ricks (ed.), *Housman*, p. 369.
9 'Cambridge Inaugural Lecture', in Ricks (ed.), *Housman*, p. 306.
10 'Swinburne', in Ricks (ed.), *Housman*, p. 290.
11 *Ibid.*, p. 454.
12 Auden, 'A. E. Housman' (1939).
13 Ricks (ed.), *Housman*, p. 370.
14 Leighton, *Victorian Women Poets: Writing Against the Heart* (London: Harvester Wheatsheaf) p. 278. Celeste M. Schenk, 'Charlotte Mew', in Bonnie Kime Scott (ed.), *The Gender of Modernism* (Cambridge: Cambridge University Press, 1996), p. 317; Kathleen Bell, 'Charlotte Mew, T. S. Eliot and Modernism', in Vicky Bertram (ed.), *Kicking Daffodils* (Edinburgh: Edinburgh University Press, 1997), pp. 13–24.
15 Marjorie Watts, 'Memories of Charlotte Mew', *PEN Newsletter* 13 (1982), 12–13, and Penelope Fitzgerald, *Charlotte Mew and Her Friends* (London: Collins, 1984).
16 Cf. Suzanne Raitt, 'Charlotte Mew's Queer Death', *Yearbook of Comparative and General Literature*, 47 (1999), pp. 71–80.
17 Jessica Walsh, ' "The Strangest Pain to Bear": Corporeality and Fear of Insanity in Charlotte Mew's Poetry', *Victorian Poetry*, 40, 3 (2002), p. 221.
18 Garber, *Vested Interests: Cross-Dressing and Cultural Anxiety* (London: Routledge, 1992), p. 13.

19 Cf. Jahan Ramazani, *Poetry of Mourning* (Chicago: University of Chicago Press, 1994), pp. 49–59.
20 Michael Millgate, *Thomas Hardy: A Biography* (Oxford: Oxford University Press, 1982), p. 470.
21 Thomas Hardy, *The Life and Work of Thomas Hardy*, ed. Michael Millgate (London and Basingstoke: Macmillan, 1984), p. 182.
22 E. g., Lytton Strachey, 'Mr Hardy's New Poems', *New Statesman*, 19 December 1914, pp. 269–71.
23 *The Dynasts* (London: Macmillan, 1912), Fore Scene, lines 2–5 (p. 21).
24 Hardy, *Life*, p. 324.
25 Von Hartmann, *Philosophy of the Unconscious*, 3 vols. in 1 (1884, repr. London: Routledge, 2000), I, pp. 246–7. Schopenhauer, *The World as Will and Representation*, trans. E. F. J. Payne, 2 vols. (New York: Dover, 1966), II, pp. 428–9.
26 Hardy, *Life*, p. 153.
27 Letter from Helen Thomas (n.d. but internal evidence suggests 1920), Dorset County Museum.
28 Thomas, 'Time's Laughingstocks', *Morning Post*, 9 December 1909, p. 2; 'Mr Hardy's New Poems', *Daily Chronicle*, 7 December 1909, p. 3.
29 Thomas, *Walter Pater* (London: Martin Secker, 1913), p. 215.
30 Review of *Des Imagistes*, repr. in *A Language Not To Be Betrayed: Selected Prose of Edward Thomas*, ed. Edna Longley (Manchester: Carcanet, 1981), p. 123. 'John Masefield and Wilfred Gibson', *Bookman*, November 1914, 51–2.
31 Thomas, *The Icknield Way* (London: Constable, 1913), p. 2.

Further reading

Fitzgerald, Penelope, *Charlotte Mew and Her Friends*, London: Collins, 1984
Holden, Alan W., and J. Roy Birch (eds.), *A. E. Housman: A Reassessment*, London: Macmillan, 2000
Howarth, Peter, *British Poetry in the Age of Modernism*, Cambridge: Cambridge University Press, 2005
McDonald, Peter, 'Rhyme and Determination in Hopkins and Edward Thomas', *Essays in Criticism*, 43, 3 (1993), 228–46
Page, Norman, *A. E. Housman: A Critical Biography*, London: Macmillan, 1985
Ramazani, Jahan, *Poetry of Mourning*, Chicago: University of Chicago Press, 1994
Richardson, Angelique, 'Hardy and Science: A Chapter of Accidents', in Philip Mallett (ed.), *The Palgrave Guide to Hardy Studies*, London: Palgrave, 2004, pp. 156–80
Ricks, Christopher, ed., 'Introduction', *A E Housman: Collected Poems and Selected Prose*, London: Penguin, 1989, pp. 7–18
Smith, Stan, ' "Literally, for this": Metonymies of National Identity in Thomas, Yeats and Auden', in Alex Davis and Lee M. Jenkins (eds.), *Locations of Literary Modernism*, Cambridge: Cambridge University Press, 2000, pp. 113–34

5

SANDRA M. GILBERT

D. H. Lawrence's place in modern poetry

A visit to Eastwood

One weekend in 1970, during a family vacation cum research summer in London, my husband and I drove up to Nottinghamshire, to explore Lawrence country. I was in the midst of converting my dissertation on Lawrence's poetry into a book, so of course I wanted to see where 'my' writer came from – although, having read Lawrence so intensely for so long, I was pretty sure I knew what I'd encounter in the 'industrial Midlands'. Nor was I shocked when, as we approached Eastwood, we found ourselves facing several large, cone-shaped mountains of darkness: 'slag heaps', we realised. This was grimy mining country indeed, and these bleak black hills were outposts of a waste land shaped by the grim technology Lawrence decried in novels from *Sons and Lovers* to *Women in Love* to *Lady Chatterley's Lover*.

Yet I was surprised to discover that these huge mounds of debris were surrounded by greenery – by flowery meadows and by the ancient forests of Robin Hood. Even in Eastwood, when we located what we decided was the original Lawrence home, we saw that the 'Backs' he'd so vividly described still sloped down toward open country. Lawrence's Eastwood, I realised now with a certainty no library research could have produced, was a geography of paradox, as marked by the juxtaposition of untrammelled nature and constricting culture as this writer's entire literary oeuvre. In fact, Lawrence's whole body of work might be seen as an effort to drag the substance of nature – the *bodies* of men and women, of birds, beasts and flowers, even of fields and hills – out from under the shadow of those slag heaps reared by the tools of reason.

And Lawrence's on-going struggle to liberate the vital substantiality of nature from the oppressive weight of culture was mirrored in a comparable linguistic struggle that marked this writer's career: an effort to find a style that would be free of what he considered verbal constraints. To this end, he wrote and rewrote draft after draft of his novels, often beginning each work anew in an attempt to achieve an oxymoronically 'spontaneous' revision. But even more dramatically he fought to find a poetics adequate to his desire for a liberation of substantial being, finally deciding, in an essay on 'Poetry of the Present' (1919), that he longed to write the 'unrestful, ungraspable poetry of the sheer present' because the 'quick of the universe is the *pulsating, carnal self*, mysterious and palpable'. Explicitly identifying such poetry with Whitman's free verse, Lawrence declared that the 'new' poetry must 'break the lovely form of metrical verse' because 'any externally applied law would be mere shackles and death', smothering 'direct utterance from the instant, whole man'. Before he made this claim, he had already begun to eschew rhyme not only in many of the poems he published about his elopement with Frieda von Richthofen Weekley, the woman who was to become his wife, but also in a number of poems he wrote during and about the First World War. Yet even what Lawrence called the 'Rhyming Poems' of his youth were marked by flexible line-lengths, experiments with dialect and straightforward narration.

'The Wild Common', the much revised piece with which this writer chose to open his *Collected Poems*, is key here for several reasons.[1] First, its title reminds us of the rural landscape so closely interwoven with the industrial gloom of the mining country. Here, below slag heaps and surrounding collieries, was a *common* ground that surged with life: 'quick sparks on the gorse-bushes', peewits overhead exultantly screaming their triumph 'o'er the ages', rabbits like 'handfuls of brown earth' leaping so that 'the hill bursts and heaves under their spurting kick', and a 'lazy streamlet' that 'wakes ... and gushes'. Perhaps at the centre of the common and certainly at the centre of the poem there's even a remnant of the pre-industrial agrarian world – 'an old sheep-dip'. But tellingly this former construct of culture has reverted to the wildness that now possesses the common, so the speaker, a 'naked lad' about to take a swim, spies his 'white shadow', a reflection dancing on the surface of the water 'like a dog on a string'.

Yet even while it celebrates the vitality of the common ground on which the protagonist takes his stand, this poem works out a careful argument between his material body and his insubstantial 'white shadow' – that 'dog on a string' which paradoxically suggests the mind or soul. Reversing an old trope in which the body is an animal controlled by bodiless spirit, Lawrence revels in casting aside his insubstantial self as he plunges into the water, proclaiming that he himself is identical with the flesh that possesses and is possessed by the wild common: 'how splendid it is to be substance, here! / My shadow is neither here nor there; but I, I am royally here!' Eventually, indeed, he declares what will be his creed throughout his career: 'All that is right, all that is good, all that is *God* takes *substance!*' (emphasis added). And by implication, the substance of all that is good is the living matter of the wild that we have in common with all life, or so Lawrence would have us believe. Equally important, once he had understood the nature of the 'direct utterance' that was at the heart of his aesthetic, for Lawrence as a poet the language in which he wrote was itself an analogue of the ground he celebrates in this verse, for the speech he came to admire was 'wild' (unconstrained, 'ungraspable', *'pulsating, carnal'*) and it was common, the shared or common tongue of the people with whom he lived.

D. H. Lawrence, T. S. Eliot and the 'essence of poetry'

Given the credo Lawrence espoused in 'The Wild Common', one of the stranger phenomena in the history of literary modernism was T. S. Eliot's curiously ambivalent obsession with this writer's work. Most notoriously, the magisterial poet-critic focused one of the moralising lectures that he delivered at the University of Virginia in 1933 (and published the following year as *After Strange Gods*) on a castigation of Lawrence's blasphemous ways. Although, he admitted, Lawrence had an extraordinary 'capacity for profound intuition', his was an 'intuition from which he commonly drew the wrong conclusions', no doubt because of an 'insensibility to ordinary social morality, which is so alien to my mind that I am completely baffled by it as a monstrosity'.[2] Still, Eliot conceded, 'Against the living death of modern material civilization [Lawrence] spoke again and again, and ... what he said is unanswerable.' Nevertheless, Lawrence had 'an incapacity for what we ordinarily call thinking', and the 'intensity' of his vision was 'spiritually sick'; indeed, as in some Gothic tale of horror, the 'demonic powers found an instrument' of great 'range, delicacy, and power' in this lamentable author.[3]

Oddly, however, in the same year that he delivered this tirade, Eliot gave another, less well-known lecture on 'English Letter-Writers' in which he quoted a statement that Lawrence made in a 1916 letter to his close friend Catherine Carswell. 'The essence of poetry with us in this age of stark and unlovely actualities is a stark directness, without a shadow of a lie, or a shadow of deflection anywhere', Lawrence had declared there. 'Everything can go, but this stark, bare, rocky directness of statement, this alone makes poetry, today.'[4] To readers of Lawrence such a definition of poetry comes as no surprise. But it is surprising that Eliot should have been drawn to it, given his revulsion against Lawrence's 'incapacity' for thinking. Yet when he produced his 'primer of modern heresy', Eliot also firmly seconded

Lawrence's view of the 'essence of poetry'. The statement in the letter to Carswell 'speaks to me', he confessed,

> of that at which I have long aimed, in writing poetry; to write poetry which should be essentially poetry, with nothing poetic about it, poetry standing naked in its bare bones, or poetry so transparent that we should not see the poetry, but that which we are meant to see through the poetry, poetry so transparent that in reading it we are intent on what the poem *points at*, and not on the poetry, this seems to me the thing to try for. To get *beyond poetry*, as Beethoven, in his late works, strove to get *beyond music*. . . .
>
> Lawrence's words . . . express to me what I think that the forty or fifty original lines that I have written strive towards.[5]

Here is an extraordinary confession, coming from the critic who penned not just *After Strange Gods* but also 'Tradition and the Individual Talent', 'The Metaphysical Poets', and 'What Is a Classic?' From youth an acolyte of the reactionary French theoretician Charles Maurras, Eliot celebrated order, maturity and traditional hierarchies; from relatively early in his career, moreover, he defined himself as 'a classicist in literature, a royalist in politics, and an anglo-catholic in religion'. Such priorities plainly shaped his belief that Lawrence's visions of 'strange gods' were blasphemous. Nonetheless, musing on English letter writers, he confronted with unusual candour his attraction to a poetics quite alien to the literary politics through which he sought to position himself in his career as a man of letters. But perhaps the ambivalence with which Eliot regarded Lawrence further illuminates the place of both poets in the history of twentieth-century English verse. For though the two never met, and though Lawrence showed little interest in Eliot, they were in some ways significantly alike; their careers were at various points intertwined from the start; and as artists they represented modes that were powerfully influential in the first half of the twentieth century, so much so that in 1951, F. R. Leavis opined that 'our time, in literature, may fairly be called the age of D. H. Lawrence and T. S. Eliot'.[6]

Among writers of their generation, to begin with, Eliot and Lawrence were both spokesmen for social metamorphoses, even though for the most part the restructurings Eliot envisioned were diametrically opposed to those Lawrence advocated. But the two men had still more in common. For instance, both moved in and out of the same Bloomsbury sets; and both were initially sponsored by that maestro of Modernism, Ezra Pound. And even some of their earliest poetic publications were entangled, for the June 1915 issue of *Poetry: A Magazine of Verse*, in which Eliot's startlingly innovative 'The Love Song of J. Alfred Prufrock' first appeared, carried also a glowing review of *Some Imagist Poets*, an anthology that had been put together by Amy Lowell but grew out of the Imagist movement Pound had defined. Here Harriet Monroe, the founding editor of *Poetry*, singled out for special praise a group of Lawrence's poems, noting that they 'are some of the finest poetry written in this century [and] of a new kind in that they could not have been written in any other century'. In fact, as if refuting in advance Eliot's argument in *After Strange Gods*, Monroe admiringly observed that 'Mr Lawrence gives us his own fire, *and cares not whether it respects rules or melts them*' (emphasis added).[7]

Close in age, both had begun seriously writing verse by the time they were twenty, and their styles were on the surface strikingly different. Lawrence's juvenilia was sentimental and Victorian in tone, offering such lines as 'the purple dreams of the innocent spring have gone' (from 'Campions', *CP*, 853). Whatever embarrassment Eliot's early efforts evoked was of a different sort. Astringent and sardonic, he presented himself alternately as a composer of *vers de société* and an urban land-scapist. His scandals, unlike Lawrence's, were scatological and misogyn-istic, as in 'The Triumph of Bullshit' ('Ladies, on whom my attentions have waited / If you consider my merits are small ... For Christ's sake stick it up your ass').[8]

But despite their differences, the two aspiring writers shared an import-ant ancestor: the late Victorian poet Algernon Charles Swinburne, whose often sado-masochistic intensity gave similar intensity to some of the strongest early poems each produced. Certainly underlying the sexual frustrations of poems from 'The Death of St Narcissus' and 'The Love Song of J. Alfred Prufrock' to *The Waste Land* was the Swinburnean fervour of the young Eliot's 'Love Song of St Sebastian' ('I would come in a shirt of hair ... And sit at the foot of your stair; / I would flog myself until I bled ...').[9] And similarly, colouring the erotic battles of Lawrence's fiction from *Sons and Lovers* to *Women in Love* and *The Plumed Serpent*, was the Swinburnean ferocity of such poems as 'Love on the Farm' ('God, I am caught in a snare! / I know not what fine wire is round my throat; / I only know I let him finger there / My pulse of life, and let him nose like a stoat / Who sniffs with joy before he drinks the blood'; *CP*, 43).

That it's appropriate to trace Swinburne's influence not just on Lawrence's poetry but on his fiction while only examining Eliot's verse underlines, however, a major distinction between the two artists. Long defined as, in Leavis's phrase, 'D. H. Lawrence: *Novelist*' (emphasis added), Lawrence began and ended his career as a poet but gained his primary reputation as a writer of fiction, and then secondarily as a travel writer, playwright, essayist, critic – and poet. Although Eliot too produced both critical prose and verse drama, his output was considerably narrower. And with the 'substructure' of prose justifying his verse, he appeared to be a more formally sophisticated artist. Why, then, did Lawrence's poetic of 'stark directness' speak so powerfully to him that he yearned to 'write poetry ... with nothing poetic about it'?

At least in part, Lawrence's vocation as novelist may have shaped both his own poetry of 'stark directness' and Eliot's surprising admiration for such an aesthetic. The novel, Lawrence once remarked, was 'the one bright book of life' and many of his most successful early poems functioned as what Whitman might have called 'sparkles from the wheel' – miniature narratives thrown off, as it were, from the novelist's workbench. Among Lawrence's early novels, for instance, *Sons and Lovers* alone inspired quite a few poems that were direct in formulation, concise, not 'poetic' in articulation – and (like much of Eliot's early work) Swinburnean in erotic energy. With its tight, imagistic focus on the 'terrible whips' of an ash tree slashing the wind outside an otherwise unidentified house, 'Discord in Childhood' examines the parallel between the terror of the tree's weird shrieking and the psychodrama of parental conflict inside the house: 'a slender lash / Whistling she-delirious rage', and 'a male thong booming and bruising' (*CP*, 36). In doing so, the poem summarizes, as if in an uncanny snapshot, the family drama that unfolds in the first third of *Sons and Lovers*.

Similarly, in a glimpse of a single moment in a romance, 'Cherry Robbers' captures the Swinburnean entanglement of the erotic and the sadistic that marks the relationship between Paul and Miriam throughout much of the novel. While succinctly exploring a parallel between the 'blood-drops' of cherries, the 'red dye' on the breasts of three dead birds who have been shot as 'robberlings', and the speaker's feelings towards 'a girl [who] stands laughing at me, / Cherries hung round her ears' and 'Offers me her scarlet fruit', the poem illuminates as in a flash of lightning the dangers implicit in desire: 'I will see / If she has any tears' (*CP*, 36–7). More tender, but marked by the same unflinching candour and the same narrative drive are the elegiac poems in which Lawrence lamented the death of the mother whose decline and demise he charts so brilliantly in *Sons and Lovers*. The very title of that book, of course, acknowledges the scrupulous introspection with which the writer dissected his own Oedipal feelings. From his cosmopolitan German wife, Frieda, he had learned a good deal about Freud, but even before there was a theory on which he could base his analysis of his own emotions he had confronted them frankly, once noting that he had always loved his mother with 'almost a husband and wife love'.[10] Thus, such poems as 'The Bride', 'Sorrow' and 'Piano' offer brief but intense insights into the processes of grieving that Freud was later to discuss from a clinical perspective in 'Mourning and Melancholia' (1917).

In the first of these beautiful lyrics, the speaker gazes at the body of the lost beloved, noting the strange dissonance of her appearance in death, and speaking like the 'lover' he knew himself to be. Yet as he gazes, his passion sees through the superficial changes of age (her 'plaits' that are 'threaded with filigree silver, / And uncanny cold') to the 'young maiden' within, the one she once was and now, in one of the paradoxes of death, once more *is*. And at the center of this vision of her, uttered with just the 'stark directness' Eliot was to admire, he embeds a synaesthetic epiphany: as his mother 'sleeps like bride', her 'dead mouth *sings / By its shape*, like thrushes in clear evenings' (emphasis added; *CP*, 101).

Continuing to trace the journey of grief, both 'Sorrow' and 'Piano' anticipate the course of loss as Freud was to outline it some years later when he defined 'the absorbing work of mourning' as a task of great magnitude which requires the griever to continually bear witness as 'Reality passes its verdict – that the object no longer exists – upon each single one of the memories and hopes through which the libido was attached to the lost object.' In 'Sorrow', as if backtracking from the vision of his mother in death that he offers in 'The Bride', Lawrence broods on the stages of her dying. The tone of his poem is controlled, even shocked, and interrogatory, beginning

> Why does the thin grey strand
> Floating up from the forgotten
> Cigarette between my fingers,
> Why does it trouble me?

Then his gaze at the cigarette smoke triggers a painful memory as he recalls how 'when I carried my mother downstairs ... at the beginning of her soft-foot malady', he often found 'a few long grey hairs' on his coat, and 'one by one / I watched them float up the dark chimney'(*CP*, 106).

Following the same course of mourning and discovery, 'Piano' also opens with a puzzling psychological experience, a singer at a concert who takes him 'back down the vista of years' till he sees himself as a child, 'sitting under the piano, in the boom of the tingling strings / And pressing the small, poised feet of a mother who smiles as she sings'. Again, the explanation of a troubling event leads further into the heart of mourning: 'my manhood is cast / Down in the flood of remembrance, I weep like a child for the past' (*CP*, 148). And though this poem, like others in the series, attempts the 'lovely form of metrical verse' that Lawrence later resolved to 'break', the common language in which its confessional candour is couched foreshadows what Eliot was to define as poetry 'with nothing poetic about it, poetry standing naked in its bare bones'.

Poetry standing naked

If even Lawrence's early, rhyming poems often appear to be 'direct utterance[s] from the instant, whole man', his later, self-proclaimed 'Unrhyming Poems' function as at least approximations of the speech of a '*pulsating, carnal self*, mysterious and palpable' – speech, as it were, of the wild common and the common wildness we all share. Interestingly, Lawrence was able to 'break' what he came to consider the chains of rhyme as his poetry grew more distant from the subject matter of his novels. From *Look! We Have Come Through!* to *Birds, Beasts and Flowers* and *Last Poems* – arguably his strongest volumes in this genre – his poems were most deeply marked not by his fiction but by the new self he felt he had achieved in his relationship with Frieda, by the crises associated with the First World War, by his critical work on *Studies in Classic American Literature* (and the travels to America) that brought him into ever closer contact with the writings of Whitman and the country that had fostered those writings, and by his final illness, a crisis in the tuberculosis from which he had long suffered that was to kill him at the early age of forty-four.

To be sure, *Look! We Have Come Through!* is a kind of narrative, 'intended as an essential story, or history, or confession', Lawrence wrote, and he supplied an 'argument': 'After much struggling and loss in love and in the world of man, the protagonist throws in his lot with a woman who is already married [and the] conflict of love and hate goes on between these two and the world around them, till ... they transcend into some condition of blessedness' (*CP*, 191). Along with a poem titled 'Manifesto' and one titled 'New Heaven and Earth', this prefatory statement suggests a theology of mystical eroticism to which Lawrence became increasingly committed. But as this belief system developed, it brought into focus a parallel poetics that helped shape what the writer was to call 'Poetry of the Present'. Rather than in 'Manifesto', the most resonant statement of this poetics appears in the book's title poem : 'Song of a Man Who Has Come Through' (*CP*, 250). Here, without ever naming the barriers through which he has come, the speaker formulates the aesthetic and philosophical parameters of the 'blessedness' he feels he has attained, noting that he has been brought to this state by an encounter with the radical otherness of the new: 'Not I, not I, but the wind that blows through me! / A fine wind is blowing the new direction of Time'.

The metaphor of wind as world-soul or *anima* breathing new life and imaginative creativity is a traditional one, appearing, for instance, as the central trope of Shelley's high romantic 'Ode to the West Wind'. But Lawrence updated it, breaking the glittering chains of Shelley's *terza rima* and casting his aesthetic in the common language of personal prayer. Confiding that as this 'fine, fine wind ... takes its course through the chaos of the world', he would be 'keen and hard like the sheer tip of a wedge / Driven by invisible blows' so that 'we shall come at the wonder, we shall find the Hesperides', he prayed to be 'a good well-head' for such wonder, longed to 'blur no whisper, spoil no expression'. But the final insight to which this worshipful incantation brings him leaps back to ancient myth and biblical epiphany. For the poet-speaker imagines that, as the wind carries him towards 'blessedness', he hears an unexpected 'knocking at the door in the night', wonders if it is 'somebody [who] wants to do us harm', and then, with mystical certainty, declares 'No, no, it is the three strange angels. / Admit them, admit them'. Either the three guardians of the Hesperides that he had earlier sought, or the three biblical messengers who visited Abraham in Genesis 18, bearing news of Sarah's marvellous fertility, Lawrence's angels deliver good tidings of great joy to the artist, who experiences himself as having 'come through' the barriers of dailiness to a realm of the visionary, as if – figuratively speaking – he had momentarily left behind the shadow of the slag heaps and re-entered a newly luminous wild common. And that the apparently simple imperative with which he concludes – 'Admit them, admit them' – is richly ambiguous ('admit them' meaning concede that they exist? Or meaning allow them to enter?) suggests the weight of significance that a poetry of 'stark directness' can convey.

If 'Song of a Man Who Has Come Through' drew on the Bible as well as Greek mythology to define the interlocking blessings of love and creative imagination, one of Lawrence's fiercest wartime poems from this period, 'Eloi Eloi Lama Sabacthani', turned to the Bible to use Christ's last words on the cross – 'My God, My God, why hast Thou forsaken me?' (Mark 15:34) – to represent the desolation of soldiers imprisoned in trenches and forsaken amidst the horror of the Front. Here, in a grotesque parody of the sacred eroticism through which the man who 'came through' gained access to the redemptive mystery of the new, the soldiers engage in unholy acts of intercourse that further alienate them from the possibilities of love. 'How I hate myself, this body which is me; / How it dogs me, what a galling shadow!' begins the speaker, a soldier at the Front, in a revision of the body/shadow dialectic that shaped 'The Wild Common'. Then he describes his bizarrely eroticised killing of an enemy:

> Like a bride he took my bayonet, wanting it,
> Like a virgin the blade of my bayonet, wanting it,
> And it sank to rest from me in him,

And I, the lover, am consummate,
And he is the bride, I have sown him with the seed
And planted and fertilized him.   (*CP*, 742)

The repetitive, conversational-seeming cadences through which Lawrence captured this speaker's despair and rage became central to the style of his later poems, most of which are works in which, as Eliot put it, poetry becomes 'so transparent that in reading it we are intent on what the poem *points at*, and not on the poetry'. For Lawrence, however, such apparently naked poetry depends nonetheless on the linguistic skill for which he had prayed in 'Song of a Man Who Has Come Through'. Most notably, this poet frequently deployed a Whitmanesque strategy of incantatory repetition (for instance, 'Like a bride he took my bayonet ... / Like a virgin the blade of my bayonet') in which grammatical parallelisms gradually modify the narrative or argument until the work is propelled towards an appropriate, if mysterious, stopping point.

Another apparently effortless technique that the poet also used throughout his later work, starting with *Birds, Beasts and Flowers*, was an often combatively conversational tone that allows the speaking voice of the poem to plunge the reader into *medias res*. 'Eloi, Eloi' begins like a casual soliloquy: 'How I hate myself, this body which is me', while a number of poems in *Birds, Beasts and Flowers* rudely address a hypothetical reader. 'You tell me I am wrong. / Who are you, who is anybody to tell me I am wrong?' begins the poet in 'Pomegranate', and then he goes on to hymn the crucial fissure in this mythic fruit: 'Do you mean to tell me you will see no fissure? ... For all that, the setting suns are open. / The end cracks open with the beginning: / Rosy, tender, glittering within the fissure'. The next poem in the collection, 'Peach', opens with an even more truculent question: 'Would you like to throw a stone at me? / Here, take all that's left of my peach', then echoes Blake's 'Tyger' in a series of not-merely rhetorical questions: 'Why the groove? ... Why the ripple down the sphere? ... Why was not my peach round and finished like a billiard ball?' As Lawrence noted in 'Poetry of the Present', the 'instant, the immediate self' that shapes 'free verse' is never 'finished, perfected'; a fruit in the form of a perfectly rounded billiard ball would belong to the 'stable, unchanging eternities' out of which this artist could no longer imagine making poetry – and he was prepared to argue with anyone who denied that the 'end cracks open with the beginning'.

Even while debating with hypothetical readers, however, Lawrence also quarreled with himself, most notably in one of his most frequently anthologised poems, 'Snake'. This parable, which once more replays the characteristic Lawrentian dialogue between conscious human reason (or spirit, 'soul', 'shadow', 'mind') and the ineffable *being* of body (flesh, substantial vitality), begins quietly enough:

> A snake came to my water-trough
> On a hot, hot day, and I in pyjamas for the heat,
> To drink there ...
> Someone was before me at my water-trough,
> And I, like a second comer, waiting.   (*CP*, 349)

But soon enough, observing that the snake is 'earth-brown, earth-golden from the burning bowels of the earth', the speaker remembers that the 'voice of my education said to me / He must be killed, / For in Sicily the black, black snakes are innocent, the gold are venomous'. And yet, he confesses, 'how I liked him, / How glad I was he had come like a guest in quiet, to drink at my water-trough'. Nonetheless, the voices of reason are insistent, even taunting, declaiming, 'If you were a man / You would take a stick and break him now and finish him off'.

Finally, therefore, the speaker hurls 'a clumsy log' towards the snake, who writhes 'like lightning' and disappears 'Into the black hole, the earth-lipped fissure' – at which the poet expresses neither triumph nor relief but deep regret: 'how paltry, how vulgar, what a mean act! / I despised myself and the voices of my accursed human education'. For, like so many other avatars of the 'quick of the universe', the snake seems to the poet a 'king in exile, uncrowned in the underworld / Now due to be crowned again'. Although in traditional Christian iconography as well as in Sicilian herpetology the snake is diabolical and dangerous, Lawrence reverses the usual hierarchy. It is his 'human education' that is 'accursed', while in its majestic otherness the snake is 'one of the lords / Of life' (*CP*, 351). Thus this brief but resonant dialogue between the teachings of reason and the intuitions of flesh ends, like so many other Lawrentian debates, in a triumph of the substance that enlivens the wild common rather than the reason that would tame, 'civilise' or exploit it.

How does such an impassioned celebrant of the substantial present that constitutes the 'quick of the universe' confront the impending annihilation of the 'carnal self' through which he knows, loves and speaks the life of each moment? This is a problem Lawrence had already begun to approach in *Birds, Beasts and Flowers* – in, for example, the richly incantatory 'Medlars and Sorb-Apples', with its evocation of the 'Orphic farewell, and farewell and farewell' of 'final loneliness' (*CP*, 281). But nowhere is this poet's dialogue with finality more naked than in some of the prayerful verses he wrote as he lay dying in the south of France. 'The Ship of Death', one of the most famous of these works, is addressed, like a sermon, to a congregation of readers. Here, drawing on Etruscan and Egyptian myths and rituals that imagine a ship bearing the souls of the dead into the unknown, the poet urges his interlocutors to 'build your ship of death, for you will need it' (*CP*, p. 717). A number of other poems in the group, however, reach beyond the immediate world of writer and reader to ask for succour from sacred intermediaries: the moon in 'Invocation to the Moon'; the airy creature in 'Butterfly' who symbolises the soul; the 'Silence' that is the 'great bride of all creation'; and, most strikingly, the paradoxical 'torches of darkness' whose powers Lawrence summons in the greatest of his last poems, 'Bavarian Gentians' (*CP*, 697).

Like 'Snake', 'Bavarian Gentians' begins modestly, with the casual observation that 'Not every man has gentians in his house / in soft September, at slow, sad Michaelmas'. But then, as the poet builds through waves of what he once called the 'continual, slightly modified repetition' that shapes not just his prose but his incantatory verse, the ordinary September gentians gradually metamorphose into magical tokens whose powers he needs to guide his passage from ordinary reality into a different world – or, more precisely, from life into death.

> Bavarian gentians, big and dark, only dark
> darkening the day-time, torch-like with the smoking blueness of Pluto's gloom,
> ribbed and torch-like, with their blaze of darkness spread blue
> down flattening into points, flattened under the sweep of white day
> torch-flower of the blue-smoking darkness, Pluto's dark-blue daze,
> black lamps from the halls of Dis, burning dark blue,
> giving of darkness, blue darkness, as Demeter's pale lamps give off light,
> lead me then, lead the way.

And as if through some sacramental alternative to conventional Christian theology, the flowers this poet addresses – denizens of the wild common out of which all life blooms – show him 'the way' down into the centre of the earth, where their bulbs will last out the winter and where life will emerge from death: the realm of darkness where 'blue is darkened on blueness' and 'where Persephone goes, just now, from the frosted September'. There, in the sightless realm where (again, paradoxically) 'darkness is awake upon the dark', the poet witnesses, or passionately hopes to witness, 'the passion of dense gloom' – the shadowy space in which 'the lost bride and her groom' will re-engender springtime.

In the nakedly hopeful yet helplessly dark dénouement of this poem, T. S. Eliot, along with other readers, would have encountered a poetry of religious mysticism 'able to get *beyond poetry*, as Beethoven, in his late works, strove to get *beyond music*'. Indeed, this 'poetry standing naked' is so plausibly prayerful that many contemporary thinkers may find it difficult to disagree with Wright Morris's assertion that 'in this world – the one in which we must live – the strange gods of D. H. Lawrence appear to be less strange than those of Mr. Eliot'.[11] But perhaps it is more important for students of Lawrence to note that here, in the downward journey of 'Bavarian Gentians', the underground origin of those slag heaps outside Eastwood – the apparently soulless mines into which the poet-novelist's father, along with countless other colliers, had been forced for decades to descend – becomes a source of regeneration whose 'torches of darkness' illuminate both the life and the language of the wild common.

NOTES

1 *The Complete Poems*, ed. Vivian de sola Pinto and F. Warren Roberts (1964; New York: Penguin, 1971), pp. 33–4; all further references in the text will be to this edition (*CP*) and page numbers will appear in parentheses.

2 T. S. Eliot, *After Strange Gods: A Primer of Modern Heresy, the Page-Barbour Lectures at the University of Virginia, 1933* (London: Faber and Faber, 1934), pp. 58–60.

3 *Ibid.*, p. 59.

4 To Catherine Carswell [11 January 1916], *The Letters of D. H. Lawrence*, Vol. II, *1913–16*, ed. George Zytaruk and James T. Boulton (Cambridge: Cambridge University Press, 1981), p. 50.

5 Quoted in F. O. Matthiessen, *The Achievement of T. S. Eliot: An Essay on the Nature of Poetry* (1933; New York and London: Oxford University Press, 1958), pp. 89–90.

6 F. R. Leavis, 'Mr Eliot and Mr Lawrence', in Frederick J. Hoffman and Harry T. Moore (eds.), *The Achievement of D. H. Lawrence* (1951; Norman: University of Oklahoma Press, 1953).

7 *Poetry: A Magazine of Verse*, VI, 3 (June, 1915), pp. 130–5 ('Prufrock'); p. 151 (Monroe on Lawrence).

8 T. S. Eliot, *Inventions of the March Hare: Poems 1909–1917*, ed. Christopher Ricks (New York: Harcourt, 1997), pp. 307, 311.

9 *Ibid.*, pp. 78–9.

10 To Rachel Annand Taylor, 3 December 1910, in *The Letters of D. H. Lawrence*, Vol. I, *1901–13*, ed. James T. Boulton, pp. 189–90.

11 Wright Morris, 'Lawrence and the Immediate Present', in Harry Moore (ed.), *A D. H. Lawrence Miscellany* (Carbondale: Southern Illinois University Press, 1959), p. 8.

6

NEIL CORCORAN

Wilfred Owen and the poetry of war

I

In 'The Owl', written in February 1915, three months before he enlisted, Edward Thomas characteristically sets himself on the open road: walking at night feeling hungry, cold and tired. When he enters an inn, though, the exterior world is 'quite barred out' except for 'An owl's cry, a most melancholy cry // Shaken out long and clear upon the hill' – and shaken out too across a stanza break, a formal prolongation dramatising the owl's effect on the poet. In fact the cry is also shaken out across English literary history, since it is explicitly distinguished from the owl's 'merry note' in Shakespeare's song. For this owl carries an echoing message 'telling me plain what I escaped / And others could not, that night, as in I went':

> And salted was my food, and my repose,
> Salted and sobered, too, by the bird's voice
> Speaking for all who lay under the stars,
> Soldiers and poor, unable to rejoice.[1]

'Salted': seasoned, but also rendered poignant or piquant. The bird's voice, the only voice we hear in this poem of human shelter and sustenance, transforms the poet's circumstances by its insistent reminder of all who lack such things, 'soldiers and poor'.

Where the owl is insistent, however, this poet is not. 'The Owl' is merely shadowed by the symbolic properties of its eponymous bird; but this voice is a wise one too, offering exemplary but disconsoling counsel, and doing so by 'speaking for' others. And, by taking their part, by speaking in their stead, the owl obviates the need for the poet to do likewise more directly. The owl is the means by which Edward Thomas both gives weight to, and avoids being weighed down by, the expectation that poets in wartime should speak for others, should take on representative status; and, avoiding that, Thomas manages also to avoid the pitfalls which might accompany such commitments: self-approval, presumption, the too easily earned satisfactions of indignation. Indeed, his co-ordination – 'soldiers and poor' – by omitting the definite article (not 'the poor') may insinuate that 'poor' is an adjective defining 'soldiers' rather than a separate category, and this may carry a political insinuation too: that soldiers might also be the poor, that poverty might have made them soldiers, even that war might be the continuation of state policy by other means. The poem's own 'most melancholy cry', in February 1915, is therefore an unemphatic but politically charged undermining of its final rhyme. This poet's voice is unable to rejoice in the imperial wartime mode of Rupert Brooke's 'The Soldier' but is also wary of the authority of representative status about to be implied and occasionally made explicit in the poems of Siegfried Sassoon and Wilfred Owen.

Just over two years after writing 'The Owl' Edward Thomas, not after all escaping what others could not, was killed; and in the intervening period he in fact spent very little time in the trenches. Many of the over 140 poems he wrote then are war poems, therefore, in a rather different sense from those of the combatant poets. Such poems as 'Words', 'Roads' and 'Rain' – monosyllabic titles which seem almost off-handedly unassertive but also hugely inclusive – are work in which the war is internalised not only as a context for consciousness and sensibility but as the very ground of these things. In 'Words' the English language must be 'worn new', an oxymoron in which 'worn' is both 'dressed in' and 'worked at': so the poem celebrates the virtue of linguistic renovation, implicitly challenging the language of a political journalism worn very old indeed – worn out – in jingoistic cliché. And 'Rain' transforms its exterior weather into an interior state of being which seems inseparable from the state of being at war, when a wrenching beatitude – 'Blessed are the dead that the rain rains upon' – introduces lines in which the unnamed war plunges thought into a form of trance. Here the language is worn new when something is worn out, in lines which waver irresolvably between prayer, personal melancholia, and universal lamentation, and do so in a limpidly fluent and self-possessed syntax at ironic odds with the desolation being given its consummate expression:

> But here I pray that none whom I once loved
> Is dying tonight or lying still awake
> Solitary, listening to the rain,
> Either in pain or thus in sympathy
> Helpless among the living and the dead,
> Like a cold water among broken reeds,
> Myriads of broken reeds all still and stiff,
> Like me who have no love which this wild rain
> Has not dissolved except the love of death,

If love it be towards what is perfect and
Cannot, the tempest tells me, disappoint.

2

It is impossible not to take stock of Thomas's poems in an essay on the poetry of the First World War, but combatant poetry nevertheless seems a special case, since the poets' responses to this unasked-for material involved them in such exceptional challenges, both aesthetic and ethical. To be an officer in charge of troops – of the 'men', sometimes referred to in poems as 'boys' – was to be made directly responsible for the suffering and death of the young, this being the inevitable consequence of orders necessarily given and faithfully obeyed. For Owen and for Siegfried Sassoon this appears to have been supportable eventually only to the extent that the anxiety, guilt or self-reproach consequent upon it was the spur to the writing of poems engaging with it. Both felt acutely their poetic responsibility, and plight, as witnesses. Owen defines this in a letter of 1917 in which he tells his mother that he has become 'a poet's poet' – he has earned the approval of Sassoon and Harold Munro – but that his poems must capture the 'look' of men at the Front, 'like a dead rabbit's': 'It will never be painted, and no actor will ever seize it. And to describe it, I think I must go back and be with them.'[2] The element of self-approval in this is bleached out when the thought becomes a promissory poem, 'The Calls':

> For leaning out last midnight on my sill,
> I heard the sighs of men that have no skill
> To speak of their distress, no nor the will!
> A voice I know. And this time I will go.[3]

And Sassoon in 'Sick Leave' expresses the guilt of withdrawal from the field by imagining 'the noiseless dead' approaching his sickbed to reproach him: ' "When are you going out to them again? / Are they not still your brothers through our blood?" '[4] The poem adds a self-recriminatory frisson to the trope of the revenant common in wartime poems (and made exceptional in Thomas's 'Roads', where 'the dead / Returning lightly dance'); and, by stopping at thirteen lines, it calls up the ghost of the sonnet, that most typical of wartime poetic forms, to suggest unfinished business, as if the business of the poem might be completed only by a return to the business of battle.

Owen's 'Spring Offensive', however, complicates the call. It recreates the lull before battle and then the attack itself before the final line of the penultimate stanza turns to the aftermath: 'Some say God caught them even before they fell'. This poem does not explicitly deny that, although the non-specificity suggests scepticism; but the final stanza asks what the survivors 'say': 'Why speak not they of comrades that went under?' The question contains bafflement, regret and even irritation, but also anxiety. This very poem, by speaking at all, is presuming to speak for those who either cannot, or who decide not to, speak for themselves. The question savingly queries the whole undertaking of Owen's work, implicitly recognising that the officer in charge, the man who has given the orders for this 'offensive', is very dubiously positioned as a spokesman for those who stay silent subsequently. The war becomes his subject while he is literally making others subject to him. The poem appears to query its own right to 'speak for', perhaps even to acknowledge that it also might seem 'offensive'; and this stress in the very undertaking is one of the several complications that enrich Owen's finest work. His poetry is the scene of his anguished examination of what it is to be a lieutenant, a *lieu-tenant*: one who holds, or stands in, the place of others. The place he holds on the battlefield is that of the commanding officer; the place he holds in the poem can only be very self-questioningly that of the private soldier.

But there are other ramifying complications in Owen's wartime poems too. An untitled, two-sentence poem brilliantly and disturbingly clarifies at least one of them:

> I saw his round mouth's crimson deepen as it fell,
>> Like a sun, in his last deep hour;
> Watched the magnificent recession of farewell,
>> Clouding, half gleam, half glower,
> And a last splendour burn the heavens of his cheek.
>> And in his eyes
> The cold stars lighting, very old and bleak,
>> In different skies.

This poem does what many of Owen's war poems do: it re-configures almost allotropically a topos everywhere in his work – a homoerotic fantasising about the faces and bodies of young men. Such continuities are apparent in Jon Stallworthy's edition which reveals how, even in the *annus mirabilis* – 1917–18 – in which he wrote most of his war poetry, he was still revising earlier work and drafting callow poems of unalloyed homoerotic fantasy, poems such as 'Page Eglantine' and 'The Rime of the Youthful Mariner'; and they are written large in Dominic Hibberd's biography.[5] In 'I saw his round mouth's crimson' these tropes are both complicated and distressed. The feeling with which the 'mouth's crimson' is gazed at is certainly erotic: the repetition of 'deepen' and 'deep' is a kind of pulsation, and the conjuration of that flush on the soldier's dying cheek carries into a strangely perturbed register the flushes of arousal which Owen would have noticed in Keats. But the poem is charged with other sympathetic recognitions too which elaborate sexual feeling into a quasi-religious 'recession' of mourning.

Indeed, the recessional hymn of the Anglican liturgy is recalled by the word 'recession', and a kind of displaced Anglicanism is never far from the tenderness of Owen's regard, as though his poem 'Maundy Thursday', probably drafted in 1915 and revised in late 1917 or early 1918, were a kind of paradigm or template for the war poems: when the crucifix is held out to the congregation for veneration, the poem's speaker kisses not the cross itself but 'the warm live hand that held the thing', the 'brown' hand of 'a server-lad'. 'I saw his round mouth's crimson' is also a poem of transferred or displaced veneration, deepening eroticism into mourning, while also disturbingly, but bravely, acknowledging the presence of erotic feeling in the context of gazing on a dying body.

'Maundy Thursday' risks blasphemy; 'I saw his round mouth's crimson' also braves risk by striving for honest record, accurate emotion, and an unflinching attempt to make language newly commensurate with horrific event. Refusing to sanitise response, it intricates suffering and reaction, victimisation and voyeurism, in a knot of intricate complexity; welling out of Owen's psycho-sexual subjectivity, it also meets the extreme demand of its historical moment. James Fenton has said of Owen's juvenilia that 'the realm of Eros was what he felt to be his great subject'.[6] In 'I saw his round mouth's crimson' and other war poems, Owen produces work in which what he felt to be his great subject, 'the realm of Eros', is forced into devastating confrontation with a subject he did not want at all, the realm of Thanatos; but this turns what he felt to be his great subject into his truly great subject, and the subject of great poems. The combination of the erotic and the representative is what makes poems such as 'Strange Meeting', 'Greater Love', 'Asleep' and 'Disabled' so emotionally complicated: poems in which a quality of yearning undermines any elegiac principle of assuagement.

'I saw his round mouth's crimson' may also, however, briefly flicker with another element apparent in Owen's war poems when it gazes into those withdrawing eyes and sees there 'The cold stars lighting, very old and bleak / In different skies'. Peter Howarth discovers the word 'indifferent' here, reading it as Owen's awareness of the soldier's unresponsiveness to his own interest; but it could also leave the man's eyes glazing over with what this poet takes to be the civilian reaction to such deaths: indifference.[7] Owen's poems are designed to shock readers out of indifference by confronting them with actuality; and some, much more obviously than 'I saw his round mouth's crimson', prominently include an element of the homiletic: notably 'Apologia pro Poemate Meo' ('These men are worth / Your tears. You are not worth their merriment'), 'Insensibility', and 'Dulce et Decorum Est'. This is one of the implications of the preface which he drafted in May 1918 for a volume he hoped to publish the following year:

> This book is not about heroes. English Poetry is not yet fit to speak of them. Nor is it about glory or honour or any might, majesty, dominion or power nor about anything except War. Above all I am not concerned with Poetry. My subject is War, and the pity of War. The Poetry is in the pity ... Yet these elegies are in no sense consolatory to this generation. They may be to the next ... All a poet can do today is warn. That is why the true Poet must be truthful.[8]

The capitalisations speak volumes: the usual motives for and prizes of war, those held in the mouths of politicians and journalists – glory, honour and so on – pale into lower case, and what stands upright is what the soldier must face, almost in the form of an apotheosised abstraction – 'War' – and what the poet has to offer – 'Poetry'. There is a politics in this, as there is in Edward Thomas's reticences; there is a revisionary aesthetics; and there is a strong sense of the poem as an act of cautionary witness. In fact, the contents list for this volume itemises not only the title of each poem but also its 'motive'; and one of the ways in which Owen was not Keatsian – as opposed to all the ways in which he was, in his youth – is his agitated certainty that poetry *should* have a palpable design upon us.[9] From this poet infinitely concerned, as his letters constantly show, with poetry, it's a self-revising gesture of the profoundest kind to declare that the poetry lies somewhere other than in the poetry; it's almost as though Owen can permit himself poetry, under these circumstances and out of this material, only when it has become something other than itself.

In an outstanding book on Owen, Douglas Kerr has shown how, in order to write these poems, he deliberately schooled himself in elegy, especially pastoral elegy; but he schools himself as a subversive.[10] Where the traditional English elegy is consolatory, assuaging grief in Christianised pastoral ('Some say God caught them even before they fell'), the truthful elegy of this war is 'in no sense consolatory'. Merging the erotic with the homiletic to create a poetry of scrupulously less deceived witness, a poetry against itself, Owen resists consolation with a more deeply distressed melancholy. Jahan Ramazani, reading Owen in tandem with Freud, makes less of the erotic than I do here, more of the poems' impulsion towards masochism, and nothing of the homiletic, but he also regards Owen as exemplifying the 'paradox' of modern elegies: that 'the best are frequently the most anti-elegiac'.[11]

'Futility' is exemplary in this way, and is also a poem in which subverted elegy and homiletic intention modify and differently focus desire. The exact intensity with which it manages this makes it, in my view, Owen's greatest poem:

> Move him into the sun –
> Gently its touch awoke him once,
> At home, whispering of fields half-sown.
> Always it woke him, even in France,
> Until this morning and this snow.
> If anything might rouse him now
> The kind old sun will know.
>
> Think how it wakes the seeds –
> Woke once the clays of a cold star.
> Are limbs, so dear-achieved, are sides
> Full-nerved, still warm, too hard to stir?
> Was it for this the clay grew tall?
> – O what made fatuous sunbeams toil
> To break earth's sleep at all?

This poem is revisionist of traditional elegy in several senses. It's a sonnet, and so a form conjuring a tradition of English lyric. But its abbreviated lines, its refusal of pentameter, make the form anxious, curtailed, self-resistant; and Owen's characteristic pararhymes (sun / sown; once / France; and so on), that influential modern invention, add to the edge and unease, the irresolution of emotion: pararhyme, Douglas Kerr memorably says, is 'a broken promise to return' – whereas traditional elegies keep their promises, and return is what they promise.[12] Some of the locations and properties characteristic of pastoral elegy – the half-sown fields, the personified rising sun, the waking from death into some form of new life – are warped in the direction of dissent and disconsolation; and, employing a standard rhetorical trope inherited from classical literature ('Was it for this?'), Owen asks one of the largest of his rhetorical questions, collapsing any elegiac solace into the ultimate insecurity of a question which is actually more than rhetorical: since, by the time 'Futility' was written (May 1918), many, both on and off the battlefield, were asking whether there was point in continuing.

'Futility' also brings to a point of pained self-revision the trope of the homoerotic gaze. The poem's opening instruction – 'Move him into the sun' – sounds like the initiation of a pastoral ritual; but it could equally be that of an officer to his men, telling them what to do with a corpse: and so Owen represents himself as both officer and poet, caught between actuality and art. But the instruction at the opening of the second stanza – 'Think how it wakes the seeds' – seems much more deeply interiorised, an instruction from the self to the self; and this is a self situated once more in the role of artful voyeur – that haunting phrase coined in a poem by a later admirer of Owen's defining his own relationship to another war and its dead.[13] Those 'limbs' and 'sides', particularised in a succession of achingly poignant epithets, might well, in another kind of poem, have been the spur to further erotic reverie. (We might even remember, with a kind of discrepant appropriateness, the camp jocularity with which Owen, in the trenches, writes punningly to Sassoon that he wants 'no more *exposed flanks* of any kind for a long time.')[14] Here, however, the eroticism is also curtailed: the licence of kissing the warm live hand in 'Maundy Thursday' has become the anguish of watching the warmth disappear forever from limbs now, just, 'still warm'; and what might elsewhere stir this onlooker erotically is in the process of becoming 'too hard to stir', except to stir this poet to the desperation and bitterness of his concluding questions. These raise Owen's exhaustion with the pieties of orthodox Christianity into a realm of almost apocalyptic weariness; a weariness which is quite a different thing, however, from resignation. 'Futility' offers, in its stabbingly eloquent economy, the spectacle of a poet in whom, under the most extreme responsiveness of obligation, everything is organised into sympathetic coherence and brought to its highest pitch of concentrated utterance. It is the exemplary combatant poem of war.

3

'Pity' is a significant word in Siegfried Sassoon's poems, and Owen was undoubtedly aided in the formulation of his preface, and altogether confirmed in his competence as a poet and in the tractability of the war as a subject for poetry, by his relationship with Sassoon, whom he met when both were inmates of Craiglockhart Hospital in Edinburgh, Owen as a consequence of 'neurasthenia' following front-line experience, and Sassoon as an alternative to standing trial for a 'declaration' against the running of the war which he made in July 1917. Not a pacifist's declaration, but, its title proclaimed, 'A Soldier's Declaration', it registered Sassoon's belief that the war had become 'a war of aggression and conquest'; it made a stand against 'political errors and insincerities'; and it blamed 'the callous complacency with which the majority of those at home regard the continuance of agonies which they do not share, and which they have not sufficient imagination to realize'.[15] This indictment was extremely brave of Sassoon, who was a quite extraordinarily impressive human being; and the fact that he also published satirical poems about the war provided Owen with a model for the way personal, non-pacifist bravery could be combined with poetic truth-telling.

Sassoon's poems take something from Hardy's *Satires of Circumstance* and comprise anecdote, reportage, invective and imitated demotic speech, and Owen learnt a great deal from work such as 'Base Details', 'The General' and '"They"'. In the last of these a 'Bishop' – and Sassoon had the bishop of London in mind – celebrates in the first stanza the fact that the returning boys 'will not be the same', after heroic transformation in battle. The second stanza, both counterpart and contradiction, then offers the boys' version of being 'none of us the same': one is legless, one blind, one lung-damaged and one syphilitic. The poem then concludes with the characteristic satirical epigram: 'And the Bishop said: "The ways of God are strange!"' Sassoon's poems typically work by such reversals of expectation, and such explosions of cliché, and they are capable of corruscatingly corrosive ironies and invective. If they seem now sometimes a little pat in their reversals, they are historically highly significant and should not be underestimated: but to witness Owen assimilating and transforming the manner in poems such as 'The Chances' is to witness poetic genius in the process of self-discovery. What begins as satire in that poem becomes less self-confident, more humanly wounded, more emotionally wrecked; and the sudden concluding phrase of reversal ('Jim's mad') has a perennial, rather than a propagandistic, desolation: satire mutates into tragedy.

In fact, whereas Owen's early letters after meeting Sassoon are effusions of hero worship (Hibberd believes that Owen was in love with him), he is, by December 1917, telling his cousin Leslie Gunston that 'Poetry with him is become a mere vehicle of propaganda': and this harsh dismissal seems a defining moment in Owen's astonishingly speedy acquisition of a sense of his own competence.[16] In 'The Chances' everything in Owen is absorptively alert and keyed to advantage; and similar effects of mastery and self-mastery are apparent in other poems too where, as Dominic Hibberd and others have shown, his early slavish indebtedness to Keats is pushed up against such things as the French Decadents, the English Georgians (especially Harold Monro) and Baudelaire. In fact, you could almost claim of Owen what Ezra Pound famously claimed of T. S. Eliot: that 'he modernized himself *on his own*'. And, given that he was in fact absorbing some of the same French influences as Eliot, it's tantalising to think that the fractures between Modernism and the 'native English tradition' may have looked very different had Owen survived the war; or, indeed, that Owen may have found a way different from Eliot's of bringing French decadence and symbolism into post-war English poetry. As it was, his accommodations, adaptations and technical inventions themselves proved deeply influential on the poets of the 1930s, a generation also necessarily sensitised to, and seeking ways to articulate, political and historical crisis (and, in some cases, homosexual orientation). And Owen continues to echo and reverberate in more contemporary poetries too. Ted Hughes's work returns insistently to the First World War, and writing in 1964 he suggests the continued relevance of Owen to an England in which that war is 'still unfinished'.[17] And for Seamus Heaney, Owen's poetry of witness has 'haunted the back of the literary mind as a kind of challenge': one met by Heaney himself in some of his work.[18]

4

I have suggested that Owen modernised himself on his own. Certainly until he met Sassoon he had no one to help him. Isaac Rosenberg, from a more poverty-stricken background than Owen – in the East End of London – nevertheless managed, by a form of short-lived patronage, to gain an acquaintance with pre-war avant-garde movements in the arts, and his poetry was supported, in a rather half-hearted way, by Ezra Pound, and by Harriet Monroe, who published him in her influential magazine *Poetry (Chicago)*. Rosenberg's forms have, as a consequence, affiliations with both free verse and Imagism. Employing Biblical and Jewish materials, and ambitiously attempting a kind of post-Blakean religio-prophetic poetry, he also had a much larger range of pre-war subject matter than Owen. For these reasons, among others, his war poetry appears less shocked into variant utterance, less alternatively galvanised, than Owen's, although the war does newly animate and sharpen what can seem a certain vatic vapidity in the earlier work. He also experiments with the same phrases and lines in different poems; and one letter poignantly promises further drafting in tranquillity: 'I will not leave a corner of my consciousness covered up, but saturate myself with the strange and extraordinary new conditions of this life, and it will all refine itself into poetry later on.'[19]

So it is a shock to learn from Vivien Noakes's superb edition that Rosenberg, a private soldier, actually wrote most of his war poems in the trenches – unlike Owen, who wrote his on leave, including the extended sick leave of his spell in Craiglockhart. Rosenberg enlisted in October 1915 and was killed on 1 April 1918; and during twenty-one months in France he had only ten days' leave. 'It is unusual,' Noakes says drily, 'for a manuscript not to be folded, torn and dirty.'[20] As a consequence, the editorial lot is more than usually unhappy, and many of Rosenberg's given texts must be regarded as provisional. Although this is one of the reasons why his

reputation has never settled in the way Owen's has, reading him is sometimes to feel that an element of folded, torn and dirty provisionality inheres
in his very aesthetic, which seems to honour, more than most, the improvisatory. We might even think that he meant something of the kind when he
wrote in a letter to Gordon Bottomley (who edited his first posthumous
volume in 1922) that his ideal was one of 'Simple *poetry* – that is where an
interesting complexity of thought is kept in tone and right value to the
dominating idea so that it is understandable and still ungraspable.'[21] This
seems to anticipate Wallace Stevens's much more famous contention that
'the poem must resist the intelligence almost successfully' and to harmonise
with T. S. Eliot's conception of the destabilising difficulties inevitably
inherent in a genuinely modern poetry. Like these, it has a quality of almost
truculently confrontational self-assurance; and it indicates that Rosenberg
was modernised, perhaps with a little help, from a very early stage. It's
remote indeed from Owen's guarded but still sometimes almost skinless
affectivity.

As a consequence, Rosenberg's poems characteristically move by ellipsis
and elision, by the melting or dripping of image into image, by abruptions
of rhythm and cadence, by unsettling and not always easily 'graspable'
syntactical transitions. His forms can jarringly convey, almost mimetically,
the actualities of trench warfare, as in 'Dead Man's Dump', in which army
'limbers' (carts or gun-carriages) 'lurched over sprawled dead'. This poem
itself lurches and jostles in its attempt to convey this exceptional grue-
someness in a fury of alliterative and assonantal linguistic wreckage ('The
plunging limbers over the shattered track / Racketed with their rusty
freight'), in biblical and other religious half-echo and allusion, in anguished
questioning, and in sudden astonishing, quasi-metaphysical conceit, as in
the likening of a bullet to a bee: 'When the swift iron burning bee / Drained
the wild honey of their youth'; which is a motivating of the inanimate as
luxuriously appalled as Owen's homoerotic anthropomorphosing in 'Arms
and the Boy': 'these blind, blunt bullet-leads / Which long to nuzzle in the
hearts of lads'.

In contrast to such poems of driven physical representation, there are in
Rosenberg much cooler poems of ironic muteness. The greatest of these,
and one of the greatest of the war, is 'Break of Day in the Trenches', a poem
of eerily disquieting calm. Here simple *poetry*, poetry in a very pure dis-
tillation, is being written, and it is a poetry in which complexity of thought,
and tone and right value are lucidly self-validating means and effects.
D. W. Harding says that suffering in Rosenberg is treated in such a way that
'no secondary distress [arises] from the sense that these things *ought not* to
be. He was given up to realizing fully what *was*'; and this appears to be at

least partly right about this poem.²² Given that exactly such secondary distress impels all of Owen's war poems and that it is actually primary distress in Sassoon, this quality makes 'Break of Day' very much the poem of a private soldier, a poem that speaks for itself and not on behalf of others, perhaps even a kind of answer to Owen's anguished question, 'Why speak not they of comrades that went under?'

The poem imagines its speaker picking a poppy from the trench parapet to stick behind his ear, when a rat from No Man's Land 'leaps [his] hand'. The rat is anthropomorphically figured as 'sardonic' and 'droll', and the speaker himself drolly rebukes the rat's treacherous 'cosmopolitan sympathies' (it crosses the lines, but the phrase is also glossed by Rosenberg's Jewishness). So – almost unimaginable thing if Rosenberg had not managed it – drollery and wit are brought to the poetry of the trenches. Complexities of thought then combine with drollery, when the dead are said to be 'less chanced than you for life' and 'bonds to the whims of murder'. So the poem plots a politics into its drollery too: soldiers in the trenches are worth less than rats; their deaths are 'murder', and not some other thing – 'sacrifice', for instance; and are governed by 'whim' and not by 'glory or honour', or even policy. So Harding is not quite right about this poem: although it makes no parade of its 'secondary distress', it certainly knows that these things ought not to be.

The poem moves to conclusion with two of Rosenberg's characteristically vast rhetorical questions – asked of the rat, and so crossing drollery with desperation, and then astonishingly inflecting anguish with recovery in a way almost jaunty in its self-presentation:

> What do you see in our eyes
> At the shrieking iron and flame
> Hurl'd through still heavens?
> What quaver – what heart aghast?
> Poppies whose roots are in men's veins
> Drop, and are ever dropping,
> But mine in my ear is safe –
> Just a little white with the dust.

This nonchalance, a desperate composure, proffers an extraordinary image: that of the trench soldier as dandy; where, previously, the cosmopolitan rat is almost a kind of Baudelairean *flâneur*, out strolling in the early morning for – the speaker says – 'your pleasure'. Yet the out-of-tune, dissonant fall of 'aghast' against 'dust' insinuates the fate of this stylish respite, and unnervingly orients the figure of the dandy – usually, of course, comic – towards tragedy. Managing such a style and such a tone at such a time and in such a place, Rosenberg is validating the authority of the aesthetic: 'Break of Day in the Trenches' learns a style from a despair by not permitting a despair to cramp, or to dictate, a style. Doing so, he also manifests a very high form of courage.

The example has been taken in: by Keith Douglas in 'Desert Flowers', his combatant poem of the Eastern Front in the Second World War, with its anxiously tributary line, 'Rosenberg, I only repeat what you were saying'; and by Michael Longley, another poet whose imagination is frequently caught up in the First World War, and whose poetry is complexly responsive to the war in Northern Ireland: 'Bog Cotton' revises the line as a tribute to Douglas, and 'No Man's Land' reads itself into the experience of a Jewish grandmother with a deferential inclination: 'I tilt her head towards you, Isaac Rosenberg'.

5

Rosenberg and Owen died in the war; Ivor Gurney survived. But his mode of survival – in mental institutions for most of his life, and constantly revisiting the war in his poems of the 1920s, preoccupied by what he calls, with characteristically perspicacious awkwardness, 'the whole craft and business of bad occasion' – offers one emblem for the way the war cannot be extirpated from psychological or cultural memory. This makes P. J. Kavanagh's devoted act of recovery of Gurney in his 1982 edition a major moment in the history of the poetry of the war, giving us in their required contexts at least two of its outstanding poems.[23] 'To His Love', written during the war, collapses a Virgilian pastoral eclogue of companionship into an urgent yearning to forget what can never be forgotten, and does so in the most jolting of enjambements:

> Cover him, cover him soon!
> And with thick-set
> Masses of memoried flowers –
> Hide that red wet
> Thing I must somehow forget.

And 'The Silent One', written several years after the war, expresses one of the worst horrors of trench warfare: having to see your friends die on the wire of No Man's Land beyond the reach of succour. The dead man commemorated in the specificity of his language and accent may stand here as an emblem for what the poets of that war managed in their own languages and accents, wearing them new; and also, since Gurney pointedly remarks the folly of military faithfulness, for the infinite waste of all the war's silent, and silenced, ones:

> Who died on the wires, and hung there, one of two –
> Who for his hours of life had chattered through
> Infinite lovely chatter of Bucks accent:
> Yet faced unbroken wires; stepped over, and went
> A noble fool, faithful to his stripes – and ended.

NOTES

1 Quotations from Thomas are taken from *The Collected Poems and War Diary, 1917*, ed. R. George Thomas (London: Faber and Faber, 2004).

2 Wilfred Owen, *Selected Letters*, ed. John Bell (Oxford: Oxford University Press, 1985), p. 306.

3 Quotations from Owen are taken from Jon Stallworthy (ed.), *Wilfred Owen: The Complete Poems and Fragments* (London: Chatto and Windus; and Oxford: Oxford University Press, 1983).

4 Quotations from Sassoon are taken from Siegfried Sassoon, *The War Poems* (London: Faber and Faber, 1983).

5 Dominic Hibberd, *Wilfred Owen: A New Biography* (London: Weidenfeld and Nicholson, 2002).

6 James Fenton, *The Strength of Poetry* (Oxford: Oxford University Press, 2001), p. 32.

7 Peter Howarth, *British Poetry in the Age of Modernism* (Cambridge: Cambridge University Press, 2005), p. 196.

8 Quoted in Hibberd, *Wilfred Owen*, p. 317.

9 *Ibid.*

10 Douglas Kerr, *Wilfred Owen's Voices* (Oxford: Clarendon Press, 1993), pp. 277–95.

11 Jahan Ramazani, *Poetry of Mourning: The Modern Elegy from Hardy to Heaney* (Chicago: University of Chicago Press, 1994), p. 69.

12 Kerr, *Wilfred Owen's Voices*, p. 295.

13 Seamus Heaney, 'Punishment', in *North* (London: Faber and Faber, 1975).

14 Owen, *Selected Letters*, p. 353.

15 Siegfried Sassoon, *The Complete Memoirs of George Sherston* (1937; London: Faber and Faber, 1972), p. 496.

16 Owen, *Selected Letters*, p. 305.

17 Ted Hughes, *Winter Pollen: Occasional Prose*, ed. William Scammell (London: Faber and Faber, 1994), p. 43.

18 Seamus Heaney, *The Government of the Tongue* (London: Faber and Faber, 1988), p. xiii.

19 Quoted in Vivien Noakes (ed.), *The Poems and Plays of Isaac Rosenberg* (Oxford: Oxford University Press, 2004), p. xlvi.

20 *Ibid.*, p. xx.

21 *Ibid.*, p. xlv.
22 D. W. Harding, *Experience into Words* (1963; Cambridge: Cambridge University Press, 1982), p. 97.
23 *Collected Poems of Ivor Gurney*, ed. P. J. Kavanagh (Oxford: Oxford University Press, 1982).

Further reading

Das, Santanu, *Touch and Intimacy in First World War Literature*, Cambridge: Cambridge University Press, 2005
Graham, Desmond, *The Truth of War: Owen, Blunden and Rosenberg*, Manchester: Carcanet Press, 1984
Hibberd, Dominic, *Wilfred Owen: A New Biography*, London: Weidenfeld and Nicholson, 2002
Howarth, Peter, *British Poetry in the Age of Modernism*, Cambridge: Cambridge University Press, 2005
Kendall, Tim, *Modern English War Poetry*, Oxford: Oxford University Press, 2006
Kerr, Douglas, *Wilfred Owen's Voices*, Oxford: Clarendon Press, 1993
Ramazani, Jahan, *Poetry of Mourning: The Modern Elegy from Hardy to Heaney*, Chicago: University of Chicago Press, 1994
Silkin, Jon, *Out of Battle: The Poetry of the Great War*, Oxford: Oxford University Press, 1972

PART THREE

Modernists

7

MICHAEL O'NEILL

The 1930s poetry of W. H. Auden

I

A virtuoso craftsman, Auden is also a poet who communicates a strong sense of an idiosyncratic personal voice. Yet this voice can seem enigmatic in its inflections. In what follows, I shall examine and compare a range of poems from his 1930s work (the term covers poems composed between 1928 and 1939) to examine three issues: whether we can see Auden as maturing beyond or falling away from his early, electrifying stylistic brilliance; whether behind the deft stylist there is a poetic sensibility capable of engagement with his subjects; and whether Auden's poetry conforms to his pronouncement in his 'Introduction' to *The Poet's Tongue* that 'Poetry is not concerned with telling people what to do, but with extending our knowledge of good and evil, perhaps making the necessity for action more urgent and its nature more clear, but only leading us to the point where it is possible for us to make a rational and moral choice.'[1]

In making that statement, Auden was judiciously asserting his freedom from agitprop ideas of art common in the 1930s, a period remarkable for its political consciousness, its sense that poetry must engage with the pressing realities of its time. Out of the window goes the High Modernist longing, beyond any fragments shored against ruins, for a vanished ideal of aesthetic and political order; in comes a feeling that the true matter for art is the state of society and the individual's relationship with the social. Long gone is 'the Poet's Party', as Auden calls it in part 3 of his witty pastiche-cum-tribute, 'Letter to Lord Byron', a party marked by its elitist disregard for 'all those cattle'; instead, as the party gives way to the hangover (of which the First World War and the Wall Street Crash of 1929 might be regarded as cataclysmic symptoms), 'the sobering few / Are trying hard to think of something new'.

2

Early Auden thinks of 'something new' by disconcerting and challenging his readers with a poetry that purges sentiment and mimes a clinical aloofness.

The poetry draws on eclectic sources to create effects of urgency and warning. Among other influences, it gathers to itself and makes a first-hand synthesis out of Laura Riding's short-lined, Skeltonic riddlings, the stressed admonitions and dislocations of Anglo-Saxon elegiac poetry, the compressed lexical and metrical adventures of Gerard Manley Hopkins's poems (published for the first time in 1918) and the uses by Wilfred Owen of forms of rhyme in which consonance goes hauntingly awry.

A tight curb is kept on feeling in the early work. 'Taller to-day, we remember similar evenings' begins with a gesture towards memory, but it leads nowhere other than a conclusion in which the poem tersely refers to 'this peace / No bird can contradict: passing, but is sufficient now / For something fulfilled this hour, loved or endured'. The feeling of 'peace' is more affirmative than is usually the case in Auden's early poetry, but the writing is guardedly vigilant. It brings into play, even as it outlaws, the idea of 'contradiction'; it acknowledges that the peace is 'passing'; even if 'sufficient now', the 'peace' is only 'sufficient' 'For something fulfilled this hour', where 'something' may understate joy or indicate 'something' only of momentary significance. If the poem refers to sexual 'fulfilment', it leaves in doubt the poet's attitude, a doubt compounded by the final three words, where the phrasing 'loved or endured' makes of love and endurance comparable states. The writing approaches the personal through the passive voice and by way of reference to alternative experience; it has a strangely displaced feel, as though one were reading a translation from a work about a culture enigmatically like and unlike our own. The line, 'It is seen how excellent hands have turned to commonness', is studiedly concerned to repudiate the first-person singular. The 'peace' attained at the poem's close is set in the context of a culture governed by forces such as 'the Adversary' that 'put too easy questions / On lonely roads'. This 'Adversary' both resembles and sends up folkloric or legendary bogeymen, and the poem's chilling rhetoric, with its possibly parodic air of authority, may mock us. It may be a form of poker-faced ridicule, as though an exceptionally clever schoolboy were mimicking his earnest elders. The verse form avoids Modernist disregard for formal punctuation, but it elongates and shrinks the iambic pentameter in accordance with feeling. In its figurative activity, its relationship with past poetry is one of indebtedness amidst novelty: that 'peace / No bird can contradict' emerges from poems by Shelley, Keats, Hardy and Hopkins in which a bird contradicts or complicates the speaker's viewpoint.

If one compares 'Taller to-day' with another love poem, this time from the mid-1930s, one can see how Auden's style changes across the decade. 'Lay your sleeping head, my love' (written in 1937) shares with 'Taller to-day' an air of decisiveness common to all Auden's poems. However oblique, however complex, an Auden poem asserts its right to exist from the start, often signalling its poetic self-confidence through a striking first line. The later poem has such formal self-confidence in abundance, organising its scalpel-sharp reflections on love, mortality and faithlessness in stanzas that achieve a gravely musical shape. Rhyme and off-rhyme serve as a marker of attempted control, of intelligence brought to bear on feeling, yet enjambment ensures that the poet's double vision unfolds as he wishes it to unfold. The poem has left behind the abruptness and reticence of the earlier poem in favour of a more subtly surprising relationship with traditional love lyric. As with the earlier poem, the addressee is likely to be male; never explicitly acknowledged by the poem, this must be inferred from what we know of Auden's biography, but may explain the feeling of exclusion transmitted by both pieces. In 'Lay your sleeping head', Auden employs the diction, tone and manner associated with tender love lyrics, but he administers a shock to the assumptions he arouses by speaking in the poem's second line of 'my faithless arm'. 'Faithless arm' disrupts tenderness, yet it creates it anew. The poet is aware that the love will not last, and that, in all probability, he will be the cause of its failure, but this awareness co-exists with a determination to acknowledge the beauty of the moment in the face of all that challenges that beauty. Even if 'the grave / Proves the child ephemeral', where the Greek-derived 'ephemeral' works to place a parallel instance of transience in a long cultural perspective, the poet still pleads on behalf of 'the living creature', asking that the lover may 'lie' in his arms. At the same time, positioned at the end of the line, 'lie' equivocates: it definitely means 'rest'; it may mean 'deceive'. Yet 'the living creature' is a phrase that only seems to depersonalise; certainly, it sees the poem's 'you' in a more generalised way, but that more generalised way is not at odds with an appreciation of the beloved's uniqueness. The stanza concludes with a recognition of the speaker's subjectivity, a recognition that is both confession and boast, as he depicts his lover as 'Mortal, guilty, but to me / The entirely beautiful'. 'But to me' does not undo the trochaic weight of the preceding adjectives, nor does it lay them aside; rather, it gathers them up into a phrase that posits an alternative, more inclusive awareness, one that values the beloved as 'The entirely beautiful', a phrase that is given a line of its own, in keeping with its glimpse of how one might view another 'entirely'.

The poem's succeeding stanzas balance tolerant disenchantment about Venus's 'tolerant enchanted slope' against the wish that 'from this night / Not a whisper, not a thought, / Not a kiss nor look be lost'. Even when Auden seems to abolish boundaries, often an image for division in his earlier work, the result is not to free human beings from the possibility of error. So, when in the second stanza he asserts, 'Soul and body have no bounds', ensuing lines suggest that human beings ricochet between eros and abstract idealism in ways that Freud might describe as sublimation and repression. But Auden's lyric achievement is to allow the significance of what he concedes to be an 'ordinary swoon' to hold its own in the face of the poem's majestically unsorrowing acceptance of our time-bound condition: 'Certainty, fidelity / On the stroke of midnight pass / Like vibrations of a bell', Auden writes at the start of the third stanza, the august nouns so many Cinderellas stripped of their finery; by the start of the fourth and last stanza, the declaration is briefer and bleaker, and yet by no means nihilistic: 'Beauty, midnight, vision dies'. The line serves as the prelude to a renewed outbreak of hope that time which deceives will also save; 'Nights of insult' will take their allotted place among friendlier 'winds of dawn'. Both love poems engage, then, with their subject, at the centre of which is human emotion; both, in their differing ways, not only seek to call up emotion but also to investigate its full human significance. Auden's earlier work always jolts and imparts a strong verbal voltage; his later 1930s work, with its mimicry of traditional formal harmonies, often lulls initially. But whether jolting or lulling, the 1930s work shares a strong impulse to 'extend our knowledge' of ourselves.

3

That knowledge concerns itself centrally with mindscapes and landscapes. In his autobiography Stephen Spender writes evocatively of Auden's 'poetic landscape of deserted mines, spies, shootings – terse syllables enclosed within a music like the wind in a deserted shaft'.[2] Auden's 'poetic landscape' in his early poems serves as an objective correlative for a sense of England as a county riven by conflict and stratification, a place where something is distinctly rotten. On the look-out for symptoms, the poetry diagnoses, often nailing its discoveries through a curt use of the definite article, the Audenesque 'the', heard in the plea that an unnamed healer should cure 'the intolerable neural itch' in one poem, or, in 'Consider this and in our time', in the mockery of 'the insufficient units' who are 'Supplied with feelings by an efficient band'. These 'units' are incapable of the sufficiency glimpsed at the end of 'Taller to-day', and the 'efficient band' taunts them with their inadequacy. The units and their like are doomed, the poem suggests, to suffer 'A polar peril, a prodigious alarm'.

This alliterative mouthful of a line zestfully plays up – almost sends up – the possibility of an apocalyptic scenario. Eliot's end-of-civilisation-as-we-know-it moments, in 'What the Thunder said', implicate us all: 'We who were living are now dying / With a little patience'. Haunted by and grieving for a coherent vision, Eliot opens his poem to surreal ghostings, snatches of gospel narrative, glimpses of hope, all conveyed in a grammar-defying sequence of juxtaposed images. When in 'Consider this' Auden imagines the disintegration of a moribund class, he does so in a language that implies an authoritative superiority on the part of the poet; if he manages to co-opt the idiom of Freud and Marx, pinpointing the psycho-social fault lines behind 'The convolutions of your simple wish', there is a gusto, a delight in the poetic performance.

That performance relies on switches of focus; verbal equivalents to wide-lens panning and sudden close-ups suggest the influence of the cinema in the opening five lines:

> Consider this and in our time
> As the hawk sees it or the helmeted airman:
> The clouds rift suddenly – look there
> At cigarette-end smouldering on a border
> At the first garden party of the year.

The syntax feels tightly wound; it makes sense, but seems to be under unusual pressure from an opening that breathes new life into the ancient injunction to 'Consider'. We must consider an undefined 'this' whose nature we assume inheres in the descriptive detail that follows, and we must consider 'this' as happening 'in our time'. This is not an admonitory poetry that stacks on the same cultural rubble-heap contemporary London and the ships at Mylae, as in 'The Burial of the Dead', the first part of *The Waste Land*. Rather, it impresses on us its relevance to an actual now.

Such relevance is the product of estranged perspective, the end of many expressive techniques in early Auden, keen to embrace the view taken by the 'hawk' or the 'helmeted airman'. The alliterative vigour of those phrases allows an older, native linguistic energy to reassert itself, one that has the effect of culturally relativising the present. A language associated with, say, Langland proves its relevance to 'our time', with the implication not that the supposed newness of 'our time' is a sham, but that it requires an intelligence familiar with earlier and other cultures as well as with the present to be brought to bear on it. The verse relishes estrangement, assuming the accents of the anthropologist exploring rituals of the tribe, such as 'the first garden party of the year'. Again, the image of the 'cigarette-end smouldering on a border' typifies Auden's ability to seize on a detail and invest it with portentous menace. At the same time he sidesteps deftly any suggestion that he is being histrionic; if 'smouldering' brings into place the idea of nursed or suppressed resentment, it is also a word that neutrally describes the dying flame of a thrown-away cigarette; and if the 'border' suggests conflict, trespass and separation in many poems by early Auden, it refers here at a literal level to a garden border.

Auden's seriousness in his early poems, indeed, links with the elusiveness of pinning down how serious he is being. F. R. Leavis objected to the 'combination of seriousness and flippancy' in *Paid on Both Sides*; but the combination is one which, in various forms, shapes the communicative inflections of many of Auden's earlier poems. Leavis thought the combination bore a relationship to 'the stultifying division in [Auden's] own consciousness'.[3] The 'supreme Antagonist' / More powerful than the great northern whale' who materialises in the second paragraph of 'Consider' bears witness, however, not to a 'stultifying division', but to a capacity for mythmaking play that energises and refreshes the verse. In its sinister yet comic invasions, the 'Antagonist' is the poet's scourge and minister, his unholy double, sharing a keen capacity to scent out illness and corruption. Auden's syntax leaves one wondering whether an initial indicative has turned into imperatives in a passage such as the following:

> Order the ill that they attack at once:
> Visit the ports and, interrupting
> The leisurely conversation in the bar
> Within a stone's throw of the sunlit water,
> Beckon your chosen out.

The positioning of 'interrupting' mimes perfectly the polite insistence of the Antagonist's intervention, while the detail of the 'bar / Within a stone's throw of the sunlit water' makes strange the slang of the privileged class, even as it loiters conspiratorially in their company. Auden's capacity to shift moods and subject positions lends the poetry an edge of imperturbable knowingness that heightens, towards the close, into a gleeful ruthlessness. In the final paragraph, Auden again addresses 'you', though this time the addressee is not the 'Antagonist' but the Antagonist's victims, the 'Seekers after happiness' destined for the poem's twinned fates of 'explosion of mania' or 'a classic fatigue'.

Auden's diction continually keeps his reader on her or his toes. The to-and-fro movement between the volcanic 'explosion of mania' and the ruefully urbane 'a classic fatigue' illustrates the pervasive dimension of lexical surprise in his poetry. In later 1930s work, the poet's political voice takes on a different timbre. 'Out on the lawn I lie in bed' significantly shifts from addressing 'you' to speaking of 'we'; it has dispensed with the harsh and dissonant compressions of the earlier poem in favour of a well-paced lyrical movement, each six-line stanza a regulated dance of rhyming octosyllabics and trimeters. At first sight, it seems a poem that does not wish to affront the traditional choir of English poetry, but to blend its voice euphoniously with it. Yet if Auden sidles up to the reader, he does so in order to deceive and disconcert. If the speaker's good fortune and luck compose the opening phase, lyric pastoral soon opens out to accommodate tragedy, warning and apocalyptic vision: all done, without an ostentatious shift in diction or tone. A key transition is the description of the moon in the line, 'She climbs the European sky'. Written in 1933, the year when Hitler came to power, the poem has no need to underscore the resonance of the adjective 'European'. As in 'Consider' Auden relies on estrangement; but whereas the hawk or helmeted airman seemed credited with powers of discernment, the moon gazes down 'blankly as an orphan': 'To gravity attentive, she / Can notice nothing here', writes Auden: it is 'we' who can or should be 'attentive' to, and yet try to hide from, the 'gravity' of a world in which 'our' worst fate is apparently to 'endure / The tyrannies of love'. Complicity in corruption is manifest in 'Consider'. In 'Out on the lawn' there is a gravely troubled acceptance of the fact that private happiness may well involve shielding the self from unpalatable historical truths. Auden brilliantly exposes the inter-dependence of personal and public in this stanza, where he speaks of how he and his friends,

> gentle, do not care to know
> Where Poland draws her Eastern bow,
> What violence is done;
> Nor ask what doubtful act allows
> Our freedom in this English house,
> Our picnics in the sun.

The stanza's tonal control is absolute; it mocks even as it sympathises; it understands even as it undercuts. 'Gentle' puns: it implies both reluctance to engage in conflict and the group's 'gentle' social status. The syntax tethers 'Our freedom in this English house' to the disinclination to 'know, / Where Poland draws her Eastern bow, / What violence is done'. The exposure of non-involvement is devastating, the more so because the poem allots the speaker's 'freedom' and 'picnics in the sun' their due. In the poem's final movement, Auden develops a conceit-like image of a revolutionary flood that will pour 'through the dykes of our content', yet he utters a secular prayer, as often in his 1930s work, that in the flood's aftermath 'this', his current happiness, may to the new 'strength belong; / As through a child's rash happy cries / The drowned voices of his parents rise / In unlamenting song'. The social reconstruction being imagined is part of the Utopian impulse that pervades poetry of the period; but Auden shows himself to be aware of engaging in such a reconstruction: the conceit works as just that, a deliberately proffered conceit, and he tactfully absents himself from the joyous future. It is less to any socialist 'strength' that the poem pins its colours, for all its devastating critique of bourgeois individualism, than to an in-between state, one in which the poet can hear the 'rash' nature of future 'happy cries' and express a latent fellow-feeling with the parental 'drowned voices'.

Earlier, in part 4 of 'It was Easter as I walked in the public gardens', a poem demanding with characteristic urgency 'the destruction of error', Auden had envisaged 'our death, / Death of the old gang' and posited as a potential symbol of renewal a de-familiarised Christ-figure, 'deep in clear lake / The lolling bridegroom, beautiful, there'. It is among his most potent images, the more powerful for resisting easy allegory; we might note, too, that even in this intermittently vengeful fantasy the poet acknowledges that 'our death', too, is necessary. In 'Out on the lawn', the 'drowned voices' include, we cannot but feel, the voice of the poem we have been hearing, a voice which seeks to present itself as 'unlamenting song', but does, in part, 'lament' a culture which at the same time it argues must be radically transformed. The poem's impressiveness is at one with its poised authenticity, its capacity to sustain unflinchingly and unmelodramatically a full awareness of the poet's divided position.

4

Towards the close of the decade, poetry's function takes centre stage in Auden's work. In 'Spain 1937' historical crisis confronts him with a challenge to which he responds with a poem that seeks, as a line from 'August for the people and their favourite islands' has it, to 'Make action urgent and its nature clear'. Yet the poem, especially as first published (Auden rewrote it several times before disowning it), is among the great 1930s poems by virtue of its fusion of near-omniscience and final existential aloneness. It might have something of the air of a superbly finished propaganda piece, all the past condensed into brilliantly compacted phrases that yield pride of place to the present. So, a series of vignettes sums up the past as a gigantic, magnificent irrelevance to what is happening in Spain in the struggle between the Republic and Franco's Fascists: 'Yesterday', Auden writes, 'the installation of dynamos and turbines; / The construction of railways in the colonial desert; / Yesterday the classic lecture / On the origin of Mankind. But to-day the struggle'. Never in all his work is the definite article so superbly equal to the task of taxonomic condensation. The 'struggle', however, tests Auden's ethical as well as his playful imagination. At one stage, as Edward Mendelson has argued, he may attempt to imply, through a sleight-of-hand involving natural images, that the decision to side with the Republic barely involves 'will' and is more the product 'of something very much like unconscious instinctive nature'.[4] So, those responding to the inner voice that Auden suggests makes up 'History', rather than any Marxist dialectic, 'Have heard and migrated like gulls or the seeds of a flower'. Yet the poem's ethical heart is the recognition that 'History' is not an 'operator', but the sum of human choices. At the close it is less Auden's omniscience that dominates our response, though we respond to the sharp perceptiveness of lines such as 'to-day the / Fumbled and unsatisfactory embrace before hurting', with its novel way of reminding us of human doubleness. Rather, it is the poet's aloneness. The final stanza has the effect of a bracing coda to many of the hopes advanced by Auden's political poetry in the 1930s, a coda that has about it a saddened undersong:

> The stars are dead; the animals will not look:
> We are left alone with our day, and the time is short, and
> History to the defeated
> May say Alas but cannot help or pardon.

The repetitions structuring the poem – of 'Yesterday', 'to-day', and 'Tomorrow' – fall away, yielding to 'our day', an interim that is ours, one charged with possibilities and the likelihood of further distress. Auden's later rejection of the last two lines, on the grounds that they 'equate goodness with success', ignores the fact that the lines betray his discomfort with any such notion.[5] The phrasing personifies History in a way that discredits personification as other than the poet's projective labelling. Auden sees personified History as hand-wringingly ineffectual, able to 'say Alas', though even the word 'Alas', denied speech-marks, seems only a mouthed act of ventriloquism, but unable to 'help' (should the 'defeated' warrant help) or 'pardon' (should the defeated require 'pardon'). The thrust of the lines is against any complacent reliance on 'History the operator' to do the work. 'Spain 1937' is, thus, concerned to 'Make action urgent and its nature clear'. It is evidently partisan, yet not propagandist; it posits the view that in any political struggle the outcome will determine the way the struggle is retrospectively seen. It does not equate goodness with success; but it does suggest that if goodness is to succeed human beings need to recognise that they have only themselves to depend on.

Despite the poet's fraught repudiations of this poem and 'September 1, 1939', each reveals Auden's concern, in lines from the later poem, to use his 'voice / To undo the folded lie'. Particular lies which 'September 1, 1939' identifies are spelled out in the trochaically light-footed, intelligent measures of the same stanza: 'There is no such thing as the State / And no one exists alone'. Auden's flair for thinking in poetry is apparent here: the two statements may seem at odds, since if there is 'no such thing as the State', does that not mean that everyone is 'alone'? Conversely, if 'no one exists alone', how do they avoid being part of a 'State'? Auden's pointed wording provokes such questions, and also the further reflection that if we subscribe to a 'State' over and above ourselves, we risk the dangerous, inhuman nationalism that is responsible for the crisis dated in the title (two days before the outbreak of the Second World War) and for the fact that 'Waves of anger and fear / Circulate over the bright / And darkened lands of the earth'. 'Circulate' implies a fluidly global connection, while the last line and a half prepare us for the notion that 'no one exists alone'.

In this poem Auden mixes elegant generalisation with a powerful communicative pressure. A medley of authorities gives the sense of the poet as well read and incisive: the second stanza alone invokes 'Accurate scholarship' as a means of telling what 'has driven a culture mad', before invoking Freudian wisdom, too. Yet it is typical of the range achieved by the poem's voice that the stanza settles for a more homespun idiom of truth-telling: 'Those to whom evil is done / Do evil in return'. The lines allude to the Treaty of Versailles and the post-war reparations enjoined on Germany. They suggest, too, amid the poem's sophisticated ability to discern and indict 'Imperialism's face / And the international wrong', a trust in robustly commonsense ethics. That *sensus communis*, however, derives from individual experience, a mode of experience which 'September 1, 1939' both exalts and mistrusts. The poem begins by presenting Auden as seemingly alone, 'in one of the dives / On Fifty-Second Street', the American English speaking of his displaced identity. Soon, though, it links his fearful uncertainty with the moral bankruptcy of 'a low dishonest decade'. Auden is at once displaced stranger and spokesman by default for this decade. He seeks in much of what follows to trace to its source the human capacity for error, finding it in the supposedly normal wish 'to be loved alone' and in the ego-forged manacles that restrict the vision of 'the sensual man-in-the-street'. Complicity in political imperfection and crisis, Auden's great theme in his 1930s poetry, reappears as a concern of the poem, a complicity whose symptom is a longing to abnegate responsibility. We are all, the poem states with rigour and sympathy, afraid 'Lest we should see where we are, / Lost in a haunted wood'. And it is in this context that Auden frames his sense of his role as a poet and builds towards a final hope. 'All I have is a voice / To undo the folded lie' introduces his definition of the role; the final hope is conveyed through the rhyming admonition (which, *pace* Auden's later self-criticism, works well in the poem) that 'We must love one another or die'. 'Die', there, means, one might suppose, less physical than moral death, a condition in which we cease to function as creatures capable of converting 'Hunger', struggle and alienation into something approaching a peaceable culture. Lest Auden seem too preacherly here, he adds in the last stanza a wryly qualified wish that he may be admitted to the company of 'the Just' dotted through our stupefied world like 'Ironic points of light'. Their capacity for 'irony' is evinced by the poem. Auden's irony is inseparable from his refusal to give way to 'Negation and despair'. If it involves simultaneous awareness of human weakness and a confession of his complicity in such weakness, it prompts a sense of human possibilities; 'composed . . . / Of Eros and of dust', he finishes the poem by expressing the desire, never absent from his best 1930s work, to 'Show an affirming flame'.

5

At the chapter's outset I posed three questions, which might be briefly rephrased thus: does Auden's 1930s work mature; does he engage with his subjects; and is his poetry able to escape didactic propaganda? It is incontestable that the earliest poems of the period, such as 'The Watershed', have a concrete and unparaphrasable warning power unmatched by any later poems. This power is illustrated by an image from the just-mentioned poem that speaks volumes about trespass and isolation: 'Beams from your car may cross a bedroom wall, / They wake no sleeper'. But the maturing intelligence of Auden's work is equally apparent, reaching a climax in the cunning, brave and eloquent defence of Yeats in 'In Memory of W. B. Yeats'. There, Auden anticipates much of the drift of his post-1930s work as he evolves a sophisticated poetics, one in which poetry 'makes nothing happen' (itself a nicely ambiguous form of words) and yet is 'A way of happening'. Often it is through his awareness of poetry as 'A way of happening' that thirties Auden achieves his fusion of emotional and conceptual engagement with his subjects: an engagement that illuminates the desperate murk at the heart of private psyches and public crises, and that fuses attention to the contemporary with a wider, longer cultural and ethical gaze. Unlike his Matthew Arnold, Auden did 'not thrust his gift in prison'; he made of it a uniquely resonant bequest to his readers.

NOTES

1 *The English Auden: Poems, Essays and Dramatic Writings 1927–1939*, ed. Edward Mendelson (London: Faber and Faber, 1977), p. 329. Unless otherwise indicated, this edition is used for quotations from Auden's work.

2 Stephen Spender, *World Within World* (1951; London: Faber and Faber, 1977), p. 52.
3 Leavis is quoted from *The Poetry of W. H. Auden: A Reader's Guide to Essential Criticism*, ed. Paul Hendon (Cambridge: Icon, 2002), p. 61.
4 Edward Mendelson, *Early Auden* (London: Faber and Faber, 1981), p. 319.
5 Auden's foreword to his *Collected Shorter Poems 1927–1957* (1966; London: Faber and Faber, 1969), p. 15.

Further reading

Hendon, Paul (ed.), *The Poetry of W. H. Auden: A Reader's Guide to Essential Criticism*, Cambridge: Icon, 2002
Mendelson, Edward, *Early Auden*, London: Faber and Faber, 1981
O'Neill, Michael, and Gareth Reeves, *Auden, MacNeice, Spender: The Thirties Poetry*, London: Macmillan, 1992
Spender, Stephen, *World Within World*, 1951; London: Faber and Faber, 1977

8

ADAM PIETTE

Keith Douglas and the poetry of the Second World War

Two books Keith Douglas carried with him during the desert campaign, as recounted in his prose memoir *Alamein to Zem Zem*, were *Alice in Wonderland* and 'a short *Survey of Surrealism*'.[1] Both are 'easily relatable', bearing an obvious relation to his experiences as Crusader tank commander in the Eighth Army. The men Douglas meets in his regiment and in the desert are odd in a manner clearly referencing both Robert Graves's *Goodbye to All That* and Waugh's satires, but indebted too to Alice's encounters with the strange beasts in her dream world. The brutal comedy of the war from Egypt to Tunisia is stylised according to the economy of Carroll's nonsense – this is a war replete with farce and nightmare jokes and booby traps, run by half-crazy, obsolete military, fought caged in fantastic machineries of death, rolling over an unreal landscape, fighting an enemy not hated but admired as reflections of the desert rats themselves. The comedy has Carrollian pathos too, sentimentality being generated by the very illogicality of this strange world:

> it is exciting and amazing to see thousands of men, very few of whom have any idea why they are fighting, all enduring hardships, living in an unnatural, dangerous, but not wholly terrible world, having to kill and be killed, and yet at intervals moved by a feeling of comradeship with the men who kill them and whom they kill, because they are enduring and experiencing the same things. It is tremendously illogical – to read about it cannot convey the impression of having walked through the looking-glass which touches a man entering a battle. (*Alamein to Zem Zem*, 16)

There is a long play on the looking-glass image, not only in the sequences of encounters with increasingly bizarre soldier-creatures in the sands, some horrifically transfigured by the lethal explosive surprises, and not only in specific allusions to Carroll (particularly Tweedledum and Tweedledee at their silly looking-glass war), but also through the extended motif of observation through field glasses that structures the curious battles after El Alamein. In the paradoxical silence created by the steady deafening noise of the tank on its way ('since the engine drowns all other noises except explosions, the whole world moves silently' (28)), seconded by the eerier silence of the dead on the sands ('the most impressive thing about the dead is their triumphant silence' (28)), it is the visual field and ambiguous objects at a distance which are the sources of the uncanny comedy of death, commented on by the militarised jargon of the coded wireless traffic heard through earphones.

Hamish Henderson was similarly struck by the looking-glass effect of the war in the desert. The two enemy armies were 'forced to live off each other', swapping equipment of all kinds. This created a weird ' "doppelganger" effect' which was 'enhanced by the deceptive distances and uncertain directions of the North African wasteland'. 'This odd effect of mirage and looking-glass illusion', for Henderson, had political consequences, since what it bore witness to was 'our human civil war, in which the roles seem constantly to change and the objectives to shift and vary'. In other words, the fluidity of relationships between objects and social forces in the desert world enabled a potentially revolutionary 'complete reversal of the alignments and alliances which we had come to accept as inevitable'. Sympathy for the dead transcended national boundaries: both Axis and Allied dead formed part of 'that eternally wronged proletariat of levelling death.'[2] The North African wasteland becomes a testing ground for the revolutionary potential of wartime, laying bare the unreal foundations of seemingly inevitable class differences, discovering looking-glass similarities between combatants from opposing sides, exposing capitalism's artificially sustained civil war.

Comradeship with the enemy, even though (or because) they are there to kill you, was not only an effect of battle as looking-glass. It had also something to do with the illogical alienation generated by warfare in late modernity. Douglas's 'short *Survey of Surrealism*' must refer to David Gascoyne's 1935 *A Short Survey of Surrealism*, the text that introduced European Surrealism to British poets. 'The most vital feature of surrealism,' wrote Gascoyne, 'is its exclusive interest in that point at which literature and art give place to real life, at that point at which the imagination seeks to express itself in a more concrete form than words or plastic images.'[3] Douglas discovered an astonishing source of surrealist energy, not in the works and stunts of the communist-psychoanalytic artists in Paris, but in the grotesque technology of the war machine at full pitch in the empty spaces of North Africa. The concrete forms taken by the imagination suddenly appear out of the emptiness, as Mk III or 88s, mere smudges on the significant horizon turning, as if *ex nihilo*, into artillery, tanks, machine-gun nests, prisoners ('The figures of soldiers continued to arise from the earth as though dragons' teeth had been sown there' (39)) . War's technology gives place to real death at that point of issue, the shot from nowhere from concealed guns. It also boosted the 'psychoanalytic' effect of the desert war on the imagination, events seeming to act out deep unnameable desires of the combatants in ways resembling Dali's paranoiac-critical method as outlined in Gascoyne's primer. Paranoia, for Dali, Gascoyne had explained, was more than persecution-mania, more 'a mental state enabling the subject, with superhuman swiftness of mind-defying analysis, to draw from the objective world a concrete proof, or illustration, of his obsessions.'[4] The superhuman swiftness of the shells acts out the secret death wish, the morbid kin-killing instincts of the armoured warriors, giving the tank commander a paranoid thrill at obsessions realised so concretely in flesh and blood and twisted metal.

But most surreal of all, especially in the Dali-like wastes of the desert, is the uncanny interpenetration of man and machine at the point of death, a cyborg sluicing together of flesh and technology. Douglas's graphic work, wash-and-ink sketches of the dead, owes something to Graham Sutherland (who illustrated Gascoyne's war poems) in both their quick squiggly technique, and also in the sensing of the monstrosity of technology, of the unreal organic forms war-metal makes. The dead bodies littering the sands in Douglas's sketches are often draped over their jeeps and tanks, or juxtaposed against weapons, the line of scribble making animals of the machines, marionettes of the dead, and generating an indistinguishable man-machine. In the text of *Alamein to Zem Zem*, the A to Z of war's landscape has as its core image variations on this embeddedness of flesh in deadly machine, especially once death has spilled blood over the vitals of gun turret. Coming across an M 13 at one point, Douglas peers into the turret and discovers a mess of body parts of two men lying 'in a clumsy embrace', one with a hole in his head, the other 'covered with his own and his friend's blood, held up by the blue steel mechanism of a machine-gun, his legs twisting among the dully gleaming gear levers' (66). The mechanics of death in an era of industrial warfare demands a consecration of technology through blood sacrifice, a sexual-democratic abandonment of the common body to the gleaming levers of the war machine.

For Douglas there was urgency in bringing prose and poetic energies into contact under the extraordinary new conditions created by 1940s war technology. This was partly due to the perceived need for a version of 1930s reportage as necessary witness: 'réportage and extrospective (if the word exists) poetry ... seems to me the sort that has to be written just now,' Douglas advised fellow-poet J. C. Hall in 1943.[5] Non-introspective reportage was demanded not only by the logic of his own poetic gift, which was naturally moving away from Donne-like modern-metaphysical verse towards a tougher semi-demotic plain style, but by the ordinary ways of feeling amongst the ranks. Writing to Hall who had asked him not to abandon the lyric in his poetry, Douglas replied that this war had no place for the 'musical and sonorous' lyric but had first to be concerned with 'the cynicism and careful absence of expectation' with which Douglas 'viewed the world': 'As many others to whom I have spoken, not only civilians and British soldiers, but Germans and Italians, are in the same state of mind, it is a true reflection.'[6]

The cynicism of the new conscript army of the 1940s accorded with both Modernist purities of technique post-Imagism and an ideological preference for democratic-demotic forms of iconoclastic reportage. The style developed by Douglas in his prose account mirrors, as in another looking-glass, the manoeuvres towards plain style in the poetry, simply because of the flat fact of this being a modernised Sassoonese, cynical, unadorned, without bullshit, developed *by the soldiers themselves*. As Douglas explained to Hall:

> if you come across the word Bullshit – it is an army word and signifies humbug and unnecessary detail. It symbolizes what I think must be got rid of – the mass of irrelevancies, of 'attitudes', 'approaches', propaganda, ivory towers, etc., that stands between us and our problems and what we have to do about them.[7]

Laced into this Kiplingesque admiration for barrack-room speech patterns are the attachments of the bourgeois intellectual in the early 1940s: Auden group left-wing disdain for elite refuges tempered by Orwellian suspicion of overtly communist identification of art and propaganda. More importantly, the statement reveals very intimate and powerful support for the democratic institution of the army itself.

The army recruit, as Alun Lewis saw it in 'Lance-Jack', was 'a migrant, an Arab taking his belongings with him, needing surprisingly little of the world's goods', liberated in the 'sudden *levelling down*', the 'possibility for change' involved in the democratic environment of the new army.[8] Government initiatives fostered this political camaraderie, in particular the work of the Army Bureau of Current Affairs (ABCA) whose fortnightly *Current Affairs* bulletins sent to army units popularised the idea of the citizen soldier, encouraging discussion of radical post-war reforms, 'the first gesture towards politicizing a British army since Cromwell's day'.[9] The move to North Africa, the first significant front after the defeats in Greece and the Far East, coincided with the entry of the Soviet Union into the war, an event which finally released the anti-fascist radicalism implicit but repressed in the real Dunkirk spirit. The army became a radical force. As Edward Thompson remembered: 'I recall a resolute and ingenious civilian army, increasingly hostile to the conventional military virtues, which became ... an anti-fascist and conspicuously anti-imperialist army.'[10] This could be a perfect description of the iconoclastic, anarchist and rebellious spirit animating Douglas's prose and poetry. Though some residual respect for the dinosaurs of the old regiment survives the satirical fire of *Alamein to Zem Zem*, the intention and drive is towards comic respect for the new power brokers of the war, the common men and their idiolect. Something of the levelling was due to the desert itself, forcing combatants down to bare essentials, life in common, men having to rely on each other for their very lives. It was in Egypt that the socialist energies of the Popular Front first re-emerged, in other words, in the form of the 'new model army' of the Eighth Army. It was in Egypt that Douglas encountered this radical democratic movement, typified by the Music for All Parliament that took place in Cairo in September 1943, 'akin', Neil Grant has argued, 'to a soviet, romantic and mutinous in character', a soldiers' parliament which had, 'rather like the Putney Debates in the English Civil War, involved soldiers debating the purposes of the war and nature of the post-war world'.[11] And, significantly, the Parliament took place in a former cinema, the base for the poets of the Salamander Society run by Keith Bullen and John Cromer which issued the influential Oasis anthologies. Georgian and Kiplingesque in spirit, the group sought, in Roger Bowen's words, 'to memorialize the soldier as amateur poet and oral historian', to counter what Cromer identified as 'obscurantist modernism', to celebrate the common purpose and cama-raderie of the troops.[12]

It was also in Egypt that Douglas encountered the poets gathered around the *Personal Landscape* journal founded by Lawrence Durrell, Robin Fedden and Bernard Spencer. Their stance was apolitical, anarchist-individualist, standing back from the war effort to examine the deep histories of precisely 'personal' experiences in wartime. Their representative poem, Fedden's 'Personal Landscape', insists on the importance of personal life and values (here figured as a Donne-like aubade) at the same time as it acknowledges that love cannot be disengaged from the ways the human body is being broken by wartime, the military inhabiting the loved one's body (the pun on 'arms'): 'I cannot disentangle your arms / From the body of the day that is breaking'.[13] The *Landscape* group were contemptuous of the war poet anthologies and looked askance at the whole idea of war poetry as a genre. Laurence Durrell wrote to John Waller with typical disdain: 'I think all this war-poet stuff is bogus and vulgar really ... the only kind of work worth while is work that wears no uniform but its own merits.'[14]

The contradiction between the radical democracy of the ABCA army and the individualism of the Personal Landscapers went more than skin-deep, however. In the gulf between the war as private catastrophe and as collective experience lies the principal set of differences structuring the war poetry of the 1940s. With the death of Yeats, the departure of Auden and Isherwood to the USA, the recruitment of Pound to the fascist cause, Modernist and 1930s political poetry had come to a halt, scuttled by the forces of reaction. The failure of the Spanish Civil War had already compromised many of the valiant gestures poets had hoped to identify with an anti-fascist poetics. The Nazi–Soviet pact had seen the Popular Front collapse into disarray. The recognition of the need, nevertheless, for service to the nation in the struggle against Hitler meant that there was little of the indignation that had energized the First World War poets. Equally, however, the mere fact that this was the second of the century's world wars also drained the culture of credulity and commitment in a curious hollowing out of rhetoric and posturing. This is what Douglas alludes to with his 'absence of expectation'. To write Second World War poetry was to write second-rate, second-hand verse belatedly in styles borrowed from the trench poets, sons imitating fathers. Douglas implies as much in 'Desert Flowers' where he admits that any poem about flowers feeding off the blood of dead men must lamely follow Rosenberg's lines on poppies in 'Break of Day in the Trenches': 'Rosenberg I only repeat what you were saying'. The repetition is more endemic than repetition of trope, however. As Douglas argued in an essay on war poetry, 'Poets of This War', the First World War hung over everything any Second World War combatant poet might care to say:

> there is nothing new, from a soldier's point of view, about this war except its mobile character. There are two reasons: hell cannot be let loose twice: it was let loose in the Great War and it is the same old hell now. The hardships, pain and boredom; the behaviour of the living and the appearance of the dead, were so accurately described by the poets of the Great War that every day on the battlefields of the western desert – and no doubt on the Russian battlefields as well – their poems are illustrated. Almost all that a modern poet on active service would be inspired to write, would be tautological.[15]

The two reasons – continuation of mass industrial warfare and repetition of descriptions of conditions and appearances – are troubled by tiny concessions to difference: the desert war's mobile character, and the fact that poets are 'modern' now. Modernity and mobility are key vectors in the cold-blooded and symptomatic writing Douglas produced late in the war. It nevertheless remains the case that the tautological nature of writing shapes and conditions the scope of individual responses to the war, if only in some twisted (and psycho-analysable) act of difficult acknowledgement of debt to the father's superior knowledge, as in Roy Fuller's 'Another War': 'Our fathers felt these things before / In another half-forgotten war'.[16]

The net effect of this set of contradictions – genuine advocacy of army democracy allied to sleepwalking indifference to ideology; desire to serve one's country merging with satirical resistance to authority; a son's sense of experiencing second-hand his father's war experience working along-side recognition of the new mass mobility and technology of the conflict – was strained at the fault line between individual experience and collective service to the war machine. The poets most dedicated to finding ways of engendering Surrealist modes in British poetry, the neo-Romantics of the anthologies collected by J. F. Hendry and Henry Treece – *The New Apocalypse* (1939), *The White Horseman* (1941) and *Crown and Sickle* (1944) and, more generally, writing in the orbit of Tambimuttu's *Poetry London* – gravitated towards a depth-psychological idiom of dream and fantasy, at times simply self-indulgent and self-privatizing. The desire to appropriate the war's violence into the language of the poem betrayed symptoms of delusion. At the same time, that desire generated some quite exceptional poetry, particularly Hendry's poem about the Blitz, *A Bombed Happiness*, that zeroed in on the struggle between free, surrealist desire and the nightmare forces of war technology. The Apocalyptic manifestoes did acknowledge a cultural change consonant with the urgency of the times – surrealism had to be reinvented as myth-creation, myth 'as a mode of release from the object-machine, whether state, system or rationalism'.[17]

Douglas can hardly be called a neo-Romantic – his choices took energy from the late plain styles of Yeats, Eliot and Auden, from the detached intensities of Bernard Spencer, from the music of Edmund Blunden, his tutor at Merton. Nevertheless, the will to read the desert war as fabulous dreamwork, to see the machines at play on the flesh of young men, to register the brutalising effects of the war's violence on the observing, desiring imagination, all this bears traces of new apocalyptic myth-making struggle with the 'object-machine' of war's states and systems. The most anthologised of his poems, 'Vergissmeinnicht', detailing the sight of a dead gunner killed on the 'nightmare ground' of a battle fought three weeks previously, gazes on the destruction wrought by the war machines on the vulnerable flesh: 'the dust upon the paper eye / and the burst stomach like a cave.' The body, even in death though, is shadowed by war technology: 'The frowning barrel of his gun / overshadowing'. The dead soldier is 'mocked by his own equipment / that's hard and good when he's decayed'.

Yet the observing eye, cruel and impersonal as it seems – its 'hard and good', Hemingway-neutral war reportage identified with the technology's overshadowing power – breaks down at the sentimental sight of a picture of Steffi, his girlfriend, and the rhetoric of unpassion shifts to lyric: 'And death who had the soldier singled / has done the lover mortal hurt'.

What Douglas has done is to acknowledge the power of the wartime object-machine in the cold form of his own mimetic-symptomatic tone at the same time as voicing resistance to the mechanical slaughter. So, in 'How to Kill', he ventriloquises a sniper, most hated of the enemy:

> Now in my dial of glass appears
> the soldier who is going to die.
> He smiles, and moves about in ways
> his mother knows, habits of his.
> The wires touch his face: I cry
> NOW. Death, like a familiar, hears
> and look, has made a man of dust
> of a man of flesh.

Here again, the looking-glass view functions as lethal technological vision – the intertwining of flesh and weaponry in the sudden drama as the scope's crosshairs 'touch' the target's face. The cold clarity of this is unnerving, especially when we consider that Douglas is using his favourite form to express the view, the six-line stanza rhyming abccba, as though his best imagination is being given to the sniper's cruel gaze. The circling in and out of the looking-glass pararhymes tracks the formal zeroing in on the victim through modern war's eyes.

Yet just as Douglas is acknowledging his own possession by the technologising violence and cool formality of the object-machine, so he also measures his resistance to it with the startlingly sentimental cross-circuit that occurs in the lines, 'He smiles, and moves about in ways / his mother knows, habits of his'. The sniper-Douglas is imagining the victim of war as mother's child, as boy, as his own boy self. The lines have a strange effect on the rest of the poem, making Death of a sudden a family member, eerily familiar, a father figure – psychoanalytic symptoms spark into life.

If such features of Douglas's poetry are understood, working double duty as both symptomatic and resistant, many of the overt contradictions in 1940s poetry, between private and communal objectives, for instance, or between neo-Romantic and classical verse, begin to fall away. The double technique is not Douglas's personal property but a feature we find in much of the best poetry from combatant poets. Alun Lewis's poems are similarly strung between private delusions and obsessions, and political function – they also dramatise their own 'militarised' neuroses, in ways so many had learnt from Auden's *The Orators*, at the same time as insisting on an ethical clearing through of feeling and compassion for fellow soldiers. In Lewis's case, the neurosis returned again and again, like the black beast of depresssion that so haunted Douglas, to the sweet lure of the death wish, 'the voice that called you / … soft and neutral as the sky / Breathing on the grey horizon'.[18] The lure is exacerbated by the war's contradictions – Lewis was stationed in India, forced to defend an empire he despised – and yet Lewis still held to the ACBA dream of the citizen soldier, 'marching light, / Enduring to the end',[19] a democratic myth to resist the machine.

Similar fears animate Douglas – his poems interrogate the colonial nature of the war in Egypt by juxtaposing the triviality of the English in Cairo ('Shall I get drunk or cut myself a piece of cake') with the poverty on the streets ('scattered on the pavement like rags'), then comparing that juxtaposition with the 'new world' of war to the west, where the machine rules:

> the vegetation is of iron
> dead tanks, gun barrels split like celery
> the metal brambles have no flowers or berries
> and there are all sorts of manure, you can imagine
> the dead themselves, their boots, clothes and possessions
> clinging to the ground.

Without comment, the poem awaits a political reading without insisting on it – the poor of Cairo mirror the dead on the ground in the desert: they are 'manure' feeding the rich fantasy world of the English on colonial holiday. What emerges from so many of the poems written in Mediterranean mode from the Personal Landscapers on is just this uncomfortable sensing of the lines of force connecting the colonial gaze on foreign peoples and landscapes and the war machine gaze on the dead.

The lines of force, for Douglas and for other combatants in Egypt and in the later campaigns of the war, in Italy and France, are imagined so closely since there was, at the heart of the conflict within the army itself, between old guard and new radical recruits, a recognition that this war would end the British Empire and its sway on the world – when Lewis shot himself on the subcontinent, there was some obscure correlation with the end of the Raj in 1947. But equally there is fear that a new empire of the object-machine might be under construction, charting the world through technology, mapping flesh and landscapes with the language of power, formal, superpolitical, informational. Hamish Henderson, another soldier-poet in

Egypt, in his astonishing *Elegies for the Dead in Cyrenaica*, can sense the new empire in the diction and rhythms of his own lines:

> Planning and execution
> recede: the preliminary inertia,
> the expectation, the lull, the relaxing and the encounter's
> suddenness recede, become history:
> > thrusts, sieges and feints
> that still blood maps with arrows
> and left dead like refuse, these are the basis
> of battle studies.[20]

The war is co-ordinated by history's bloodstained map, an academic exercise securing the destruction of the dead as commodities. With Douglas, the same recognition of the primacy of planning, execution, historical distance as mapping of flesh pertains in the analysis of the war machine's formal patterns of power. The nightmare sequence 'Landscape with Figures' (perhaps partly a rebuke to the *Personal Landscape* crowd with their Greek nostalgia) maps the battle from impersonal heights ('a pilot or angel looking down / on some eccentric chart'), like Walter Benjamin's Angel of History, only seeing the destroyed machines ('useless furniture ... sand vehicles / squashed dead') like insects on the desert floor. But the poem shifts perspective to the soldier on the ground who moves in 'like Thomas', 'to poke fingers in the wounds' and discovers 'monuments, and metal posies':

> on each disordered tomb
> the steel is torn into fronds
> by the lunatic explosive.

Instead of the human dead, though, the walking observer is infected by the vision of the angel of history, can only respond to the beauty of the ripped metal, constructing an elegy not for the useless dead men, but to the broken machines.

The many anti-elegies written during the war form a genre all of their own and are shaped by the clashing forces being analysed with such acuity by Douglas's deranged observer. The conscripts drawn in to the war were forced into this strange elegiac space which privileged the war machine, to the extent of offering up their own imaginations (based on broken elegies to their own doomed bodies) to the quasi-sacred technologies of death. The most prescient of the conscript writers was Sidney Keyes, an Oxford poet like Douglas in being on the fringes of the neo-Romantic revival, but closer in spirit to the sacrificial rhetoric of the neo-Christian revival spearheaded by Charles Williams. In the essay 'The Redeemed City', written for the *Dublin Review* in October 1941, Williams talks movingly about the 'law of bearing one another's burdens' in the necessary combat between the Allies (representing the City) and the Axis (the Infamy).[21] This Tolkien-style combat needed soldier conscripts ready to sacrifice themselves in an act of interchange, an offering of imaginations and bodies as substitutes for the souls of brethren and enemies. The interchange had its counterpart in poetry, with preference for a poetry of medievalising, Rilkean, Yeatsian, Lawrentian and Jungian symbolism dwelling on the necessary death wish. Keyes was to die in the desert war and, again like Douglas, had a premonition he would not return. The premonition merges into morbid death wish, fashioned, significantly, as service to war technology:

> all must face the sun, the red rock desert,
> And see the burning of the metal bird.
> Until you have crossed the desert and faced that fire
> Love is an evil, a shaking of the hand,
> A sick pain draining courage from the heart.[22]

Eliot's mysticism of the red rock desert is crossed with the desert war and the strafing Luftwaffe to create a latterday quest narrative, designed to offer up the conscript body and mind to the surveillance and firepower of the war's technology, new god of this world.

The imagining of the battleground as spectacle, as theatre, is related to this machinic-sacrificial fantasy – Douglas's second poem in the *Landscape with Figures* sequence imagines the dead as 'stony actors' 'crawling on the boards of the stage like walls'. The war machine reduces the spectacle of death to a performance of flesh's subservience to mechanical history, but also what is being imagined, proleptically, is a spectacular society based on lethal commodification of the human body, subjecting it to the object-machine. The mapping of the bodies of soldiers is also a scripting of actors within a digestive system – one of the last poems Douglas wrote before being killed in Normandy imagines the huge army of soldiers awaiting embarkation as '[a]ctors waiting in the wings of Europe', 'just little pieces of food / swirling in an uncomfortable digestive journey'.[23] That machine of consumption reduces the soldier body to a unit in the control system of the larger body of the machine ('the sucking mouth of the day that swallowed us all / into the stomach of a war'), a system Douglas intuited, in the last sections of *Alamein to Zem Zem*, as informational. The concept returns to the prose like a virus, linked clearly by Douglas to the ability of those trained by the military to turn the 'mind's eye' into a military map ('the coloured lines advance across the map of his mind' (108)): 'it may mean he misses important information' (109); 'Near here, we knew from our information four 88s were sited' (112); 'I could report no more than I had already reported. But this information had clearly made no impression' (118). The motif turns round an incident where Mousky ignores Douglas's warning and sends men in carriers to their deaths in search of 'information' ('bring back some information', he tells his doomed men (118)).

This was written in 1943, the year cybernetics was born in the States, the year Turing completed Colossus at Bletchley and the year atomic weapons began to be built in the States. Cybernetics began as a theory of the relation of organic to mechanical systems in order to minimise human error in negative feedback systems; specifically it began as an MIT problem-solving study based on the need to be able to chart missile trajectories.[24] Caught up in the control system of the war machine, monitoring missiles and their trajectories, Douglas's imagination registered the draw of the human into servomechanical 'negative feedback' relationship to the flow of information, *matériel*, firepower. His poetry and prose reflects on the looking-glass sights, scopes and maps being generated by the machine, understands the servomechanism that flesh is heir to in war's informational battle studies, and serves notice of the empire of the object-machine to come.

Again, his example should point us to other poets who bore witness to this nightmare change: Alan Ross on his destroyers, his great narrative poem about the 1942 Battle of the Barents Sea, 'J. W. 51B: A Convoy', written after the war, linking the unreality induced by 'radar / And Asdic and RL 85 slowly revolving' to the image of the crew in deep sleep (26). G. S. Fraser's 'Journey' watches the planners not only moving men around the world, but mapping their very insides, inhabiting basic responses with the ghosts summoned within the body by technological forces:

> Mappers of nerves, who graph our play and toil,
> Who aim the rifle, fire, and the recoil
> Hits not their hearts, as our own crimes had done,
> These armoured men, of metal and of steel,
> With rubber hands and fluorescent eyes,
> Who act, but who neither think nor feel,
> Whom we poor poets curse.[25]

It is this recognition of the rule of the object-machine in the new world inaugurated by the Second World War which links, finally, the combat poetry of the conflict to the many poems issuing out of civilian suffering. In the poetry of J. F. Hendry, in particular, we discover the same intuition of the machinic, dreamt here in fine apocalyptic poetry, sensing the shadowy relations linking Blitz and the future atom bomb through tropes of formal pattern, molten metal, a 'naturalized' war machine in the skies:

> Here artist and scientist concur to admire
> A formal pattern of battle, where herring-bone squadrons

Elude the swaying bars of light, and white fire
From London's living furnace, flung up like a tilted cauldron,
Splits the atom of doom.[26]

That same formal pattern of the war machine that killed Hendry's wife in the Blitz (celebrated in the heart-breaking elegy *The Orchestral Mountain* of 1943) is seen bombing men to their death on the shores of Italy in Hendry's own war poem, 'Sicilian Vespers', with its extraordinary account of the invasion of Sicily in 1943. The lines 'whipped-up snakes of action swarmed / round soldiers in the allegory of crystal' visualise, as through some looking-glass, weaponry's mechanical-organic forms within warfare's 'crystal' formal patterns of engagement.[27]

It is in their inaugural and collective response to the new war machine of the twentieth century – at work in the world in all warfare states since – that the poems of the Second World War retain their power and courage, shocking us still, well beyond the artificial divisions of rival poetry schools and their advocates.

NOTES

1 Keith Douglas, *Alamein to Zem Zem*, ed. Desmond Graham (London: Faber and Faber, 1992), p. 98.
2 Hamish Henderson, *Elegies for the Dead in Cyrenaica* (London: John Lehmann, 1948), pp. 11–12.
3 David Gascoyne, *A Short Survey of Surrealism* (1935; San Francisco: City Light Books, 1982), p. 61.
4 Gascoyne, *A Short Survey of Surrealism*, p. 101.
5 Letter to J. C. Hall, 10 June 1943, Keith Douglas, *The Letters*, ed. Desmond Graham (Manchester: Carcanet, 2000), p. 287.
6 Compiled from a series of airgraph letters sent to Hall in August 1943 by Desmond Graham. Douglas, *The Letters*, p. 295.
7 *Ibid.*, p. 294.
8 Alun Lewis, 'Lance-Jack', *Collected Stories*, ed. Cary Archard (Bridgend: Seren Books, 1990), p. 64.
9 Max Beloff, *Wars and Welfare* (London: Edward Arnold, 1984), p. 264.
10 1978 *New Statesman* article quoted in the introduction to David Edgar's and Neil Grant's *Vote for Them* (London: BBC Books, 1989), p. 5.
11 *Ibid.*, p. 6.
12 Roger Bowen, '*Many Histories Deep*': The Personal Landscape *Poets in Egypt, 1940–45* (London: Associated University Presses, 1995), p. 47.
13 *Ibid.*, pp. 46–7.
14 Quoted Roger Bowen, ' "The Artist at his Papers": Durrell, Egypt and the Poetry of Exile', *Twentieth Century Literature*, 33, 4, Laurence Durrell special issue, Part II (Winter 1987), 468.

15 'Poets in This War', written May 1943, first published in 1971 in the *Times Literary Supplement*. Quoted by Sebastian Knowles, *A Purgatorial Flame: Seven British Writers in the Second World War* (Bristol: Bristol Press, 1990), p. xviii.

16 Roy Fuller, 'Another War', *Collected Poems* (London: Faber and Faber, 1966), p. 55.

17 J. F. Hendry, 'Writers and Apocalypse', in J. F. Hendry and Henry Treece (eds.), *The New Apocalypse: An Anthology of Criticism, Poems and Stories* (London: Fortune Press, 1939), pp. 9–10.

18 Alun Lewis, 'For Edward Thomas', in Howard Sergeant (ed.), *Poetry of the 1940s* (London: Longman, 1970), p. 15.

19 'Infantry', in *ibid.*, p. 16.

20 Hamish Henderson, 'Sixth Elegy: Aroma', *Elegies for the Dead in Cyrenaica*, p. 35.

21 Charles Williams, 'The Redeemed City', in Anne Ridler (ed.), *The Image of the City and Other Essays* (Oxford: Oxford University Press, 1958), pp. 102–9.

22 Sidney Keyes, 'The Wilderness', in Michael Meyer (ed.), *The Collected Poems of Sidney Keyes* (London, Routledge, 1988), p. 118.

23 Keith Douglas, 'Actors Waiting in the Wings of Europe', in Desmond Graham (ed.), *The Complete Poems* (Oxford and New York: Oxford University Press, 1978), p. 117.

24 Julian Bigelow, Arturo Rosenblueth and Norbert Wiener, 'Behavior, Purpose and Teleology', *Philosophy of Science*, 10, 1 (January 1943), 18–24.

25 G. S. Fraser, 'Journey', *Scottish Arts and Letters*, 1 (1944), 37.

26 J. F. Hendry, 'Midnight Air-Raid', *The Bombed Happiness* (London: Routledge, 1942), pp. 15–16.

27 J. F. Hendry, 'Sicilian Vespers', in Iain Sinclair (ed.), *Conductors of Chaos: A Poetry Anthology* (London: Picador, 1996), p. 90.

Further reading

Bowen, Roger, '*Many Histories Deep': The Personal Landscape Poets in Egypt, 1940–45*, London: Associated University Presses, 1995

Glover, Jon, 'Person and Politics: Commitment in the Forties', *Poetry Nation*, 3 (1974), 69–80

Graham, Desmond, *Keith Douglas, 1920–1944*, Oxford: Oxford University Press, 1974

Kendall, Tim, *Modern English War Poetry*, Oxford: Oxford University Press, 2006

Knowles, Sebastian, *A Purgatorial Flame: Seven British Writers in the Second World War*, Bristol: Bristol Press, 1990

Silkin, Jon, 'Keith Douglas', *Agenda*, 19, 2–3 (Summer 1981), 49–50

9

EDWARD LARRISSY

Languages of modernism:
William Empson, Dylan Thomas,
W. S. Graham

If one wishes to understand the attitude to their craft of British poets of the mid-twentieth century, the influence of T. S. Eliot, both in his poetry and his criticism, is one of the most important facts to consider. This is true even where that influence is mediated or qualified, but in the case of William Empson it is direct and avowed. Empson's *Seven Types of Ambiguity* (1930) and *The Structure of Complex Words* (1951) are developments of Eliot's shift away from 'personality' and 'emotion' towards the discovery of feelings of which the identifiable components of the poem were the only true gauge. A more proximate influence on Empson's thinking was his Cambridge tutor, I. A. Richards, but Eliot lies behind Richards too and is a more pervasive point of reference for poets.

The revolution that Eliot wrought in the reading and criticism of poetry can best be illustrated by a compilation of assertions from the essays collected in *The Sacred Wood*. In the best-known of these, 'Tradition and the Individual Talent' (1919), he states that 'The poet's mind is ... a receptacle for seizing and storing up numberless feelings, phrases, images, which remain there until all the particles which can unite to form a new compound are present together.'[1] The word 'compound', in evoking a scientific analogy, suggests that 'impersonality' which Eliot lauds in the essay, and this consorts well with another implication: the poem becomes an object – a variegated object, compounded of different elements, but an object nevertheless. As such, it can be understood and analysed. In the essay (1919) on *Hamlet* from the same volume, Eliot makes an assertion which extends the definition of the 'compound': 'The only way of expressing emotion in the form of art is by finding an "objective correlative"; in other words, a set of objects, a situation, a chain of events which shall be the formula of that *particular emotion*; such that when the external facts are given, the emotion is immediately evoked.'[2] The 'formula' makes, or perhaps is, the 'compound'; and when the different components are put together in the right way, the 'particular emotion' will be evoked as a direct result, and without the requirement for any statement about how one is feeling. There is an analogy with the formulations of other Modernist writers, most obviously with Joyce's concept of 'epiphany'.

Eliot was an influence on the criticism produced in the dynamic Cambridge English Faculty of the 1920s and 1930s. The following formulation from I. A. Richards's *Principles of Literary Criticism* (1924) is quite similar in import to Eliot's pronouncements, and that is no accident:

> To make the work 'embody', accord with, and represent the precise experience upon which its value depends is [the artist's] preoccupation ... and the dissipation of attention which would be involved if he considered the communicative side as a separate issue would be fatal to most serious work.[3]

The 'compound' that embodies the precise experience or emotion may be analysed and specified by the critic. And it was to this exercise that Empson brought an unparalleled clarity of purpose and thoroughness of execution.

In *Seven Types of Ambiguity*, he refers to the popular assumption 'that what the poet has conveyed is no assembly of grammatical meanings, capable of analysis, but a 'mood', an 'atmosphere', a 'personality', an attitude to life ...'[4] He goes on to speculate that '[t]his belief may in part explain the badness of much nineteenth-century poetry'. Empson, by contrast, assumes that 'atmosphere' is the consciousness of what is implied by the meaning. He proceeds to engage in a virtuoso analysis of Macbeth's speech, 'Come, seeling Night' (III.ii.50). In particular, he fastens on the lines 'Light thickens, and the Crow / Makes wing to th' Rookie Wood.' He refers to the associations of 'thickens' with blood which have already been established elsewhere in the play. He then makes explicit the associations which radiate from the idea of the rook: it is ill-omened; and there is a distinction between *rook* and *crow*, the former social, the latter solitary. Macbeth is in the position of the solitary crow. The way he describes his rejoining society simultaneously figures his intention to murder, his sense of distinction from the mass of his subjects, and his fear of his own solitude. Empson also tries to show how the sounds of the words contribute to the overall effect, with clicking sounds being reminiscent of footsteps in a wood at night.

The technique is analytic, and while there may indeed be 'atmosphere' in these lines, it is the sense of embodied thought and feeling that Empson prizes, rather than a belief that good poetry must always make the hair stand on end. The dissection of 'atmosphere' is congruent with an attitude to poetry which takes ideas and intellection to be a natural, even if not a necessary, part of it. In this yet again Empson is true to the influence of Eliot, who, in his essay 'The Metaphysical Poets' (1921), had spoken of a malign 'dissociation of sensibility' which had divorced thought from feeling in much poetry written since the late seventeenth century.[5] The metaphysicals, however, pre-dated this catastrophe: John Donne, Eliot implies, felt his thought immediately as 'the odour of a rose'.[6] In the same spirit, the modern poet would be able to bring together the experiences of falling in love, the sound of the typewriter, the smell of cooking and reading Spinoza. This formulation is actually yet another version of the 'compound', or the 'formula'; but one needs to weigh the full implications of the idea of reading Spinoza. Empson's poetry, in its 'conceited' character, conforms with Eliot's sense that intellection was a natural part of poetry, and in particular with his high valuation of the metaphysicals. Leaving aside the question of Eliot's influence, it is in any case on record that Empson claimed that he 'definitely was not bitten by Donne until Cambridge and it became clear I wanted to write argumentative poetry'.[7] As with Eliot's account of the metaphysicals, intellection may well comprise 'wit', and witty conceitedness is a marked characteristic of Empson's poetry. This is where the play on meanings touches on that other interest of his, ambiguity.

It seems appropriate therefore to find a way into the texture of Empson's poetry at the stylistic level. Yet as so often, there is a link between style and substance, and one of Empson's most celebrated poems, 'This Last Pain' (CP, 52–3), is apt for the illustration of style, substance and link. The poem begins with a summary of the doctrine of the 'beatific vision': that is, the teaching of the Church Fathers that the cruellest punishment of doomed souls was that, before being consigned to Hell, they would be able to see and feel for a moment the bliss experienced in Heaven by the blessed. As Empson puts it, 'This last pain for the damned the Fathers found: / "They knew the bliss with which they were not crowned."' Much of the subsequent development of this idea is comprised in the following two lines: 'Such, but on earth let me foretell, / Is all, of heaven or of hell'. This is congruent with Empson's well-known and strongly professed atheism, but it also ascribes a perverse structure to the human experience of happiness. Yes, the only happiness is to be found on earth; but it is acquired only at a distance, so to speak, and always just before being snatched away. It is really this conception of the true condition of human life which is subject to development and conclusion. The following stanza indicates the development: 'Man, as the prying housemaid of the soul, / May know her happiness by eye to hole ...'. It also provides a conveniently rich example of the uses to which Empson puts ambiguity. As for the general idea, it is close to the conclusion of the first stanza: that we only know happiness temporarily and at a remove. But the proof of the pudding, with Empson, is in the ambiguity, which is structural. 'Man' appears to be separate from 'soul', as an inferior being, a housemaid. Is it his own soul from which he is separate, or some larger entity: the soul of the world, perhaps? There is a sense in which both are true: the implication is that, just as man is not entirely identified with the sacred in the universe, so he is not at one with the part of himself that aspires to such identification. In any case, man knows the happiness of the soul by peering through a keyhole at her bliss. But the very fact that it is something that can be peered at in this way suggests that the soul's happiness contains elements that are not as 'pure' as most people think: at the very least, something to be savoured in privacy and isolation. But there is another ambiguity: it is not clear whether 'her' happiness is that of the housemaid or the soul, since both qualify as antecedent nouns. If it is the housemaid's happiness that man may know, it is precisely a prurient satisfaction of curiosity which is the most blessed experience to which humanity can aspire. One must, however, toy with both readings, which in any case are not entirely incommensurate with each other. The effect is of a fundamental investigation of the human condition, one which embodies the suggestion that there can be no unified explanation of it, and which forces the reader to confront the deep-rooted influence of sexuality, power and selfishness in those high matters we had thought were the province of the 'soul'.

In other words, this poem indicates that 'ambiguity' is more than a matter of double meanings: it may be essential to experience. Nor is it likely to be 'double' only. As Empson himself says about the meaning of his poem 'Bacchus', 'the notion is that life involves maintaining oneself between contradictions that can't be solved by analysis; e.g. those of philosophy, which apply to all creatures, and the religious one, about man being both animal and divine' (CP, 290). Note that these are given as examples: they are not the only contradictions involved in life. Furthermore, not only do both philosophy and religion comprise their own contradictions, they must be to some extent in contradiction with each other, since what applies to all creatures cannot apply to a creature half divine.

Empson's meditation on contradiction is as compact with implication as many examples of ambiguity in the poems. Faced with the situation he describes, he is inclined to suggest that 'it may be that the human mind can recognize actually incommensurable values, and that the chief human value is to stand up between them'.[8] However, as Christopher Ricks has noted, this leads to an ironic danger: that one may accord an 'absolute status' to the rejection of absolutes.[9] It is a danger of which Empson was aware. Speaking of the 'embarrassing' way in which Richards, Ogden and Wood appear to posit 'Absolute Beauty' in their *Foundations of Aesthetics*, Empson remarks that: 'It is a familiar paradox; any serious attempt at establishing a relativity turns out to establish an absolute. ...'[10]

This was a danger signalled in the very first pages of the powerful collection with which Empson first attracted notice, *Poems* (1935). Its epigraph, reprinted in the *Collected Poems* of 1955, is Empson's 'synthesized translation' of the Buddha's Fire Sermon, which evokes the weariness occasioned by the empty fires of passion consuming the unenlightened life. Enlightenment, indeed, is true freedom from these things, for one becomes 'weary of the feeling which arises from the contact of the visible, be it pleasure, be it pain' (*CP*, 3). These constitute a major example of life's contraries, and possess an analogy with what Empson refers to as 'contradictions'. But the Buddha goes on to specify that one also grows weary of the visible, 'be it neither pleasure nor pain'. This implies that one should seek 'non-attachment' even to those states of mind where one would have thought there was no attachment in any case. John Haffenden's notes to this epigraph run to several pages (*CP*, 138–52) and make it clear that Empson did not regard the epigraph as a key to his work. Yet John Wain raised the obvious question, why he should therefore continue its apparent sway by reprinting it in the 1955 collection. Empson conceded that he 'perhaps should not have put it at the front'. He does not feel that the life-denying attitude makes people any better. Yet 'it has a quieter kind of merit'. This merit is partly to do with the stance of the Buddha, beyond both contraries and the rejection of contraries, which mirrors the uncommitted stance for which the poet strives. It also has something to do with the way in which the Buddha's depiction of the human condition reflected the fears of a writer who could not accept the consolation proffered by the Christian story of salvation.

Indeed, Empson's poems are full of intimations of mortality. One of the finest, 'To an Old Lady' (*CP*, 24), develops the conceit of comparing a still arresting old woman to an exotic but 'cooling' alien planet – or to one who inhabits such a planet. So Empson not untypically connects the facts of individual mortality to a scientifically informed view of cosmic entropy. A stark paradox, framed around the contradictions noted earlier, structures one of the central thoughts of the poem: the old lady is related to the divine by being on another planet, for other planets, unlike ours, are given the names of gods. However, 'Our earth alone given no name of god / Gives, too, no hold for such a leap to aid her' This could be because her contact with the divine is something with which the modern observer, understanding the fatuity of faith, cannot empathise. Or it could be that the poem momentarily concedes that she, like us, is really of the earth and is gloriously exiled from the harsh truth about humanity. This compound ambiguity is typical of Empson.

Another poem about the inevitable approach of death concentrates on the waste which presages and prefigures it. 'Missing Dates' (*CP*, 79) is a villanelle, the repetitiveness of whose form mimics the sense of time as unredeemed repetition. Yet again, a sense of life's contrarieties is central to its thought:

> Not to have fire is to be a skin that shrills.
> The complete fire is death. From partial fires
> The waste remains, the waste remains and kills.

The three conditions outlined here contain echoes of the Buddha's Fire Sermon, but they are more sharply differentiated in their unsatisfactoriness: not to have fire, a position not fully outlined by the Buddha, is to be empty. The complete fire is death, a claim with which the Buddha would agree, but which here takes on, by contrast with lack of fire, a sense of grand if terrifying excess. Partial fire kills by the slow but relentless accumulation of toxic waste but is presumably the condition of most of humanity. It also suggests an affinity with that position, poised between alternatives, which seems Empson's recommendation for an approach to life. The poem thus develops an alternative view of his own favoured stance: a negative contrary, exhibiting his capacity to doubt even his commitment to sagacious uncommittedness.

The verse form of 'Missing Dates' is highly pondered and memorably sonorous. It is easy to forget, adverting necessarily to Empson's intellectuality, those stylistic features of his poetry which go beyond, even as they help to support and embody, the argumentative. It is not only the conceit that Empson shares with the metaphysicals: he also deploys rhetorical figures to structure an argument and he has a good ear for the music of a line, qualities evident in the concluding stanza of 'This Last Pain':

> Imagine, then, by miracle, with me,
> (Ambiguous gifts, as what gods give must be)
> What could not possibly be there,
> And learn a style from a despair.

The 'then' is an example of rhetorical connectedness: this is the conclusion of the preceding argument. The sentence is cast in the imperative mood: only a strong conclusion dares to start with a command. The command itself takes on added force from the alliteration on 'm' ('Imagine', 'miracle', 'me'), as does the next line, with its hard 'g' alliteration. While the 'm' in the first line might seem to suggest the dreamlike, it is arguable whether or not it is onomatopoeic, but it does draw together imagery and miracle in such a way as to suggest that the former is miraculous. The connection with 'me' reinforces the essential subjectivity of such a state of mind: one which, in order to share, we might have to submit to some pressure from another person, in this case the speaker of the poem. The most notable thing about verbal music in Empson is the way in which it operates as an autonomous means of linking ideas and images.

Empson's poetry, then, is an intense amalgam of intellection and feeling involved in a passionate scrutiny of the contradictions of human life; and considered from a technical point of view, it offers an appropriate and absorbing intensity of artifice. In these respects it is similar to the work of a poet whom Empson profoundly admired – Dylan Thomas. Empson would have no truck with the notion that Thomas heedlessly threw his feelings onto the page, regardless of their sense. In his review of Thomas's *Collected Poems* he says of the obscurity of the early poems that 'they hit you before you know how, but that is no reason for not wanting to know how'.[11] This is similar to the argument for analysing 'atmosphere', and it certainly implies that Thomas's meaning can be analysed. On Empson's account, Thomas would have agreed, and ironically enough, in the same terms as were employed by his critics. This is clear from his 'Poetic Manifesto', which appeared in the *Texas Quarterly* in 1961. Based on replies given to a research student's questions in 1951, it is thus a late work.[12] Thomas speaks of the influences on his work, and claims that the earliest of these, 'that first made me love language', were 'nursery rhymes and folk tales, the Scottish Ballads, a few lines of hymns, the most famous Bible stories and the rhythms of the Bible, Blake's Songs of Innocence and the quite incomprehensible magical majesty and nonsense of Shakespeare heard, read, and near-murdered in the first forms of my school.'[13] The 'nonsense' is not as approved as it might appear to be, for it is a product of the inadequacy of school education. That Thomas has no abiding respect for the irrational is underlined by his response to the attempt to enlist him in the Surrealist movement. Thomas disagrees 'profoundly' with the Surrealists' method, because they juxtapose words and images with 'no rational relationship', whereas he believes that poetic images 'must go through all the rational processes of the intellect'.[14]

Yet the issue shows how, even in his own day, Thomas was often regarded as an irrationalist. His Romantic themes, combined with the incantatory reading offered by his sometimes repetitive rhetoric and rhythms, made him seem a natural ally for neo-Romantic poets such as those of the New Apocalypse, including Henry Treece and Vernon Watkins.[15] Yet Thomas did not repay their admiration. He would have prized John Goodby's estimate that 'the naïvely Romantic response to postwar conditions of the New Apocalypse poets bears little resemblance to the dense complexity and lucid control of Thomas's poems'.[16] Arguably, Thomas has been the victim of an ill-considered response, motivated partly by the vagaries of literary fashion, partly by class and national prejudice, partly by the accident of his happening to die just as the Movement was initiating a reaction against the New Apocalypse poetry with which his work had been misleadingly identified.

It is Thomas's themes which should be associated with Romanticism, but no serious critic can conclude that this proves him an irrationalist. His poetry offers a celebration of the fecundity of the natural cycle, combined with an awareness of death's inexorable place therein, and a visionary interpretation of that cycle in terms of its birth, flourishing, renewals, fading and final end. An aspect of the tentative myth Thomas constructs consists of the presence within it of what threatens life and creativity. If that sounds Blakeian, one may feel that Thomas's own avowal of the early influence of Blake is indeed accurate.[17] At the same time, as is true also of Blake, the myth, if that is not too strong a term for the tendencies in his work, has a strongly Christian basis.

But as for his style, Empson's admiration was indeed procured for 'dense complexity and lucid control', and for the conceited and metaphysical character of the complexity. The way in which Blakeian themes are con-veyed in a metaphysical style is epitomised in 'There Was a Saviour'.[18] This poem describes a tyrannical god, reminiscent of Blake's Urizen, who can only hold sway over his subjects while they are enslaved in their own minds. When one escapes from his control, one emerges into a state of innocent sexual love. The saviour has his own kind of truth, though his excessive adherence to it turns it into something else: 'crueller than truth'. This appearance of truth is related to other ambiguities: while the saviour has a 'golden note', it turns repetitiously 'in a groove', so that what might have appeared positive becomes suspect in such a way that the very word 'golden' accrues some of the more negative connotations of gold: that it glitters, that it represents superficiality.

The internalisation of this tyrant's control is memorably conveyed at the end of the first stanza: 'Prisoners of wishes locked their eyes / In the jails and studies of his keyless smiles'. To be the prisoner of a wish is not quite the same thing as being simply the prisoner of the saviour: it is to have been reduced to the state of wishing rather than acting in the first place. In that case, one becomes blind to a range of things: to the fruits of satisfied desire, but also to the nature of the imprisonment itself. Jails and studies com-pound physical and mental enslavement, as Blake might have depicted. But the fact that these are constituted by the saviour's 'keyless smiles' suggests a psychological domination no less damaging for its apparent subtlety. The 'keyless' smiles are certainly not liberating, but they are also unnervingly hard to decode or find the 'key' to; and this is presumably a technique for unsettling the saviour's victims. But they are also smiles that do not show the white teeth resembling a piano's keyboard, and thus they are closed, ungenerous and probably at best insincere, at worst a disguise for viciousness. Finally, although the 'saviour' has a 'golden note', it is out of 'key', and thus not attuned to the harmony of things, which is a condition one would expect in a genuine saviour.

These lines are broadly characteristic of much of Thomas's work and do not conform to the caricature sometimes drawn of him. It is easy to see why he elicited the admiration of Empson. The two poets might be further compared in their use of ambiguity. With Thomas, as for Empson, the device merges with the topic of life's contradictions: for instance, there are those who appear to be saviours but are actually murderers in virtue of their very narratives of salvation. Yet for Thomas this is a recurring kind of contradiction, fastening him more securely to a repeated structure of thought than is the case with Empson. That repeated structure, as already suggested, is a fundamentally Romantic, and often Blakeian, one. Thus, in 'Fern Hill' (*DTCP*, 134–5), we are informed that 'Time held me green and dying / Though I sang in my chains like the sea'. Here, time is both the basis of the singing and the perpetrator of the ambiguous limitations which are necessary to any formed expression. Time is also the principle of death. Thus it is that, as with the 'saviour', we are presented with a phenomenon of dual aspect. On the one hand, Time is the impetus of the natural cycle; on the other, its terminus. Yet unlike with the 'saviour' there is a life-giving aspect to it. Contemplating the radiant pastoral imagery, and the 'lamb white days' of the child in the country, one feels, alongside that of Blake, the influence of the Wordsworth of the 'Intimations' Ode. However, one only needs to think of how one might isolate the destructive form of Time as a separate figure to see how it might indeed be related to the 'saviour' and other life-denying figures in Thomas's verse. This shows how he is not really offering different kinds of cycle, but rather playing with the attitudes appropriate to different stages and positions in the same one. Thus, in addition to the opposition of life and death, what is thought life-enhancing may in fact be destructive, and what is thought destructive may be the agent of a frightening but necessary process of liberation. Such cyclical patterns, stretching between contrary poles, and either fundamentally identical or exhibiting strong parallels with each other, repeat themselves over and over in Thomas. Since they revolve around a quasi-mythical representation of the great themes of life, death and sexuality, they may sometimes give rise to the thought expressed by Neil Corcoran that, for all their 'glamour and charm', they are 'elaborate tautologies'.[19] They certainly court this danger, and that only underlines the difference from Empson already suggested: that where his ambiguities open onto numerous points of view, Thomas's grand Romantic themes offer a sharply defined and repeated structure. This, rather than incoherence, is the identifying feature of Thomas's neo-Romanticism.

W. S. Graham is himself often seen as a neo-Romantic, and one who in his earlier work was overly indebted to Thomas. They were friends, and Graham's first book, *Cage Without Grievance* (1942), was published by David Archer's Parton Press, which had also brought out Thomas's first collection. Graham sometimes felt that he might be overfond of what he himself saw as the 'rich clutter of language' in Thomas, and aspired to something more than that.[20] That something was the 'TECHNIQUE OF MENTAL VERSE', by which he meant that, alongside the manipulation of sound, the poet had a craft for handling ideas. He explains this in terms of the way in which metaphors, and the links between metaphors, further a rich complexity of meaning.[21] And, while it is true that Graham's early poetry can be self-indulgent, in the way that it is often claimed that Thomas's is, precision is necessary here also. Graham's earlier poetry, that of *Cage Without Grievance*, *The Seven Journeys* (1944) and *2nd Poems* (1945), is sometimes reminiscent of the Thomas of 'Altarwise by Owl-light'. But no more than with Thomas is this because we are confronted by free association. As with Thomas at his least successful, the poem can be the result of too much care of the wrong kind. Calvin Bedient offers a number of examples of unsuccessful writing by Graham, accurately claiming that 'This is the poetry of the whirligig, the words spinning so fast that the imperial order of the world, its arrangement of time and death, is lost in the blur.'[22] He quotes the first verse of 'Let Me Measure my Prayer with Sleep':

> Let me measure my prayer with sleep as an
> Infant of story in the stronghold eyelid
> Left by a hedge with a badge of campions
> Beats thunder for moles in the cheek of spring.[23]

Bedient assumes that the lines are supposed to make sense, and decodes them thus: 'So prayer will consist of a dream inspired by a glimpse of nature (the hedge) and joyfully participating in its fertility (beating thunder for moles).'[24] This seems right, though Bedient would presumably not have regarded it as an exhaustive explication. Thus, that prayer should be measured with sleep suggests the moderating influence of dreams, even as they further a prayer which is formed by the waking mind, but which may perhaps be too insistent at that level. So dream is protective, and this is why it is said to occur within the stronghold of the eyelid. What it protects is the innocent imagination of one who is like an 'Infant of story'. But the dreaming imagination is itself protected by Nature, for the hedge is also protective. This is the emblem of a creativity quietly gestating potential, and it is fitting that it should wear the apparently insignificant but eye-catching 'badge of campion', a flower whose pinkish violet petals make a startling contrast with the hedgerows where it grows. The imagination still at some level deals with the actual, for while it is in a dreaming sleep, it 'Beats thunder for moles' – moles who are under the hedgerow where the infant sleeps. And since the infant is sleeping on the ground, its cheek is on the ground. So it is cheek-to-cheek with Nature, and the thunder of the pulse in its head is heard by the moles, which is to say by a representative part of Nature, a part to be found in its very depths. The overall idea is thus of a reciprocal relationship between Nature and Imagination.

As with Thomas, then, the effect is of an intense compression of multiple meanings into a charged metaphorical space. Whatever one may think about the aesthetic effect, there is more to say about it than can be summarised in terms of metaphor. For a whole poem constructed in this way, while it certainly does not look like a representation of everyday thought, does look like some kind of – strange, exalted – representation of thought. It is as if Graham were depicting an intense mode of imaginative apprehension poised between the connection-making power of dream and the ordering faculty of consciousness. This concern with presenting a mode of poetic consciousness is typical and forms a central strand in the continuity between the earlier Graham and the later, though the later becomes more and more sensitive to the role of language in consciousness, and thus in the poem.

This investigation of consciousness is connected to a thoroughly Modernist sense of impersonality. In particular, Graham does not see imaginative consciousness as identical with the mundane self or ego. Along with this goes an impersonal sense of the poet as craftsman with language:

> The most difficult thing for me to remember is that a poem is made of words and not of the expanding heart, the overflowing soul, or the sensitive observer. A poem is made of words. It is words in a certain order, good or bad by the significance of its addition to life and not to be judged by any other value put upon it by imagining how or why or by what kind of man it was made ('Notes on a Poetry of Release', *Poetry Scotland*, No. 3, July 1946).[25]

In Graham's later work, the poet as linguistic craftsman and the poet as explorer of imaginative consciousness coalesce. Thus it is that two of the most arresting poems in *Implements in their Places* (1977) are 'What Is the Language Using Us For?' (*NCP*, 199–204) and 'Language Ah Now You Have Me' (*NCP*, 207–9). One common element in both titles is lack of control by the ego. Indeed, language as the medium for a fundamental exploration of a wider and deeper self may lead to places that surprise and unsettle the ego:

> Language now you have me
> Trying to be myself but changed into
> The wildebeest pursued or the leo pard ...   (*NCP*, 208)

Appropriately, Graham is often, as Corcoran puts it, 'improvisatory and impulsive'.[26] Indeed, the rigour with which he is these things can, as his work develops, start to resemble thinking aloud, or the attempt to make a poem out of something so similar to thinking aloud that it remains only just on the right side of the shaping faculty:

> In from the West a fine smirr
> Of rain drifts across the hedge.
> I am only out here to walk or
>
> Make this poem up. The hill is
> A shiny blue macadam top.   (*NCP*, 202)

Even these lines, though, confirm that the world does exist for Graham; and in his finest poem, *The Nightfishing* (1955), he makes the sea an emblem of the way in which the world of Nature, irresistibly strong, can also be so protean in appearance as to prove a fitting emblem of the interrelationship of world and interpretation. The extraordinarily dense, detailed, precise and inventive descriptions of the sea can be appreciated simply for their virtuoso fidelity, but in the end have to be understood in a wider symbolic light.

A significant fact about composing an essay on Empson, Thomas and Graham is the ease with which one may construct a linear account, moving from one to the next, picking up the same themes, and observing how these are exemplified differently in each. This is because each enacts a Modernist emphasis on the poet as rational and impersonal craftsman with words. In their particular expression of this emphasis, in terms of metaphor and word play capable of rational interpretation, they reveal their indebtedness to the revolution in poetics wrought by Eliot. It is only once this fact has been established that one can proceed to specify Thomas's poetry as neo-Romantic in its themes, and Graham's as neo-Romantic in its exploration of the imagination at work.

NOTES

1 T. S. Eliot, 'Tradition and the Individual Talent', *The Sacred Wood*, 2nd edn (London: Methuen, 1928), p. 55.

2 T. S. Eliot, 'Hamlet and his Problems', *The Sacred Wood*, p. 100.

3 I. A. Richards, *Principles of Literary Criticism*, 2nd edn (London: Kegan, Paul, Trench, Trubner, 1926), pp. 26–7.

4 William Empson, *Seven Types of Ambiguity*, 3rd edn (London: Chatto and Windus 1953), p. 17.

5 T. S. Eliot, 'The Metaphysical Poets', *Selected Essays*, 2nd edn (London: Faber, 1934), p. 288.

6 *Ibid.*, p. 287.

7 Quoted in William Empson, *The Complete Poems*, ed. John Haffenden (London: Allen Lane, 2000), p. xlii. Future references given in the main text as *CP*, followed by page number.

8 William Empson, *The Structure of Complex Words* (London: Chatto and Windus, 1951), p. 421.

9 Christopher Ricks, 'Empson's Poetry', in Roma Gill (ed.), *William Empson: The Man and His Work* (London and Boston: Routledge and Kegan Paul, 1974), p. 150.

10 William Empson, *Argufying: Essays on Literature and Culture*, ed. John Haffenden (London: Chatto and Windus, 1987), p. 212.

11 *Ibid.*, p. 392.

12 Dylan Thomas, 'Poetic Manifesto', in Walford Davies (ed.), *Dylan Thomas: Early Prose Writings* (London: J. M. Dent and Sons, 1971), pp. 154–60.

13 *Ibid.*, p. 157.

14 *Ibid.*, p. 159.

15 [J. F. Hendry, ed.], *The New Apocalypse: An Anthology of Criticism, Poems and Stories* (London: Fortune Press, 1939).

16 John Goodby, '"Very Profound and Very Box-Office": The Later Poems and *Under Milk Wood*', in John Goodby and Chris Wigginton (eds.), *Dylan Thomas* (Basingstoke: Palgrave, 2001), p. 201.

17 Edward Larrissy, *Blake and Modern Literature* (Basingstoke: Palgrave, 2006), pp. 51–5.

18 Dylan Thomas, *Collected Poems 1934–1953*, ed. Walford Davies and Ralph Maud (London: Dent, 1988), pp. 104–5. Subsequent references are given in the main text as *DTCP* followed by page number.

19 Neil Corcoran, *English Poetry Since 1940* (Harlow: Longman, 1993), p. 44.

20 Undated letter to Edwin Morgan [*c.*1950], W. S. Graham, *The Nightfisherman: Selected Letters of W. S. Graham*, ed. Michael Snow and Margaret Snow (Manchester: Carcanet, 1999), p. 118.

21 Letter to William Montgomerie, 20 August 1944, *The Nighfisherman*, p. 20.

22 Calvin Bedient, *Eight Contemporary Poets* (New York: Oxford University Press, 1974), p. 162.

23 W. S. Graham, *New Collected Poems*, ed. Matthew Francis, foreword by Douglas Dunn (London: Faber and Faber, 2004), p. 24. Subsequent references are given in the main text as *NCP* followed by page number.

24 Bedient, *Eight Contemporary Poets*, p. 162.

25 Graham, *The Nightfisherman*, pp. 379–80.
26 Corcoran, *English Poetry Since 1940*, p. 53.

Further reading

Bedient, Calvin, *Eight Contemporary Poets*, New York: Oxford University Press, 1974
Constable, John (ed.), *Critical Essays on William Empson*, Aldershot: Scolar Press, 1993
Corcoran, Neil, *English Poetry Since 1940*, Harlow: Longman, 1993
Davies, Walford (ed.), *Dylan Thomas: New Critical Essays*, London: Dent, 1972
Gill, Roma (ed.), *William Empson: The Man and His Work*, London and Boston: Routledge and Kegan Paul, 1974
Goodby, John and Chris Wigginton (eds.), *Dylan Thomas*, Basingstoke: Palgrave, 2001
Lopez, Tony, *The Poetry of W. S. Graham*, Edinburgh: Edinburgh University Press, 1989

PART FOUR

Later modernities

10

STEPHEN REGAN

Philip Larkin: a late modern poet

On 20 March 1942, aged nineteen, Philip Larkin wrote to his friend, Jim Sutton, excitedly announcing his admiration for D. H. Lawrence: 'I have been reading "Sons and Lovers" and feel ready to die. If Lawrence had been killed after writing that book he'd still be England's greatest novelist'.[1] Larkin's own ambitions as a fiction writer came to fruition a few years later with *Jill* (1946) and *A Girl in Winter* (1947). The two novels suggest a full alertness to the range of Modernist experimentation in the writings of Lawrence and such contemporaries as Virginia Woolf and Katherine Mansfield.[2] Modernist fiction of the first few decades of the twentieth century encouraged Larkin to move beyond realistic depiction into a symbolist evocation of a less tangible subject matter, including obscure dreams and desires. A similar trajectory can be found in the poetry from the 1940s onwards. The sudden shift from downbeat empiricism into visionary symbolism, an opening out from the securely known into the utterly unfathomable, was to become a hallmark of his work, giving a complex charge to many of his best-known poems, including 'The Whitsun Weddings' and 'High Windows'.

Larkin's enthusiasm for the fiction of Lawrence and Woolf might come as a surprise to those categorising his work as avowedly anti-modernist. An even greater surprise awaits anyone looking back to Larkin's earliest poems, since these show beyond doubt that the dominant influence was T. S. Eliot. 'The Ships at Mylae' is a free-verse composition, echoing *The Waste Land*, in which Larkin addresses his mock-hero in the peremptory manner with which Eliot summons the enigmatic Stetson: 'Stanley! / You who serene from unsung argosies / Gazed on the mounting foam!' The Stanley poems take their inspiration from Eliot's Sweeney poems, skilfully adopting their ironic tone and supercilious detachment. 'Stanley en Musique' and 'Stanley et la Glace' are written in the lean quatrains of 'Sweeney Among the Nightingales' and their comically pretentious French titles recall poems written by Eliot under the influence of Baudelaire and Laforgue.

Larkin appended a note to 'Stanley en Musique', mildly chastising himself for the indulgence in half imitating, half parodying, the author of *The Waste Land*: 'Eliotian but amusing'.[3]

Eliot's influence goes well beyond the ironic depiction of the hapless Stanley. A fractured sonnet, 'Street Lamps', deftly catches Eliot's nocturnal landscapes: 'When night slinks, like a puma, down the sky, / And the bare, windy streets echo with silence, / Street lamps come out, and lean at corners, awry'. Even more impressive is Larkin's mastery in 'Erotic Play' of the kaleidoscopic perspective and the pervasive irony of 'La Figlia Che Piange'. Many years later Larkin was to label himself 'the Laforgue of Pearson Park', but these early poems suggest that he thoroughly absorbed the techniques and effects that Eliot had learned from the French poet: the subtle modulations of tone, the disorienting perspectival shifts, and the achievement of a serene impersonality.[4] Although particular poems by Eliot function almost as blueprints for Larkin's precocious juvenilia, the results are not weakly derivative. Far from constructing pale imitations of Eliot's Modernist experiments, Larkin absorbs and assimilates within his own repertoire of effects a set of linguistic registers and rhetorical contrivances to be deployed later with immense technical assurance. What Larkin learns from Eliot very early in his poetic apprenticeship is a way of writing in which the play of consciousness itself seems to enter the poem and become the motivating subject.

The myth that Larkin's poetic instincts were profoundly anti-Modernist stems mainly from two sources: his declared dislike for Parker, Pound and Picasso in his introduction to *All What Jazz* (1970) and his apparent championing of an 'English line' in *The Oxford Book of Twentieth-Century English Verse* (1973). Larkin's association with the 'Movement' in English poetry during the 1950s and 1960s also created an impression that he stood for a return to certain qualities displaced by Modernist experimentation: lucidity, accessibility, rationality. The remarks on Charlie Parker and modern jazz have too often been taken out of context and read as a blanket condemnation of all modern art. Larkin vehemently objects to what he sees as 'irresponsible exploitations of technique in contradiction of human life as we know it', complaining that Modernism 'maintains its hold only by being more mystifying and more outrageous: it has no lasting power'; but the direction of his own work, especially in the 1970s, suggests that Modernist writers such as Lawrence, Joyce, Yeats, Eliot and Woolf, if not Pound, did have lasting power.[5]

When Larkin was asked to edit a new Oxford anthology of poetry, he substituted the words 'twentieth-century' and 'English' for 'modern' to distinguish it from its predecessor, *The Oxford Book of Modern Verse*

(1936), edited by W. B. Yeats. As with the introduction to his jazz criticism, his concern was that 'modern' might be too readily equated with 'modernist' in a narrowly experimental sense. The anthology gives some prominence to an English tradition, with Thomas Hardy as one of its principal representatives, emerging at the end of the nineteenth century and interrupted by the First World War. At the same time, the volume gives substantial coverage to the Modernist poetry of T. S. Eliot, D. H. Lawrence, W. B. Yeats and Basil Bunting, adding a good number of poems by Irish writers other than Yeats, including James Joyce, Austin Clarke and Louis MacNeice. Commenting on his choice of poets, Larkin admitted that the language of the Georgian poets was 'stale', and that 'It was Eliot and Yeats, and perhaps even Pound, who sharpened up the language'.[6]

To suggest that Larkin's attitude to Modernism was one of unqualified hostility is to miss the point that his own practice as a poet frequently embraces the devices associated with Modernist experimentation: linguistic strangeness, self-conscious literariness, radical self-questioning, sudden shifts of voice and register, complex viewpoints and perspectives, and symbolist intensity. These tendencies are clearly marked in Larkin's early poems, including those that were to appear in *The North Ship* (1945) and *The Less Deceived* (1955), but they are even more pronounced in his most iconoclastic, stylistically diverse collection, *High Windows* (1974). Rather than simply rejecting Modernism, Larkin learned from its example, adopting and refining its preoccupations, modifying its concerns in the light of the changed political and social circumstances of the late 1930s and 1940s. Not surprisingly, the immediate example of the poets of the 1930s impressed on Larkin the need for a socially responsive, ethically vigilant writing, and it also provided the model for a properly 'modern', as distinct from 'Modernist', poetry.

If Larkin was ready to die after reading Lawrence, he felt much the same after reading early Auden. He reserved his highest praise for *Look Stranger!* (1936), remarking to Sutton, 'When I read stuff like this I tend to fold up and die'.[7] In a preface for his 'Chosen Poems' of 1938–41, he commented that 'almost any single line by Auden would be worth more than the whole lot put together'. Noting the 'increasing traces of the Auden manner', he confided that what he had aimed to capture was Auden's 'ease and vividness'.[8] The 'manner' is evident in topical sonnets such as 'Observation' and poems of social commentary such as 'Midsummer Night, 1940'. Larkin's verse drama, 'Behind the Facade or "Points of View"', written in 1939, is modelled on Auden's collaborative efforts with Christopher Isherwood in *The Ascent of F6* and *The Dog Beneath the Skin*. What was to prove most decisive and enduring was Auden's 'seamless wide-angled vision'.[9] This panoramic mode gives life to some of Larkin's most impressive work, including 'Here' and 'The Whitsun Weddings'.

In 1963, Larkin summed up the influence of Louis MacNeice for his own generation, suggesting that, because his poems were not recommended 'in the same breath as those of Eliot and Auden', perhaps 'the secret taste we formed for them was all the stronger'. Larkin applauds the brilliant perceptions of MacNeice the town observer: 'his poetry was the poetry of our everyday life, of shop-windows, traffic policemen, ice-cream soda, lawn-mowers, and an uneasy awareness of what the news-boys were shouting'.[10] MacNeice's rhythmic enumeration of everyday things is vividly captured in Larkin's 'cheap suits, red kitchen-ware, sharp shoes, iced lollies' in 'Here', while his satirical vision of social types is neatly emulated in the clustering compound adjectives in the 'dog-breeding wool-defined women' and 'car-tuning curt-haired sons' in 'Show Saturday'.[11] Larkin finds the more durable aspect of MacNeice's legacy in his articulation of pain and loss: 'Against the sombre debits of maturity that his later poetry so frequently explores ... he set an increased understanding of human suffering, just as against the darkening political skies of the late Thirties he had set the brilliantly quotidian reportage of *Autumn Journal*.'[12] The combined influence of Auden and MacNeice pointed Larkin towards a poetry vigilantly responsive to the changing moods and attitudes of its time, and strikingly up to date in its rendering of the contemporary social milieu. If it wasn't exactly Modernist, it was nevertheless impeccably modern.

Larkin's own account of his poetic development in the 1940s plays down the Eliot–Auden phase and explains the maturing of his sensibility, rather too simply, as a sudden turning from the intoxicating music of Yeats to the chastening pathos of Hardy. In the introduction to the re-issue of *The North Ship* in 1966, Larkin claims that Yeats was a potent influence between 1943 and 1946, when he rediscovered Hardy by reading 'Thoughts of Phena At News of Her Death'. As an illustration of the transformation in his work, he points to the poem 'Waiting for breakfast, while she brushed her hair' (written in December 1947 and not included in *The North Ship* until 1966), commenting that it 'shows the Celtic fever abated and the patient sleeping soundly'.[13] Some of Larkin's most distinguished critics have argued to the contrary that the Yeatsian inspiration persists, manifesting itself in moments of high rhetoric and transcendental yearning. Andrew Motion claims that Larkin's most impressive work is generated by the tension between the empirical mode of Hardy and the symbolist mode of Yeats. Seamus Heaney acknowledges moments of intense illumination and epiphany in the poems, while Tom Paulin draws attention to their recrudescent Yeatsian imagery and idiom.[14] The effect of this criticism in the 1980s and 1990s was to shake up a poetic reputation that had come to be seen, too easily, as old-fashioned and to reconstitute Larkin's role in the making of modern poetry.

Looking back at the poems in *The Less Deceived* (1955), generally considered the collection in which Larkin found his own distinctive voice, it is not difficult to see why some readers believed that he was attempting to bypass Modernism and to re-instil in English poetry qualities of lucidity lost since the early twentieth century. F. W. Bateson praised the 'perspicuity' and 'finish' of the poems, noting how they seemed to derive from a 'rational system of human values and obligations' recalling the 'equipoise' and 'correctness' of Pope and Gay.[15] Larkin's avuncular wit also suggested to some readers a determined effort to write as if Modernism had never happened. The title of the opening poem, 'Lines on a Young Lady's Photograph Album', would seem to indicate a rather conservative poetic temperament, modestly establishing continuity with a contemplative mode of writing common in England at least as far back as the eighteenth century. The poem is much more modern than its title suggests, however, not least in its arch formality and rhetorical posturing. The young lady is constructed in various guises, as Tennyson's 'sweet girl-graduate' and then (with a provocative transvestite touch) 'in a trilby hat'. The speaker's not-so-furtive aside ('Faintly disturbing, that, in several ways') gives away its post-Freudian, post-Lawrentian orientation. This is one of a number of early poems by Larkin in which sexual desire threatens 'control'.

As Steve Clark points out, 'Lines on a Young Lady's Photograph Album' is riddled with sexual puns of a kind that make it more Baudelairean than Augustan.[16] The album, 'at last ... yielded' and 'once open', is much more of an emblem of seduction and voyeurism than its initial 'distraction' seems to suggest. Some of the puns are so cunningly disguised that we might easily miss them, 'however hard we yowl across / The gap from eye to page'. Here, it is not just that the clever enjambment between stanzas might claim our prior attention; it is also that the peculiar word 'yowl' calls for recognition. It is in keeping with the poem's playful preoccupation with its own medium that it should employ a word that is essentially imitative (of the sound of an animal) to record the painful exactitude of an imitative medium (photography) in a poem that is, itself, imitative of a well-established poetic tradition. 'Lines on a Young Lady's Photograph Album' is not some naive copy of a once-fashionable genre, but an astutely modern poem that raises problematic questions about desire, imagination and truth. It sets up expectations of delicacy and polite tradition, but it quickly undermines these to the point where it becomes a parody of the kind of poem it purports to be. If the vocative address, 'But o photography! as no art is', seems reminiscent of an older lyric poetry, it is also self-consciously anachronistic in the manner of Eliot's ironic apostrophes ('O City city') in *The Waste Land*. The apostrophising is also ambivalent. Is the poem lamenting the fact that photography falls short of art in being so uncompromisingly faithful to life or praising the way in which photography exceeds all other arts in its commitment to truth?

Too often, Larkin has been presented as a simple apologist for a Kodak aesthetic of the post-war years, as if the achievement of an art 'in every sense empirically true' was his ultimate manifesto. 'Lines on a Young Lady's Photograph Album' tends towards an aesthetic perspective altogether more complex and enigmatic. The closing stanza appears to be praising a photographic art that truthfully preserves the past, but the mood is not entirely celebratory: 'It holds you like a heaven, and you lie / Unvariably lovely there, / Smaller and clearer as the years go by'. 'Holds' might offer a welcome security, but it also hints at a less comforting sense of fixity, and this ambivalence is borne out in the rather odd, uncertain simile 'like a heaven', in the blunt pun on 'lie', and in the peculiar adjectival qualifying of 'lovely' (neither 'invariably' nor 'unvaryingly', but 'unvariably'). Everything here makes for tentativeness. If photography has the virtue of showing things as they are, it will in time remind us of our diminishing selves, bringing into focus what is irretrievably lost.

'At Grass', the closing poem in *The Less Deceived*, might also seem to typify a stubborn anti-Modernism and a preference for diction and syntax harking back to an eighteenth-century literary formality. Alvarez singled out the poem for criticism in his introduction to the Penguin *New Poetry* anthology, complaining that it smacked of 'gentility', and Heaney noted its pastoral, elegiac qualities, remarking that it might well have been subtitled 'An Elegy in a Country Paddock'.[17] The poet who provides the blueprint for Larkin's shadowy elegy, however, is not Thomas Gray, but W. B. Yeats. The poem's five stanzas, written mainly in iambic tetrameter, are skilfully modelled on 'The Wild Swans at Coole'. Yeats's 'brimming' water finds a delicate verbal echo in 'Dusk brims the shadows', helping to fill out the parallel twilight setting, while the retrospective distance is reduced from nineteen to fifteen years. Just as Yeats's elegiac lyric finds sanctuary in Coole Park in the aftermath of Easter 1916, Larkin's poem offers contemplative solace in the post-war years. 'At Grass' wistfully catches the glory and excitement of English summer race days, so that the pathos of retired racehorses might readily be identified with feelings of diminished national power or 'post-imperial *tristesse*'.[18] At the same time, there is a positive sense of relief and release at the end of the poem, complicating any political reading too readily equating its postcolonial vision with regret. For all its well-crafted alliteration and enjambment, the poem works essentially through an accumulation of realist, metonymic detail, prompting David Lodge to see this and other Larkin poems as evidence of a widespread hostility to Modernism in the 1950s.[19] But where the poem makes its modernity most evident is not in its structural or figurative modes so much as in its tentative perceptual processes and its refusal to offer comprehensive statements of truth. The opening line quietly sets up what was to become a characteristic concern in Larkin's poems with the problem of seeing clearly and judging rightly: 'The eye can hardly pick them out / From the cold shade they shelter in'. The poem's vocabulary is one of 'seeming', its vision a matter of imagined felicity, in which the horses gallop 'for what must be joy'. In the very moment of apprehending its cold pastoral, the poem declares its own provisionality, so that any reading of 'At Grass', either as a fable about growing old or as an allegory of national decline, must take into account its overriding concern with the fallibility of perception and the incompleteness of knowledge.

'Deceptions', effectively the title poem of *The Less Deceived*, ought to alert us in the plurality of its title, not just to the blind desire of the rapist and the bitter anguish of his victim, but also to those forms of deception attendant on any effort to know and recreate the past. The poem has been read too simply and crudely as a callous and sadistic turning away from female suffering to an ironic identification with the self-deceived assailant. What hinders any decisive reading is the problematic frame of reference: a quotation from Henry Mayhew's *London Labour and the London Poor*, in which a young woman's words are transcribed by a Victorian social commentator. The suggestion that the event in question is already 'textualised' is re-emphasised in the allusion to Ophelia's sense of betrayal in *Hamlet*: 'I was the more deceived'. The distance involved in trying to recover the truth of the event is not just temporal; it has to do with the multiple distortions and falsifications that accompany the written records by which we seek to know the past. The poem opens with what looks like a confidently empirical rendering of the tastes and sights and sounds that the woman might have experienced, but it quickly becomes aware of its own erratic reading. The intriguing simile at the end of the opening verse paragraph – 'Your mind lay open like a drawer of knives' – is both painfully exact and strangely imprecise, hinting at exposure and a sharp sense of pain, without entirely clarifying the terms of comparison. The image seems well intentioned but self-consciously adroit. The speaker's admission, 'I would not dare / Console you if I could', is not some heartless withholding of sympathy, but a recognition of his own limited perspectives and his own capacity for self-deception. If the poem points to the desolate outcome of violent desire, it also recognises the difficulties of knowing and understanding the past through its textual remains.

The colloquial tenor of Larkin's poems often disguises their progressively modern stance on questions of truth, knowledge and belief. 'Church Going' is a case in point. The plain-speaking, commonsense agnosticism of the speaker is apt to appear quaint, and while this has encouraged readings that see him as a descendant of Eliot's Prufrock, it draws attention away from the poem's sheer quality of wonder. The speaker's being 'at a loss ... wondering what to look for' suggests more than a lukewarm interest in metaphysics. The question of 'what remains when disbelief is gone' is radically unsettling; it clearly suggests an intellectual and poetic advance over the Hardyesque agnosticism with which Larkin is sometimes associated. It also prompts a fresh look at a number of early poems which explore the troubled border between life and death, prompting some urgent questions about the very nature of existence. One of these is 'Going', written in 1946 and included in the unpublished typescript *In the Grip of Light* under the title 'Dying Day'. The riddle-like nature of this short lyric only adds to the bafflement of its epistemological anxieties. The evocation of 'an evening coming in' is familiar enough as an image of death, but the poem quickly renders the failure of the senses and the terrifying prospect of abandonment. The 'going' in this instance is not the diminished attendance at church services, but the slipping away of consciousness itself.

The slightly later 'Days' (written in 1953 and published in *The Whitsun Weddings*) is another ontological riddle that points to a pervasive interest in fundamental questions of being. 'What are days for?' has a childlike simplicity, but trying to solve the question involves the priest and the doctor in what are purportedly matters of soul and body. As Terry Eagleton points out, the poem turns on a troubling ambivalence that has to do with the curious long gowns of the priest and the doctor and the unexplained nature of their running across the fields.[20] Existential dilemmas abound in Larkin's poems, though the manner of their expression sometimes gives them the appearance of casual, commonplace observations. 'Ignorance' is forthright and candid in its account of the strangeness of knowing nothing and of never being sure of what is right or real or true. The italicised colloquial responses are a way of asserting a shared and common dilemma – '*Someone must know*' – but the poem is resolute in conveying an utter sense of bewilderment about why we exist at all.

Two of the most imposing poems in *The Whitsun Weddings* – the opening poem, 'Here', and the title poem – declare their modernity most obviously in their meticulously detailed rendering of a changing post-war English landscape. The 'seamless wide-angled vision' so much admired in

Auden is now directed from a railway carriage window at the variegated scenes constituting a new England, a country recovering from the constrictions of the war years and sensing a revived economic prosperity. In both poems, however, the impression of modernity is filtered through a particular consciousness – that of the sceptical, alienated intellectual, not entirely at home in the new social order – and in both poems there is a search for some way of integrating that consciousness within a sustaining culture. If 'Here' confronts the extremes of existential loneliness, 'The Whitsun Weddings' offers a utopian glimpse of achieved community. The swerving verbal activity in 'Here', the absence of any obvious subject or personal pronoun in the opening lines, and the repeated insistence on 'here' all prepare us for the philosophical shift from 'here' as a recognisable place to 'here' as a state of being. The perception of an individual freedom beyond social obligations and restraints lifts the closing lines into a moment of heightened lyrical beauty, but it carries with it the chastening truth of its own impossible realisation: 'Here is unfenced existence: / Facing the sun, untalkative, out of reach.' The poem's arrival at a geographical margin is also an arrival at a linguistic margin. If 'untalkative' suggests a condition of silence, it also brings with it a Wittgensteinian recognition of that which cannot be talked about. The poem does more than evoke the attractions of solitariness; it looks out at an awe-inspiring emptiness. It acknowledges the urge for transcendence and simultaneously confronts the limitations of language and consciousness.

'The Whitsun Weddings' is often regarded as the showcase poem of Movement writing in the 1950s and 1960s, elegantly crafted and empirically grounded. The railway journey from Hull to London has elements of social documentary that once again point to the current popularity of photography and film, but underlying the superficial comedy of the weddings is a profoundly mythic and anthropological interest in rituals and rites of passage. What links the poem to its Modernist precursors, including *The Waste Land*, is its search for some redeeming vision amidst the seeming chaos and contingency of contemporary civilisation. Whitsun provides the opportunity for revelation and insight as the sceptical speaker repeatedly adjusts his attitude to the presence of the newly married couples with whom he shares his journey. Rather than insisting on its own empirical certitude, the poem draws attention to the perspectival nature of knowledge and the fallibility of perception. 'The Whitsun Weddings' is a quest for a unified vision and a shared system of belief in a desacralised world, but it is also a quest for social integration. The closing stanza acquires an articulate energy as the acceleration of the train and the tightening of brakes convey both the impulse towards a shared sense of endeavour and its gradual dissolution.

The final image of 'an arrow-shower / Sent out of sight, somewhere becoming rain' keeps open the possibility of fulfilment, allowing sacramental suggestions to linger alongside the more secular associations of rain with disappointment and desolation.

J. R. Watson, in one of the first critical essays to take Larkin's metaphysics seriously, claims that the poetry 'celebrates the unexpressed, deeply felt longings for sacred time and sacred space' that persist in modern culture. Frequently, the primitive, ritualistic aspects of Larkin's poems carry a regenerative charge that suggests continuity with a good deal of Modernist art. Watson reminds us of Mircea Eliade's claim that 'the fundamental myth is that of the proximity of paradise', and the point is well made in relation to 'High Windows', however much that poem shrugs off contemporary substitutes for heaven.[21] The speaker's ironic response to the sexual freedom of the 1960s – 'I know this is paradise' – reverberates throughout, prompting the thought of high windows and the sublime apprehension of infinite nothingness beyond. Few modern poems demonstrate so well the post-structuralist insistence on the ultimate gap between word and world and the elusive nature of the transcendental signified. Where Larkin's distinctive modern voice is heard most clearly, however, is not just in the poem's overt preoccupation with questions of epistemology, but in its shift from the grim colloquialism of the first four stanzas to the symbolist luminosity of the closing lines.

'High Windows' led some to wonder if Larkin was acquainted with French symbolist poetry. '*Hautes Fenêtres*, my God!' Larkin guffawed in an interview when asked about his interests in non-English poetry.[22] Barbara Everett's brilliant analysis of 'Sympathy in White Major' shows just how extensive the influence actually was. Everett helpfully suggests that Larkin's parodic perspective on French symbolism perhaps makes him a *post-modern* (if not *postmodern*) poet, in more than just a chronological sense.[23] That parodic instinct is so widespread in the poems of *High Windows* as to suggest another dimension of postmodern art: its unashamed eclecticism and penchant for pastiche. In the 1950s Larkin had carefully concealed the extent of his debt to his own modern contemporaries, claiming to dislike casual allusions in poems to other poems and poets, but in a broadcast in August 1972 he was explicit about the attractions of writing 'different kinds of poems that might be by different people'.[24] The urge to be different from himself produces in his later poems an astonishing range of voices, allusions and literary echoes. Along with poems ostentatiously modelled on works by other authors, there is a collision of styles and generic possibilities. The occasional pleas and imperatives suggest that there is room, too, for a more partisan poetic voice at the end of Larkin's career, one more inclined to dogma than disinterestedness. In the end, though, it is this hectoring, anxious and sometimes vehement voice that gives the final poetry a quality and appeal far exceeding the attractions of a purely playful and pluralistic postmodernism. Larkin never abandons the vision of an integrated culture, even though that vision is sometimes provocatively conservative and nostalgic. Larkin's poetry is a late modern poetry of anguished self-questioning and perplexity, a poetry brazenly confronting the extremes of existence. One of the great ironies of modern literary history is that Larkin should have been berated for a lack of 'urgency' by his earliest critics.[25] There is no voice more urgent in late twentieth-century poetry.

NOTES

1 *Selected Letters of Philip Larkin 1940–1985*, ed. Anthony Thwaite (London: Faber and Faber, 1992), p. 32.

2 For a detailed and persuasive account of Virginia Woolf's influence on Larkin's poetry and fiction, see Stephen Cooper, *Philip Larkin: Subversive Writer* (Brighton: Sussex Academic Press, 2004).

3 Philip Larkin, *Early Poems and Juvenilia*, ed. A. T. Tolley (London: Faber and Faber, 2005), p. 21.

4 *Selected Letters*, p. 460.

5 Philip Larkin, *Required Writing: Miscellaneous Pieces 1955–1982* (London: Faber and Faber, 1983), p. 297.

6 Philip Larkin, *Further Requirements: Interviews, Broadcasts, Statements and Book Reviews*, ed. Anthony Thwaite (London: Faber and Faber, 2001), p. 96.

7 *Selected Letters*, p. 28.

8 Larkin, *Early Poems and Juvenilia*, p. 361.

9 Larkin, *Further Requirements*, p. 329.

10 *Ibid.*, p. 18.

11 Quotations from Larkin's poems, other than those included in *Early Poems and Juvenilia*, are from his *Collected Poems*, ed. Anthony Thwaite (London: Faber and Faber, 1988).

12 Larkin, *Further Requirements*, p. 18.

13 Larkin, *Required Writing*, p. 30.

14 Andrew Motion, *Philip Larkin* (London: Methuen, 1982); Seamus Heaney, 'The Main of Light', in *The Government of the Tongue* (London: Faber and Faber, 1988), pp. 15–22; Tom Paulin, 'She Did Not Change: Philip Larkin,' in *Minotaur: Poetry and the Nation State* (London: Faber and Faber, 1992), pp. 233–51.

15 F. W. Bateson, 'Auden's (and Empson's) Heirs', *Essays in Criticism*, 7 (1957), 76–80.

16 Steve Clark, ' "Get Out As Early As You Can": Larkin's Sexual Politics', in Stephen Regan (ed.), *Philip Larkin* (Basingstoke: Macmillan, 1987), p. 115.

17 A. Alvarez (ed.), *The New Poetry* (Harmondsworth: Penguin, 1966), p. 25; Seamus Heaney, 'Englands of the Mind', in *Preoccupations: Selected Prose 1968–1978* (London: Faber and Faber, 1980), p. 166.

18 Blake Morrison, *The Movement: English Poetry and Fiction of the 1950s* (Oxford: Oxford University Press, 1980), pp. 82–3.

19 David Lodge, 'Philip Larkin: The Metonymic Muse', in Regan (ed.), *Philip Larkin*, pp. 71–82.

20 Terry Eagleton, *How to Read a Poem* (Oxford: Blackwell, 2007), p. 126.

21 J. R. Watson, 'The Other Larkin,' *Critical Quarterly* 17, 4 (1975), 351, 354.

22 Larkin, *Required Writing*, p. 69.

23 Barbara Everett, 'Philip Larkin: After Symbolism', *Essays in Criticism*, 30 (1980), 227–42.

24 Larkin, *Further Requirements*, p. 92.

25 Alvarez (ed.), *The New Poetry*, p. 28.

Further reading

Booth, James (ed.), *New Larkins for Old: Critical Essays*, Basingstoke: Macmillan, 2000

Booth, James, *Philip Larkin: The Poet's Plight*, Basingstoke: Palgrave, 2006

Bradford, Richard, *First Boredom, Then Fear: The Life of Philip Larkin*, London: Peter Owen, 2005

Corcoran, Neil, *English Poetry Since 1940*, London: Longman, 1993

Motion, Andrew, *Philip Larkin: A Writer's Life*, London: Faber, 1993

O'Neill, Michael, 'The Importance of Difference: Larkin's *The Whitsun Weddings*', in George Hartley (ed.), *Philip Larkin 1922–1985: A Tribute*, London: Marvell Press, 1988, pp. 184–97

Regan, Stephen, *Philip Larkin*, Basingstoke: Macmillan, 1992

Swarbrick, Andrew, *Out of Reach: The Poetry of Philip Larkin*, Basingstoke: Macmillan, 1995

I I

M. WYNN THOMAS

R. S. Thomas and modern Welsh poetry

In *The Unbearable Lightness of Being in Aberystwyth*, a zany noir spoof of Raymond Chandler, Malcolm Pryce has his private eye, Louie Knight, buy a ticket to Nantyronen that includes 'admission to the Iago Prytherch "home-stay"'. Having reached his destination, he is guided by signs such as 'You are now entering Iago Prytherch Country' and 'The bald Welsh hills' to the hovel ('Warning: spittled mirth') where Iago himself huddles.[1] Parody of this order is an inverted tribute to the power of the early R. S. Thomas to recreate the human and physical landscape of rural, upland Wales in the very image of his own obsession. He gave that obsession a name, Iago Prytherch, and a local habitation, Prytherch country, as broodingly mapped as Faulkner's Yoknapatawpha County.

If Dylan Thomas was the definitive poetic talent of pre-Second World War Wales, then it was this other Thomas, culturally, politically and poetically his polar opposite, who became the defining poetic talent of post-war decades. It is therefore with a shock that one realises that R. S., who fully blossomed only after Dylan's death in 1953, was in fact a year older than his namesake. But whereas the quintessential South Walian was a prodigy, who had completed a corpus of remarkable lyrics by the age of eighteen, the North Walian was by his own admission a late developer, both as a poet and as a man, an emotional retardation he blamed on his snobbishly genteel mother's possessiveness. And while his poetic development was impeded by his lingering attachment to the variously Romantic poems in Palgrave's *Golden Treasury*, he saw it, too, as ultimately deriving from the immature sensibility cultivated in him by her. Iago was therefore the tutelary spirit not only of a breakthrough poetry but also of a personal maturation that took the form of a narcissistic adult's belated encounter with the Reality Principle. That encounter was traumatic, and the fixity of R. S.'s poetic attention, for a quarter of a century, to the figure of Prytherch is the measure of the depth of his psychological fixation.

In naming Iago the product of 'the bald Welsh hills', and catching him 'docking mangels, chipping the green skin / From the yellow bones with a half-witted grin / Of satisfaction',[2] Thomas was confronting his naked, unaccommodated nature. It was in harsh tune with the cruel, post-Darwinian natural world from which Iago could find no hiding place, as neither could his creator in the faux-Celtic nature idylls of misty writers like Fiona Macleod (the Scotsman William Sharp), or in the nostalgic Welsh ideology of the 'gwerin' (the naturally pious and cultivated rural folk) – although the remnants of such dreams did linger on in poignant counterpoint to Iago. Those hills were the defining feature of the symbolic geography Thomas shared with influential cultural anthropologists and Welsh-language intellectuals of the period who saw the upland regions as the refuge of ancient autochthonous Welshness while the valleys and coastal lowlands had long been overrun by invaders. No more bitter self-indictment could therefore be imagined than Thomas's when, in 'Invasion on the Farm', he named himself as an invader, and thus put himself in the company of the despised colonisers, from the voyeuristic Romantic seekers of the picturesque, to the Birmingham blondes and the Elsan culture of the holiday caravanners he so witheringly derided.

While Thomas served a brief pre-war apprenticeship producing late-Georgian poetry for publication in outlets such as the *Dublin Magazine*, he really emerged into (incomplete) maturity with the small-press publication of his first collection, *The Stones of the Field*, in 1946. And whereas his original pan-Celticism had taken the form of a passion for Macleod and the early Yeats, in its developed form it was expressed as a creative response to Patrick Kavanagh's *The Great Hunger* and the new Scottish poetry of Hugh MacDiarmid. Although, to the very end of his life, he believed that, apart from Eliot, only two twentieth-century poets, W. B. Yeats and Wallace Stevens, had possessed the supreme genius of decisively altering poetic expression, he recognized in the later 1940s that the new Irish, and particularly Scottish, writing showed that English could be changed into a language appropriate for use by non-English writers. The poems of his early maturity need accordingly to be valued as a deliberate language experiment – in being about Iago, his land and his kind, they are also about language itself. It, too, had to be reborn of the 'bald Welsh hills', since Thomas believed that, in order to be expressively answerable to their subject, wordscapes had to be moulded out of the very matter of the landscapes whose physical and cultural realities they attempted textually to mediate. Iago is often construed, and constructed, as a geological outcrop, or viewed as embodying 'the land's patience and a tree's / Knotted endurance' (*CP*, 12). But it is through language he bulks large. Filling the inner ear, the sonically dense words and obtrusive tropes seem to fill space: 'if you could choose/To wrest your barns from the wind and the weather's claws' (*CP*, 16) . This was the period when Thomas was painstakingly making himself fluent in Welsh, a process that may well have meant he found his native English was defamiliarised, its peculiar grain and texture rendered newly visible and thus palpably available for his purpose.

Certainly to read the early poetry is to become aware that the medium's thickness is the message. Just, for instance, as Iago is famously first seen 'penn[ing] a few sheep in a gap of cloud' (*CP*, 4) so this is language occupying a liminal space between the Welsh language and mainstream English. Drawing on the example of Austin Clarke with Irish English, Thomas attempted to use complex assonantal and alliterative patterns approximate to Welsh *barddas* in order to render English 'foreign' to its ordinary self, bent out of 'true' by the invisible gravitational pull of another language. In this respect, the early poetry is a would-be declaration of linguistic independence, the counterpart of a burgeoning cultural and political nationalism characteristic of many young Welsh writers' reaction against the Anglocentric character both of wartime Britishness and the centralist Britain of the post-war welfare state. And in this period he held hopefully to the belief (later bitterly repudiated, in obedience to the linguistic politics of Saunders Lewis) that English, too, could become a self-fashioning language not only of Wales but of Welshness.

But the language also works to different effect. On first reading, the striking succession of vivid tropes that constitute an early Thomas poem can seem the equivalent of Cubist multi-perspectivism, the three-dimensional definition of an object in space:

> The same garments, frayed with light
> Or seamed with rain, cling to the wind-scoured bones
> And shame him in the eyes of the spruce bids.
> Once it was ignorance, then need, but now
> Habit that drapes him on a bush of cloud
> For life to mock at, while the noisy surf
> Of people dins far off at the world's rim.   (*CP*, 39)

But subsequent readings lead to a very different impression, of an endless process of substitution, an indefinite deferral of any definitive access to essence. This poetry is the definition of Iago's inalienable mysteriousness rather than the solution of his mystery. An obsession is, after all, by definition, inexhaustible. And thus the unspoken subject of the early poems is the power and impotence of language. By turns bestially mute and eloquent in the alternative green language of nature, Iago repeatedly witnesses to the inefficacy of Thomas's poetry. So many of the poems feature a fascinated mention of eyes – eyes which, whether sharp and 'bright as thorns' or impenetrable as pebbles, invariably fail to register the faintest recognition of the poet's anguished concerns. And so Iago is simultaneously materialised and dematerialised. It may therefore be no accident that in successive printings one word (italicised below) in the early poem 'A Peasant' oscillated between two forms: 'churning the crude earth / To a stiff sea of *clouds/clods* that glint in the sun' (*CP*, 4): earth and the etherial thus become endlessly interchangeable. Iago is not to be simplified to any single, self-consistent set of meanings. Both brute creature and child of nature, he is endlessly contradictory, embodying the Gordian knot of Thomas's psychic anxieties.

In creating Iago, Thomas displays his mastery of the grotesque, that byproduct of *kulturkampf* that had become the default genre of Welsh writing ever since it was notoriously patented in 1915 by Caradoc Evans, in his short-story collection *My People*. This physically gross Iago, who gobs into the fire, is the most unlikely spirit of place, the grotesque *genius loci* of the border uplands that brought Thomas to his senses by speaking so brutally plainly to his previous fastidiousness. Passively obedient to his mother's wish that he enter the priesthood, he first entered upon what became his genuine vocation in the border parishes of Chirk and Hanmer, before coming to Manafon as a naively eager young priest to a mortifyingly unresponsive people. He came with prospects, expecting to find the culturally healing and nourishing Welsh heartland so long romantically imagined as secreted in the distant mountains variously viewed from Birkenhead, Anglesey, Bangor and the border railway line. No wonder that the most prominent syntactical marker of the early poetry is the abrupt biblical imperative that brooks no evasion. 'Behold,' 'Look,' 'See,' all have a double significance. For a Thomas faced with a stolidly unresponsive flock, they are a preacher's didactic strategy infused with the urgency of a last effort to prevent psychic disintegration. But they are also a manual of self-instruction: 'He, too, is a man like you' – like the old Lear, the cossetted Thomas, faced with Iago, self-laceratingly recognises that 'I have ta'en too little care of this.'

Song at the Year's Turning, the volume that brought him to English attention, was published two years after Dylan Thomas's death in 1953. It was the end of an era, because it was the real end of the 1930s, and of a generation of talent that had produced the first body of anglophone work distinctively Welsh in character. This literature, whose house journal was Keidrych Rhys's periodical *Wales*, was thus a rival, and threat, to the Welsh language literature, its senior by almost 1,500 years, that had been the traditional carrier of Welsh national identity. The resultant civil war tortured R. S. Thomas throughout his life while adding the sharp creative edge of guilt to his poetic handling of English. As for Dylan's death, following close on the likewise premature deaths of Alun Lewis and Idris Davies, it left only Vernon Watkins and Glyn Jones to work through their full maturity in the afterglow of the comet. And Dylan's epigones as they were, the new talents emerging – Dannie Abse, Leslie Norris, John Ormond – found they were yesterday's men before ever they had reached their youthful today. They were left to wrestle insubstantially with the shadow of his fame, whereas R. S., as Dylan's contemporary, had enjoyed the advantage of framing his own, alternative, poetic discourse before world renown had rendered Dylan's charismatic. R. S. could express distaste, amused and contemptuous by turns, for the jumped-up boyo who had pandered, in colonised South Walian fashion, to English stereotypes of the colourful Welsh windbag. But in taking the title of his 1953 volume from 'Poem in October' Thomas was in fact enacting his poetic relationship to his renowned namesake in different terms, of simultaneous tribute, expropriation and displacement.

More than Dylan Thomas's equal in experimental daring was Lynette Roberts, whose long five-part war poem *Gods with Stainless Ears* was introduced as written from the Laugharne that Dylan made famous. Sharing David Jones's passion for studding poetry with arcane words whose etymology sediments a complex cultural history, she produced an electrifyingly strange poetry, filmic in character, that, like the later experimental writing of John James, is only now beginning to be appreciated, not least by poets searching for Welsh antecedents alternative to the stylistically and culturally conservative R. S. Thomas. Herself a cultural exotic, raised in Argentina as the daughter of parents of distant Welsh descent, educated in England and resident in a Welsh coastal village, Roberts was multicultural and drew upon her learning with all the inspired eccentricity of genius. She sets her long poem in 'St Cadoc's estuary', and sees it shadowed by 'Homeric hills', before evoking its 'migrat(ing)' quagmires that 'draw victim eyes with lustre sheen, suck / Confervoid residue from gillette veins.'[3] The peculiar exactness of the description becomes apparent when one discovers that 'Conferva' are green algae. Wanting to convey the invasion of the natural world by the mechanical rhythms of military preparation, she writes of how 'Into euclidian cubes tempered air is planed' (47), the pun in the last word vividly suggesting the way an aircraft's sound affects space. And in commemorating the three-night blitz on Swansea she moves from sinister lyricism as 'Night falling catches the flares and bangs / On gorselit rock', to a mad wish to 'Snip up the moon sniggering on its back / For on them [the rippling waves of the bay] sail the hulls of ninety wild birds / Defledged by this evening's raid: jigging up / Like a tapemachine the cold figures February / 19th, 20th, 21st. A memorial of Swansea's tragic loss' (57). By the end, therefore, the scene has turned into a movingly grotesque pastoral.

Another emergent post-war poet not overawed by Dylan Thomas was Roland Mathias, who became notable for work of singularity and integrity. His is a learned, cerebral poetry, 'bleak with conscience' and thus forbiddingly faithful to the moral injunction to 'lay the action bare'. There is no hiding place in his poems, least of all for language, which is subject to the most rigorously sceptical oversight, lest it lead seductively to the careless talk that could cost spiritual life. He laboured to construct 'the strong, remembered words, the unanswerable / Texts against chaos'.[4] As the phrasing suggests, his poetic was consciously puritanic. In his stern masterpiece, 'Brechfa Chapel', a passionately respectful commitment to the Welsh Dissenting tradition he knew R. S. Thomas had dismissed emerges in a condemnation of the 'militant brabble' – the Cromwellian echo is pointed – of the black-backs, those waterbirds signifying modern complaisant, louche society. A historian by training, Mathias sought to ground himself not only in Welsh Nonconformist history but also in the cultural matter of Wales, thus becoming, like the Welsh Anglican R. S. Thomas, an influential figure both in critiquing the secularisation of a people for whom religion had been a seemingly indispensable constituent of nationhood, and in researching the new historical terms adequate for ensuring national continuity. If class had, for many Welsh writers of the thirties, been the defining marker of identity, then Welsh nationality was to become the marker for several of the most important writers of the post-war decades.

Mathias's search for historically lost ground was, of course, predicated on the opposite experience of radical cultural dislocation, an experience not only angrily lamented but also inscribed as a harlequinade of stylistic improvisation in the poetry of T. H(arri) Jones for whom Wales offered only 'a broken landscape of regrets'. But for his untimely death in Australia, Jones might have gone on to develop a poetry of multiple selfhood, in the manner of John Berryman, one of his heroes. As it is, his body of work is largely a theatre of imitation too questing to be pastiche, an exercise in sometimes enabling literary ventriloquism. 'The sensual landscape in his mind' was at once that of the female body he guiltily found so physically and poetically irresistible and that of the rocky Welsh uplands where he had been grimly raised and whose physical and puritanical harshness had marked him for life. Exile brought him costly liberation, as he acknowledged in 'Back?', a notable poem angrily addressed to an R. S. Thomas he viewed as stern guardian of Jones's own lost patrimony of belonging and in the image of whose early poetry Jones produced some of his most moving poems of personal recollection. It ends with the doubtful consolation of 'the waves, of water and of fern / And words, that beat unendingly / On the rocks of my mind's country', and so identifies rootlessness as ironically the root of his own work of grounding his lost landscapes in language.[5]

Had Jones but known it, Thomas was himself an exile – sentenced, in more than one sense, to a lifelong internal exile and to making his home, too, only in poetry. Out of place in Manafon, he moved to Eglwys-Fach only to find not a heartland Welsh community but one infiltrated by culturally arrogant English settlers, most conspicuously the retired senior military officers who dominated parish affairs. His poetry became correspondingly unsettled, encompassing distant reflections on his Manafon experience and waspish poems about his more intolerable parishioners. Dependent on obsession, his imagination displayed withdrawal symptoms following the geographical and psychological distancing of Iago. And while his local hatreds enabled him to focus another obsession, the colonial subordination of Wales, he ultimately lacked the satirist's cool accuracy, born of the indispensable talent for combining burning anger with a chip of ice in the heart. The most searingly memorable of his Welsh jeremiads are perhaps those most clearly originating in personal hurt and confessing to a disturbing self-disgust: when supplemented by the bitter squibs in *What is a Welshman*, these state-of-the-nation addresses (finally collected in *Welsh Airs*) stood clearly revealed as the lightning strikes produced by the electrically charged air of the 1960s – the watershed decade of post-war Welsh cultural and political history. The period is thick with key events, personalities, organisations and developments – 'Tryweryn' (the Westminster-decreed 'drowning' of a valley to supply Liverpool with water); Saunders Lewis's radio address forecasting the imminent death of the Welsh language; the Free Wales Army; the attack on water pipelines; the Welsh Language Society and its peaceful law-breaking campaigns; the 'quisling' Secretary of State for Wales, George Thomas; the election of Gwynfor Evans as the first-ever Plaid Cymru MP; the infamous (to R. S.) Investiture of the Prince of Wales; the gradual institutionalisation of Welsh national difference through the growing powers of the Welsh Office and the establishment of the Welsh Arts Council; and the launch of *Poetry Wales* (later followed by Poetry Wales Press, subsequently Seren Books) as the instrument of cultural change.

Disillusioned by the compromises involved in the mainstreaming of nationalist politics, Thomas instead identified passionately with the dramatic acts of civil disobedience of the language campaigners, and vehemently denied the possibility of an English-language Welsh poetry (or identity) even as a new, richly talented generation of Welsh anglophone poets, mostly emerging from the industrial south Thomas so despised, began to form a broad front with Welsh-language writers and activists to produce a culturally committed, sometimes explicitly engagé, poetry. Sympathetic to this, Jeremy Hooker, settled in Aberystwyth, was reactively stimulated to produce *Englishman's Road*, a fine meditation on his identifying relationships to his own native place in Hampshire, while by invoking the traditional Welsh model of the 'bardd gwlad' (local and occasional poet), the Falstaffian Harri Webb used popular verse performance in pubs and clubs as a means of mass mobilization. In the humorous 'Ianto Rhydderch Tch Tch' the egalitarian socialist Webb imagined a reply to the snobbish condescension of R. S. Thomas by an Iago-like figure who finds 'It [takes] all my idiot peasant strength / To be polite to him.'[6] Webb's example as impassioned spokesperson for the colonised and capitalistically exploited industrial proletariat that Thomas had slandered as not Welsh was followed by Nigel Jenkins and by Mike Jenkins, who dedicated his talent to articulating (sometimes in local dialect) the experiences of a post-industrially derelict Merthyr. This work of mapping post-industrial South Wales was differently undertaken by the sardonic John Tripp, who had a keenly jaundiced eye for the detritus of urbanised living.

Two major figures – Tony Conran and Gillian Clarke – were also products of the 1960s awakening and confirmed admirers of Thomas's cultural politics. Conran is probably post-war Wales's 'strongest' poet, in the Bloomean sense that he is incisively, massively and uncompromisingly original. Over five decades of single-minded work, including a body of translations from the Welsh and devoted to the complex poetic imagining of Wales, he has evolved an integrated personal, social and historical myth on which his sophisticated late modernist, anti-capitalist poetic is based. His most magisterial work is *Castles*, a sequence of poems layered with allusions and tracing, from the period of Roman occupation to the present, the oscillation of Wales between identification with centralist British imperialism and the assertion of a separate, anti-colonial identity. The hewn voice of Conran's poetry is complemented by the intuitive fluidities of Clarke's, who feels her sensuous way along her lines and is attuned to the songlines of the subconscious. Finding in the published work of Sally Roberts Jones and others belated licence at the end of the 1960s to be a woman poet, Clarke seemed a mature poet from the outset, assured in her instancing of a female (as opposed to feminist) poetic that privileged an emotionally insinuating rhythm and a probing discourse, using tropes like sonic radar for mapping the deep sea floor of feeling. She both feminises and universalises a range of interconnected subjects, from the intimate and domestic to the social ravages of foot and mouth, from the natural world to green issues and from Welsh history to international events. And part of her aim has been to insert female experience into the contemporary and historical matter of Wales.

But several important writers were determinedly deaf to the 1960s' call to the national colours, and extremely sceptical of R. S. Thomas's concerns with political and cultural commitment. 'I keep short boundaries holy'[7] became the motto of Leslie Norris, a poet who was to draw first upon his melancholy-sweet memories of boyhood Merthyr and then on a spectrum of responses to the natural and human worlds in a beautifully nuanced, quiet-voiced and frequently elegiac poetry that owed much to the example of yet another (semi-)Welsh Thomas, Edward. Rejecting the siren song of the 1960s to Welsh exiles to return 'home', Norris spent most of his life in Sussex and latterly in Utah, carefully cultivating, like Dannie Abse, the divided allegiances he felt nourished his imagination. Abse, indeed, created a major body of work out of a stance that resourcefully equivocates between semi-detachments and multiple attachments, advertising himself as both Welsh and Jewish, doctor and poet, in the process of delicately tracing the elusive ambiguities of human being and personal identity. He treats profound subjects such as man's amphibious nature and mysterious existential circumstancing with the most attractively light of touches, having a shrewd 'Jewish' understanding that they may best be addressed through the haunting obliquities of humour, fable and fantasy. Far less well known, though undeservedly so, is Abse's friend, John Ormond – director of a classic film portrait of R. S. Thomas – the best of whose poetry is a complex study in an apolitical aesthetic. In a tour de force of poetic performance, 'Certain Questions for Monsieur Renoir', Ormond marvels at 'La Parisienne', 'Who wears that blue of smoke curling / Beyond a kiln, and blue of gentians, / Blue of lazurite, turquoise hauled // Over the blue waves' – an excited response to the vocabulary of a single colour which epitomises Ormond's sense of poetry as the language of amazement.[8]

With Abse, Ormond wrote, we are 'always on the haunted brink of what might be revealed'.[9] The same is true of the later poetry of an R. S. Thomas who, with the appearance of *H'm* in 1972, had clearly found his next, and last, necessary obsession. The volume's punning title itself epitomised Thomas's approaches to his elusive God for the remaining thirty years of his long life. Rumination, dismissive ejaculation, these and a range of other possibilities are contained in a word which is itself haunted by the central absence of that single letter, 'i', which would turn it into a referent confidently identifying and substantiating the deity. Language is thus self-reflexive here, in the way it continued to be in Thomas's last poetry that spans some ten volumes almost wearyingly devoted to the contemplation of an oxymoronic God. His mind informed by his virtually daily reading of Kierkegaard, Thomas drew upon the New Theology, from Bonhoeffer through Tillich to Robinson, and the New subatomic Physics as popularised by Paul Davies, to produce postmodern tropes suitable for exploring the 'God-space'. As a means of savagely critiquing the Christian practice of speaking of God by speaking of man in a loud voice, he lyrically fabricated fantastic mental universes analogous to those of Borges, likewise a creator of great metaphysical fables.

Borges was fascinated by the God Script, and haunted by the biblical account of Christ's writing invisibly on the ground with a stick. What had he written? How could one read the writing of God? And how could one write God? These were also Thomas's concerns. Even to call his remarkable collection of late poems a 'body' of work is misleading, although its cumulative power is undeniable, because, for Thomas (as for the Eliot by whose *Four Quartets* he was undoubtedly mesmerised), any poem paradoxically devoted to defining the infinite was necessarily provisional and self-cancelling. And all tropes were conceits – absurd figurative extravaganzas silently admitting to being mere, self-regarding, mental constructs. Nor were sentences, the supposedly reliable building blocks of printed utterance, to be trusted: Thomas's line breaks are cunningly contrived to show how plain statement can suddenly turn into equivocating expression revealing the Janus face of human experience of the divine. Man, in this late poetry, seems frequently to be double-crossed by a God who had, after all, been crucified on a cross the arms of which, as Thomas wryly noted, pointed in two diametrically opposite directions. This cross was, in Protestant iconographic tradition, always left empty – signifying, for this consciously doubting Thomas, the possibility not only of Resurrection but also of terminal divine absence. His unorthodox Christology is nowhere more vividly apparent than in his characterising of Christ as the stitch incurred in the side of a callously laughing God, almost as though the Son were the Father's reflex action of pity in the face of His Creation's suffering.

'And the dogfish, spotted like God's face, / Looks at him, and the seal's eye- / ball is cold' (*CP*, 224), wrote Thomas, the lines bleak with acknowledgement of the divinely created world's impersonal ferocities that left his poetry drying 'on the rocks / Of a harsh landscape under an ailing sun' (*CP*, 224). From the beginning he had known that his was 'no friendly God' (*CP*, 11), as he had put it in his first volume, *The Stones of the Field*, its title a desolate phrase from the Book of Job. 'Christen me, christen me, / The stone cried' (*CP*, 216), he wrote in another poem, acknowledging the difficulty of Christianising a post-Darwinian universe, whose savagery was inseparable from that beauty which nevertheless gleamed irresistibly out at Thomas as what he wistfully called 'the rainbow of your coming and going'. This rainbow is not so much the biblical sign of God's forgiveness of human sin as the sign of His forgiveness of Himself for his botched creation. Because if there were bright fields to which Thomas turned 'aside like Moses to the miracle / of the lit bush' (CP, 302) there were also moorlands, where not only was 'the air rarified / as the interior of a cathedral // expecting a presence' but there were the harriers' 'claws of fire, / quartering the bare earth' (CP, 513). And in the face of this Thomas could sometimes only respond with one word that might be taken both as his poetic and as the epitaph of his vulnerable, peregrine self. In a poem called, ironically (with its glance at the Johannine Gospel), 'The Word', Thomas imagines a pen suddenly materialising in his hand and a god directing him to 'Write what it is to be / man'. He finds a word taking flesh, as it shapes itself under his hand on the blank page, the one word 'lonely'. And moving to erase it he is stayed by hearing 'the voices / of all those waiting at life's / window' crying out loud: ' "It is true" ' (CP, 265). In his attenuated later poems, Thomas can seem the Giacometti of modern poets.

Thomas's choice of poetic (but not political) isolation in his last remote fastnesses at Aberdaron and elsewhere was made easy by the appearance, mostly from the South Wales industrial communities and conurbations he so lamented and despised, of a number of new poets. Several of these were disenchanted with his talk of the soul of Wales, let alone of human being. With their preference for travelling light, without the baggage of national culture, and their interest in the casual kaleidoscope of human experience, they were the forerunners of the postmodernism that many of their Welsh successors, like Stephen Knight and Oliver Reynolds, would enthusiastically embrace.

The dismantling of industrial communities during the Thatcher years, the reactive miners' strike at a time when social mobility was problematising class allegiance, campaigning from Greenham to the Green Movement: these and other issues entered into poetry from the 1970s onwards, when Wales was establishing its first (Welsh Arts Council-funded) separate publishing base and the public mind was silently haunted by the devolution issue resolved only in 1997 with a vote for a Welsh National Assembly. At the same time, the internationalising of experience by ease of travel was accompanied by the dissolving of the traditional social fixatives of individual and national identity.

The popular vote against political devolution in 1979 effectively silenced some notable older poets of the Thomas politico-cultural persuasion, like Raymond Garlick, but licensed younger writers to diversify. While Oliver Reynolds' 'To whom it may concern' is a witty spoof letter from the

Secretary of State for Wales advising the recipient of the government's new enlightened policy of removing the Rhondda unemployed to better prospects in 'Falkland fawr and Falkand fach', his poem about learning Welsh implicitly critiques Thomas's old notions of language-identity as it makes its way through a maze of puns ('declenched teeth';'Welshing on the language'; 'learn about roots') in the direction of a new multicultural 'language' poetry suitable for the refractions of modern identity.[10] Similarly, in *Flight Patterns* (1991), John Davies mixes casual aperçus ('isn't the point of travel to keep / going') with keen perceptions of the mirages of modern movement ('bulging in heat, / cars wobble like toads') and reflects on 'breeched / defences, ways of living blown'. An admirer of R. S. Thomas's concern with centredness, Davies takes as his theme the ambivalent experience of 'losing ground' and the modern gamble on the game of change: 'Flight paths converge, / fade out, as sky measures gain and loss'.[11] The transatlantic flight paths that concern Davies also fascinate other US-minded poets like Duncan Bush and Tony Curtis, who based 'The Deerslayers' on twenty-four plates by the American photographer Les Krims. Its opening – 'A delta of blood from the leaking mouth' – captures the ambulance-chasing side of an imagination artistically excited by the immolation of a racing-car driver in 'so much pain he heard his screams like music': it is the aesthetic of suffering. A post-war child trying to expiate his non-combatant's guilt by repeatedly exploring war experiences, Curtis can be swaggeringly macho – as when he treats his son to a display of his prowess at removing ivy: 'as we axed and ripped the tentacles / it slacked its biceps, unclenched its fist'. But if he sometimes aspires to belong to the Hemingway school of writing, he can also disarm with vulnerably raw emotion. As he leaves his dying father in Singleton Hospital, 'the lift drops / like a flat stone through water'.[12]

The poetry of Robert Minhinnick, Green activist who is an impassioned objector to the would-be-Green Thomas's arrogant human appropriation of landscape, is vivified by living on the dangerous edge of experience. What he tellingly likes about unemployed teenagers in their punk gear ('parched boots bracketed with lime / And studs like quillets') is that 'they warm themselves on language hot as rum'. His writing tenses to release 'the thwarted energies of quiet streets' and to isolate the quirky quiddities of people ('that woman whose eyes are a lizard's / Lidless bulge').[13] Very differently attractive are the poems of Jean Earle that bathe the world in a calm evenness of perception. Her love-affair with light is ecstatically consummated in 'The Woollen Mill'.

Seventy-one before she published a volume, Earle was understandably not attuned to the liberationist concerns of gritty feminist writers like Penny

Windsor, or the sensuous poetics of Hilary Llewelyn Williams, richly seen in *The Tree Calendar*. Settled in west Wales, Llewelyn Williams is in part a poet of discovered place, as is Ruth Bidgood in the rural uplands of Powys, where, as community remembrancer, she pays devout attention to verbally exhuming past lives, and Christine Evans in R. S. Thomas's Llŷn where, fascinated by the way the mundane quietly and shyly offers us glimpses of its transfigured self, she occasionally reveals herself to be at heart an alchemist of the imagination. Not for Evans the gimlet eye and tart tongue of Sheenagh Pugh as she scours out the innards of individuals, or exposes the quirkiness in the human politics of relationships and situations.

Still developing writers include Owen Sheers, Deryn Rees-Jones, Sarah Corbett, Samantha Wynne Rhydderch and, most electrifyingly, Pascale Petit, whose debut volume, *The Zoo Father*, elaborates an exotic baroque myth for handling the otherwise unbearable subject of a father's habitual abuse of his daughter. But undoubtedly the most arresting and impressive poet to have appeared over the last twenty years is Gwyneth Lewis, the only young poet on whom R. S. Thomas, always personally (and sometimes poetically) a great poison-dropping upas tree to other talents, bestowed the dubious benediction of his friendship. Born in Cardiff, the birthplace of an R. S. Thomas who spent his life living down the fact that he had been born in a 'foreign' city, the comfortably bilingual Lewis is able to turn her own urban, cosmopolitan experience of living between languages and cultures into a distinctive poetics. It is suitable both for addressing the distinctive bicultural (and incipiently multilingual) condition of contemporary Wales and for brilliantly mediating general postmodern concerns with performative identity, the heteroglossic self and the radically ungrounded nature of language itself. By these methods she is able to continue the late R. S. Thomas's poetic efforts to probe the frontiers of human intelligence's language-bound apprehensions of a metaphysical reality. In describing (in 'Illinois Idylls') a failed attempt to track to source a whip-poor-will's song (she is baffled by 'the ventriloquism of distance'), Lewis enacts her own bilingual self's failure to will itself into cultural singularity of being.[14]

One of the earliest, and most resiliently resourceful, exploiters, like Lewis, of modern Wales's multilingualism to create, out of his passion for the language poetry of the twentieth-century's Euro-American avant-garde, a poetic flow chart of national experience, is Peter Finch, in some ways Wales's Edwin Morgan. Having early complained that 'to live in Wales // Is to be mumbled at / by re-incarnations of Dylan Thomas',[15] Finch went on to a long, and only partly adversarial, fascination with R. S. Thomas, and has constructed a remarkable open-ended on-line work that is the apotheosis of innumerable published attempts by significant Welsh poets to talk back to Thomas in poems explicitly or implicitly directly addressed to him. A mixture of mockery and of admiration, of elegy and celebration, it is, in its exuberant inventiveness, a supreme postmodern tribute to the incorrigible life in poetry of one whom 'mad [Wales] hurt into poetry'.[16] Six years after his death, Thomas is now, again like Auden's Yeats, 'given over to unfamiliar affections' – and, yes, occasionally 'punished' critically, too, 'under a foreign code of conscience'.

NOTES

1 Malcolm Pryce, *The Unbearable Lightness of Being in Aberystwyth* (London: Bloomsbury, 2006), 135–7.
2 R. S. Thomas, *Collected Poems* (London: Macmillan, 1993), p. 4. Hereafter *CP*.
3 Lynette Roberts, *Collected Poems* (Manchester: Carcanet, 2005), p. 45.
4 Roland Mathias, *Collected Poems* (Cardiff: University of Wales Press, 2002), p. 223.
5 T. H. Jones, *Collected Poems* (Llandysul: Gomer Press, 1977), p. 181.
6 Harri Webb, *Collected Poems* (Llandysul: Gomer Press, 1995), p. 141.
7 Leslie Norris, *Collected Poems* (Bridgend: Seren, 1996), p. 115.
8 John Ormond, *Selected Poems* (Bridgend: Poetry Wales Press, 1987), p. 75.
9 'An ABC of Dannie Abse', in Joseph Cohen (ed.), *The Poetry of Dannie Abse* (London: Robson Books, 1983), p. 126.
10 Oliver Reynolds, *Skevington's Daughter* (London: Faber and Faber, 1985), p. 63.
11 John Davies, *Flight Patterns* (Bridgend: Seren, 1991), pp. 30, 35, 39.
12 Tony Curtis, *Selected Poems* (Bridgend: Poetry Wales Press, 1986), pp. 67, 23, 36, 98.
13 Robert Minhinnick, *The Looters* (Bridgend: Seren Books, 1989), p. 14.
14 Gwyneth Lewis, *Parables and Faxes* (Newcastle upon Tyne: Bloodaxe Books, 1995), p. 19.
15 Peter Finch, *Selected Poems* (Bridgend: Poetry Wales Press, 1972), p. 15.
16 Available at www.peterfinch.co.uk/depot.htm

Further reading

Brown, Tony, *R. S. Thomas*, Cardiff: University of Wales Press, 2006, Writers of Wales Series
Conran, Tony, *Frontiers in Anglo-Welsh Poetry*, Cardiff: University of Wales Press, 1997
Walford Davies, Damian (ed.), *Echoes to the Amen: Essays After R. S. Thomas*, Cardiff: University of Wales Press, 2003
Thomas, M. Wynn (ed.), *The Page's Drift: R. S. Thomas at Eighty*, Bridgend: Seren Books, 1993
Thomas, M. Wynn (ed.), *Welsh Writing in English*, Cardiff: University of Wales Press, 2003

12

LINDA ANDERSON

Gender, feminism, poetry: Stevie Smith, Sylvia Plath, Jo Shapcott

In November 1962, three months before her death, Sylvia Plath wrote to Stevie Smith: 'I better say straight out that I am an addict of your poetry, a desperate Smith addict.'[1] This addiction had been fed by her experience of listening to the recordings that Smith had made for the British Council with Peter Orr a year earlier, a task that Plath was now similarly engaged in. In the interview with Orr that Plath recorded concurrently she noted that her own recent poems were written by being spoken aloud and how 'wonderful' the new development was of 'recording poems, of speaking poems at readings, of having records of poems'.[2] That Plath was particularly impressed by the sound of Smith's poems – whether we mean by that Smith's remarkable reading of her own poems, or the way the poems themselves indicate the spoken voice – is confirmed in an article that Plath had written earlier in the same year for the *London Magazine* where Smith is grouped alongside Lowell, Roethke and Bishop as poets who seem to invoke the physical production of voice:

> The poets that I delight in are possessed by their rhythms as by the rhythms of their own breathing. Their finest poems seem to be born all-of-a-piece, not put together by hand: certain poems in Robert Lowell's *Life Studies*, for instance, Theodore Roethke's greenhouse poems; some of Elizabeth Bishop and a great deal of Stevie Smith.[3]

The word 'possession' echoes the 'addiction' which Plath had light-heartedly confessed to Smith. The sense of the poet or person surrendering to some other force suggests a Romantic tradition of poetic inspiration; however, this tradition, with its exulting of the masculine subject, could also work to re-inscribe feminine subordination: 'I married a real poet, and my life is redeemed: to love, serve & create.'[4] Smith, in contrast, was unenthusiastic, if friendly, in her response, claiming she wrote poetry only 'sometimes' and 'practically never read a word'. At the same time she depicts in quirky vignettes both an elusive bookseller, who is 'shy – just sends books and the a/c', and herself, secluded in her house – 'I camp upstairs most of the time with my aged Aunt, she is 90!' – as self-contained figures, who seem far removed emotionally and physically from the spell-binding effects of a powerful 'other'.[5] The two poets spoke about meeting but never actually met. However, this tantalisingly brief conjunction of two of the most significant women poets of the twentieth century raises interesting questions about what they might share *as* women and more generally how gender produces common strategies in terms of the poetic 'voice'; it also allows us to ponder their national and generational differences, already apparent in their contrasting epistolary styles and personae.

Inside history

Alison Light has pointed out how difficult it is to connect female writers – who are traditionally positioned 'outside history' – to narratives of national identity. In Smith's case, Light argues, this difficulty leads to a curious paradox whereby the local effects, idioms and accents of her poetry can be allowed to be recognisably 'English', whilst the place accorded to her as a poet remains marginal and unrepresentative.[6] A reviewer of her *Selected Poems* noted in 1962 that 'there is simply nowhere to put her', an opinion which has been repeated by many critics since.[7] In an influential essay, written on the occasion of the posthumous publication of her *Collected Poems*, Seamus Heaney talked about the importance of bringing to Smith's poems 'an ear aware of the longueurs and acerbities, the nuanced under-statements and tactical intonations of educated middle-class English speech'. Later in the same essay, however, despite his attempts to secure for her a serious reputation as a poet, he capitulates, admitting 'in the end the adjective has to be "eccentric"'.[8]

Smith's own response to the 'problem' of her cultural place was char-acteristically both commonsensical and combative: 'But I'm alive today, therefore I'm as much part of our time as everybody else. The times will just have to enlarge themselves to make room for me, won't they, and for everybody else.'[9] Here Smith seems to have recognised that her 'eccentricity' was in part, at least, a product of a normative definition of her 'times' and its cultural traditions which relegated whatever did not seem to fit to the margins. Never a feminist – 'why have poems by women only?', she wrote in a review of an anthology of women poets in 1968 (*MA*, 180) – she nevertheless can be seen as offering an uncompromising challenge to the hierarchy of literary forms, and to a dominant discourse which erases dif-ferent kinds of speech. Parody, pastiche, nonsense, ballads, nursery rhymes were just some of the sources for her poetic performance, which always seemed to seek to foreground an unacknowledged continuity between written and spoken forms of language, and between oral and literary traditions. At the same time her drawings, never simply illustrations for the poems, suggest not only another dimension of meaning, beyond language, but also a continuity between doodling – the playful desire to inscribe rudimentary or unintegrated energy or meaning in a transitional space – and literature. Her presence as a literary figure from the 1930s to the 1970s (she died in 1971), bringing a darkly ambivalent vision to domestic and suburban existences, should make us question, as she did, the adequacy of our cultural narratives and versions of national consciousness which depend on drawing a division between public and private life. In terms of this chapter, the fact that her gender and her Englishness seem deeply implicated in each other allows us to arrive at a more varied and inflected notion of the gendered subject. To put this another way, given that Smith and Plath both used voice and performance as strategies in their poetry in ways which are arguably to do with gender, why do they still sound so different?

'I rather like the idea of death'

When Smith began to write in the 1930s Britain had largely retreated from that assertive rhetoric of national and imperial destiny which had carried it into war in 1914. Nationalism had been replaced by an idea of English- ness – used uncritically as a metonym for nationhood – which was quieter, more introspective and private, and which found its embodiment in the suburban 'little Englander', who cultivated a love of 'home and hobbies', and who nostalgically extolled the beauty of rural England. Whilst, as Alison Light has pointed out, this in many ways constituted a feminised idea of the nation, for women the period also coincided with the achieve- ment of full citizenship (suffrage was granted in 1928), and the opening up of new possibilities for education and employment. A degree of disturbance – particularly in terms of the organisation of gender roles – underlay the assumption of the 'ordinary' and the 'domestic' as a focus for national life.[10] Perhaps, from this point of view, it is not insignificant that when Smith summed up her portrait of a quintessentially English suburban family life, she makes no mention of the woman and apparently positions herself as narrator/observer on the outside: 'And behind the fishnet curtains in the windows of the houses is the family life – father's chair, uproar, dogs, babies and the radio' (MA, 104).

Smith never married and seems to have felt she could not manage 'a deux love' (MA, 303). Despite being briefly engaged to Eric Armitage, she was finally frightened by his conventionality, and the threat to her creativity which marriage seemed to pose. Instead she found domestic comfort and enduring warmth living with her 'lion–aunt', never leaving the family home in Palmer's Green that she moved into with her mother and sister when she was four. This 'house of female habitation', as Smith calls it in her famous poem, is a refuge, yet firmly embedded in those values of the national character of 'sternness and reserve' that she also mocked elsewhere.[11] Indeed Smith routinely pictures characters in her poems who are deeply inhibited by their national upbringing, for instance, 'the intellectual Englishman' who cannot give way to 'emotional extravagance' in 'Oh, If Only ...' (CP, 290) or the Englishwoman in 'The English Visitor' who is not 'less sorry', only 'brought up differently' (CP, 305). This double attitude of closeness or identification and distancing in relation to national characteristics was central to Smith's writing: she recognised she was in flight from something which was also inescapable. Entering the public sphere, the world of work – though thus avoiding the entrapment of matrimony – was also to imbibe another set of incompatible values, and, as the Second World War loomed, a shameful complicity in national history. Her surrogate Pompey Casmilus, in her bleak novel *Over the Frontier* (1938), finds herself in uniform, her gender subsumed, having to acknowledge her own guilty sharing in the masculine project: 'I know now from whom I hold my commission, and am sick with the weight of its fatality, but how escape, who have so much involved myself, too actively promoted his designs?'[12]

Romana Huk has stressed the fact that Smith's many strategies of resistance in her writings do not issue from an alternative 'place' or gesture towards a different future; Huk quotes from an unpublished broadcast from 1961 where Smith talks admiringly about 'the feeling of courage without hope and resistance without belief'.[13] Though she loved life, as Smith told Kay Dick, it was only because she kept herself 'well on the edge': 'I couldn't commit to anything'.[14] If ideologies, romantic ideals and belief itself were all suspect to Smith, who feared the power of homogenising discourses to drown out individuality, she is nevertheless also implicated, unable to separate her 'self' from the contemporary voices and meanings which constituted her. Her struggle, as Huk points out, is with language but from a place *within* it. This is part of the point of her most famous poem 'Not Waving But Drowning' where the man's gesture of 'waving' – with its sense of breezy cheerfulness, also perfectly captured by the expressly English word 'larking' – signals his death as well, and where the narrator as witness, ambiguously drawn into the first person and the masculine gender in the last stanza, seems to share in his subjecthood and his fate (CP, 303).

Smith often turned to death in both her life and her writing as a last resort, exploring its finality and mysterious otherness, but also its power to offer a way out of life's suffering if necessary.[15] She reported herself as dealing with the traumatic separation from her family through illness when she was eight by invoking the thought of suicide and this paradoxical coping strategy seemed to be useful to her as an adult as well; thoughts of death could provide empowerment for her in moments of despair, thus sparing her the need to act: 'This is the simplest of all thoughts, that Death must come when we call, although he is a god' (MA, 110). Smith made only one, probably not serious, attempt to kill herself, which resulted in her, happily, being pensioned off from her job.

Her preoccupation with death, however, could be seen as having a historical, as well as personal, resonance. Britain had to confront the vast scale of its death toll in the trenches after the First World War and the destabilising aftermath of absence and grief; both society and its subjects could be said to be carrying death within them through a prolonged and traumatic period of mourning. In Smith's poem 'Edmonton, thy cemetery ...' the numbing repetition of 'the countless countless dead' confounds the basis of religious belief with its offer of future happiness (CP, 404), whilst that turn to spiritualism which became so popular in this period is mercilessly parodied in 'Mrs Simpkins' where the gullible and superficial Mrs Simpkins ironically drives her husband to suicide by offering him a 'simple' vision of the same life continuing after death. Frequently death features in Smith's poetry as a kind of layered figure, combining trauma with fortitude; death can call forth the same kind of stoicism which was part of the national rhetoric and which Smith admired her country for during the Blitz. In poems such as 'My Heart Goes Out', where death is both 'end and remedy' (CP, 368), or 'Come, Death (2)', the poem she wrote at the end of her life, where death is summoned as 'the only god' (CP, 571), Smith's turning to death becomes a positive act, an emboldening of the spirit, or, as she put it herself, 'a proud thought' which can 'puff one up' (MA, 112).

Yet, the pervasiveness of the death drive in Smith's poetry also seems to have had another function, one more obviously linked to gender. If that repeated linking of death with the feminine in Western culture has been, as Elizabeth Bronfen has extensively demonstrated, a way of repressing the threat of otherness to the stability and unity of the (masculine) subject,[16] then the imagining of death – and moreover a death that is energised and in movement – becomes a way for a woman writer of questioning the limits of signification and bringing her own uncanny presence back into the text. In her poem, 'Do Take Muriel Out', which seems initially to be repeating the need for romance to enliven a woman's life, the desired partner turns out to be death, and moreover a death which can propel her beyond those stifling interior spaces of Palace, home and room (*CP*, 250). Smith remarked on how one 'one wants that idea of Death, you know, as something large and unknowable, something that allows a person to stretch himself out' (*MA*, 113). Typically, she uses a confiding voice – 'you know' – to push beyond the boundaries of the social, and to question the distinction between the known and the unknown. The invocation of dreams or dream states in Smith's poems is frequently coupled with riding, harnessed to a repressed yearning for an untethered spaciousness which may turn out to be death ('In My Dreams', *CP*, 129). In her famous poem 'I rode with my darling' she refuses the masculine 'reasonable' advice to turn back but goes on instead, beyond even the stance exemplified by the fortified tower and which she herself endorsed of 'resisting without belief', beyond the last traces of her cultural script, the literary and fairytale traces. The poem ends with unanswered questions, drawn from Smith's own life, and a bleak sense of negation which could be death, offering no reward for the speaker's determined and lonely journeying into uncharted territory (*CP*, 260). However, the space is not empty, but rather silent – 'All, all is silent in the dark wood at night' (*CP*, 260). Is it necessarily beyond speech?

The contrary stance

The importance of the performative dimension of Smith's poetry has been frequently noted and, in answer to the question above, is crucial to thinking about how her poems can generate meaning beyond the text, can speak from that nowhere which marks the woman poet's vanishing point, her deathly identification, within the system of cultural signs. Smith uses a range of voices in her poetry which mimic social attitudes and codes. At the same time, her poems often enter into an intertextual dialogue with other poems – 'Childe Rolandine' (*CP*, 331), for example, or 'The Word' (*CP*, 542) – calling up a literary heritage, which, whilst inescapable, cannot wholly speak the woman's plight. Language is almost always parodic in Smith's poetry – as is her use of form – and vividly conveys how dependent identity is on the discourses which make it up. However, parody is always a double discourse, a combining of imitation with resistance, and Smith's arch style establishes a complex writing position for herself, a contrary stance,[17] where she can gesture to another silent subtext, repressed and unspoken. Luce Irigaray famously used the term 'mimesis' to indicate how the woman, through mimicry, can play out roles within discourse but still remain 'elsewhere'. Without any specifically feminist intent, Smith could also be seen as employing a similar strategy of resistance in her work, using voices which are circumscribed by language, but which she also exceeds and is not totally absorbed by. So Miss Pauncefort – an incongruous contemporary matronly figure whom Smith represents in a drawing placed above the poem – may confound her audience with her unintelligible song – 'Sing Tirry-lirry-lirry down the lane' – but Smith's rendering of her obstinate repetitiveness, leaves open the question of what it means and who is being silly here, the audience or the 'songster' (CP, 30).

Smith's own performances of her poems became an important feature of her later career and contributed to the dramatic rise in her popularity in the 1960s. She seems to have created an effect of dissonance in these readings, either though her appearance and her childlike mode of dressing – sometimes in pinafores and white stockings – or the way she stressed or even sang her poems. As with Miss Pauncefort, her audience was sometimes destabilised, unsure of how to respond. Norman Bryson has commented on the effect she had on him as a student in 1965:

> The dominant tone was of cheerfulness exaggerated, as if the rise and fall of a cheery, vernacular voice were pushed higher and lower and became a stylized sing-song that wasn't cheerfulness but had an alienated relation to cheerfulness ... the performance was unnerving because it was so excessive ... the meaning of the words was set aside in the performance. And the motives for this were entirely unrevealed: this seemed almost the main point. It was as though what was being dramatized was a state of being so pent up, so much without outlet, that emotions couldn't have, any longer, any appropriate objects.[18]

Bryson's insightful account allows us to recognise the ways in which Smith seems to have intended her own performance of the poems to exceed the text, to open up a gap between the words and their orality, thus suggesting another dimension of meaning. That unlocated energy which Bryson comments on picks up a similar effect created by her 'doodling', and could suggest pre-oedipal drives uncontained by language, could point towards the unregulated body which remains 'alienated', outside signification. In her poem 'To Carry the Child' the subject is figured as split between adult and child:

> But oh the poor child, the poor child, what can he do,
> trapped in a grown-up carapace,
> but peer outside of his prison room
> with the eye of an anarchist?   (CP, 437)

Smith, dressed like a child, seems to have brought precisely this sense of anarchy to her performances, unleashing a disturbing humour which questions the stability of the adult subject and undermines the fixity of written forms. In her extraordinary poem 'The Donkey', she concludes with the line 'I aspire to be broken up', and looks to an abject animal, the donkey, and death's 'odder anarchy' to break through the constraining pattern of adult subjecthood (*CP*, 535). For all that her poems also lament the impossibility of escape – except through death – her voicing of contrary aspirations both within the poems and in her energetic, uncanny performances, enabled a moment of disruption, the force of which has yet to be fully appreciated.

Crossing the water

Smith's consciousness of exile, expressed by her in almost metaphysical terms, did not relate to the experience of spatial and cultural dislocation. Indeed her life, in that sense, was, to an unusual degree, static. Turning to Sylvia Plath, however, a very different sense of exile emerges, and a powerful feeling, existing alongside the conflicts embedded in gender, of living as an outsider, without any secure sense of cultural belonging. Plath came to England as a Fulbright Fellow at the University of Cambridge in 1955. Apart from the two years when she and Ted Hughes tried to establish their careers in the States, she lived in England, both in London and in Devon, until her death in 1963. Within this narrative of transatlantic crossing, a complex set of responses emerges, and a critique and longing which could just as easily attach itself to either place. In 1957 she wrote to her mother about the 'flat, clever, colorless' poems published by 'the old Guard' in England which she contrasts with the 'color, life and vigor' of writing in America. She then goes on to express her hope that 'Ted will come to associate America with the growing acceptance and publishing of his writings. England is so stuffy, cliquey, and plain bad, bad.'[19] It was difficult for Plath to disentangle England from ideas of tradition and class, and a literary heritage she often felt excluded from; even its landscape was refracted through previous representations – 'like an engraving out of Dickens' (*LH*, 493). Living in Devon, she could feel like the 'American girl', an outsider, who did not fit into the tight, gossipy networks of village life (*J*, 637). Earlier, however, looked at from America, England had been a place of desire which demanded an 'artistic leap' (*J*, 148), a wager with herself to find 'myself: my man and my career' before returning home (*J*, 270). The period living with Hughes in America from 1957 to 1959 was a time of opposing desires, but eventually they became convinced that they had to make their home in England: 'Ted will be best there' (*J*, 464). To a friend she amplified this, admitting that the decision was not as straightforward for her as the 'homesick' Hughes and would leave her feeling 'a good bit in exile'.[20] Plath often expressed her own conflicting aspirations and needs in terms of the different cultural pulls. America could exert a pressure to conform: 'I find myself horrified at voicing the American dream of a home & children' (*J*, 411), yet its commercialism, whilst 'crass and crude' could also energise (*J*, 346) and moreover offered a level of material comfort – electrical goods – much missed by Plath as a young mother in a more austere and uncomfortable England. England, however, became the place which showed 'hospitality' to her poems and writing (*J*, 529). Separated from Hughes, she resisted her mother's advice to return to America, fearful of the loss of independence, and the collapse of the 'considerable reputation' she had built up in England (*LH*, 467). Indeed the final year of her life reveals the degree to which she had found a place in British cultural life, with invitations to record programmes from the BBC and the British Council. However, it was as an American she thought she spoke: 'As far as language goes I'm an American, I'm afraid, my accent is American, my way of talk is an American way of talk, I'm an old-fashioned American.'[21]

'A ship in a bottle'

The word 'old-fashioned' is significant and hints at the way America is also historical for her, a place which she knew best in the 1930s, 1940s and early 1950s, and which held her childhood memories. In her memoir 'Ocean 1212-W' she reveals how the English seascape can never match her memory of the sea of her childhood: 'The geography is all wrong.' However the 'exile' she writes about is rapidly re-situated in a particular moment of her personal history, and connected to a sense of losing her place within her family history after the birth of her brother: 'I trudged off on my own, in the opposite direction, towards the forbidding prison.'[22] Estrangement, one could argue, is Plath's major theme, and created an inner topography which her situation in England could both accentuate and return her to; England's very distance from familiar landscapes and sounds could replay deep patterns of inner remoteness and exclusion. In her 'Bee Poems', for instance, written in 1962, Plath produced tense dramas out of her own experience of foreignness in her Devon village, which are also mediated – and intensified – through her awareness of gender roles. In 'The Bee Meeting', for example, she is aware of her difference, exposed as she is in her 'sleeveless summery dress', but is equally disturbed at the possibility of her identity being covered up and of being assimilated into the group: 'Now they are giving me a fashionable white straw Italian hat / And a black veil that molds to my face, they are making me one of them'.[23] The narrator imagines different scenarios for an event which she can only guess at, removed as she is from the common understanding of it. Her inability – both social and psychological – to join in, opens up another space of identification for her, the disturbing place of victim, like the bees, of the villagers' increasingly sinister intent. This common formation in Plath's poetry makes the place on the outside both cold (white) and deathly but also the residual site of an (oedipal) narrative of murderous feelings. In 'Stings', written just three days later, the narrator's alienation and fear of incorporation is more obviously expressed in relation to other women: 'I stand in a column / Of winged, unmiraculous women ... Will they hate me / These women who only scurry' (CP, 214). She seems closer to the man, the 'great scapegoat', who, while carrying the burden of sin, nevertheless betrays her. Her identification with the queen bee at the end of the poems has frequently been read as enabling her triumphant escape from domestic enclosure in 'the mausoleum, the wax house'; however, its defensive positioning – not male, not female – and the apocalyptic imagery – 'red / Scar in the sky, red comet' – which could also be read as bringing a violent history back into the poem, should make us question what or who she can become.

In other poems, red is frequently associated with war – the 'soldier colour' of the sky in 'Wuthering Heights' (CP, 167) echoing the metaphor of the 'Redcoats' in 'Cut' which appear 'out of a gap' (CP, 235), and not only opens a wound in her flesh but cuts across the difference between the individual body and history. In 'Elm' Plath takes a traditional emblem of the English countryside and fuses it with contemporary images of violence: 'I have suffered the atrocity of sunsets. / Scorched to the root / My red filaments burn and stand, a hand of wires' (CP, 192). Plath's use of metaphor works to defamiliarise ways of seeing which, within English culture, have been taken for granted: 'The sheep know where they are' (CP, 167). She shifts the ground by linking nature with history and revising the very terms in which the natural world has been imagined. At the same time history is also invoked with the force of a repetition which replays – without ever getting beyond – trauma.

In Plath's most widely anthologised and controversial poem, 'Daddy' (1962), historical and personal narratives become conflated in a way which is profoundly unsettling and has often elicited anger. Robin Peel helps us to complicate a reading which sees Plath as simply appropriating the Holocaust by drawing attention to how the Adolf Eichmann trial (1961–2) was contemporary with her inception of the poem, and could well have revived other memories of the Holocaust as it was reported in her childhood. Collapsing the categories of public and private, however, the poem no less collapses the past and present and the distance – geographical and national – that keeps them apart. The figure of the father is estranged and inaccessible because he is both distended across the whole continent of America, and has his indeterminate origins in a Germany whose violent history begins to take over the poem. In her interview with Peter Orr, Plath complicated her American nationality by referring to the family history of immigration from Austria and Germany.[24] In terms of this poem, the father's insertion into another history, in another continent, disturbs the narrative sequence and begins to undo the spacing and separation on which the symbolic function of language and identification depends. The narrator is either alienated by a language which is foreign to her and which splits and nullifies her identity – 'Ich, ich, ich, ich' – or regresses into the rhyming pattern of infantile speech (you/do/Achoo). The ending of the poem, for all its attempt at finality, cannot secure separation, for that final 'through' is also a ritual or performance, to be endlessly repeated, and reverberates with the earlier desire for communication – 'the voices just can't worm through' (CP, 224).

Plath's struggle with the figure of the father is also a struggle with the authority invested in the symbolic father, and a tradition and language she felt alienated from. The maternal function, however, was also problematic, and if not figured in terms of a debased domesticity, was explored through the body and voice, and an abject, fragmented subjecthood. In 'Elm' the tree breaks away from its status as symbol to speak in a voice that is feminine; however, that 'other' voice or voicing of otherness, is variously described in terms of 'nothing', 'madness', or a violent 'shriek' (CP, 192), and linked to nightmares, darkness and the uncanny. In 'Medusa', the speaker struggles to dissociate herself from the engulfing shapelessness of the mother's body which 'steamed' to her 'over the sea'; she attempts to give the maternal definition through a series of images which meta-morphose into each other, offering little protection. Ultimately the speaker, as at the end of 'Daddy', cannot sustain the difference between closeness and distance: 'There is nothing between us' (CP, 226). If Plath's 'American' voice was one way of interpellating herself into a culture and tradition which also had the power to silence, it also carried within it, as she says in 'Ocean 1212-W', 'a breath', which could be either her own breath or 'the breath of my mother'.

Plath's career has frequently been read in terms of an emerging selfhood, which was triumphantly realised in the later poems: 'Ariel and the later poems give us the voice of the (real) self.'[25] The attempt to read the later poems through a history of 'crossing' between countries, cultures and genders suggests nothing could ever be settled for Plath, and that her voice always had to be in dialogue with an absent, overwhelming or repressed other. Her enthusiasm for Stevie Smith's poetry and in particular Smith's use of voice in this period of her life indicates an attraction to performance and the double or uncertain perspective it could enable. Like Smith, she could deliberately use the figure of death that culture seemed to have assigned the woman and represent it as a form of presence, rather than absence ('Edge') or try – despite the danger – to make her inspiration travel outside the limits of her 'place' ('Ariel'). However, Plath's transatlantic history gave her a different linguistic range, a more apocalyptic sense of her times and engendered performances, which, as Deryn Rees-Jones argues, while they tried to get beyond the personal, could double back on her, become forms of 'acting out'.[26]

Motherland

Neither Smith nor Plath speak simply and directly from a female or feminist perspective. Both, whilst aware of the constrictions placed on them as women, used different identifications – used the mobility and power of voice and performance – to move between masculine and feminine positions, destabilising the unity and coherence of the poetic 'I', and escaping her fixing in the muted or deathly place of the feminine. However, it has been the argument of this chapter that we cannot speak about sexual differences without also attending to the other discourses through which the subject is constituted. The extent to which 'belonging', with all its different resonances of exile and problematic affiliation, has gone on being an issue for contemporary women poets is well illustrated by one of the most significant, Jo Shapcott. Although Shapcott is more likely to acknowledge Elizabeth Bishop as an influence, she uses Surrealist imagery and humour, personae, voice and explorations of the abject through animals or the body, in ways which recall aspects of Smith and Plath. She has, moreover, an acute sense of the burden of nationality, and inner exile. In her poem 'Phrasebook' the Englishwoman can only represent herself by drawing on multiple disparate linguistic codes which do not provide a sense of wholeness. In another poem, 'Motherland', itself a translation, Shapcott explores her sense of distance from a notion of national identity while experiencing the impossibility of being 'nothing', or retreating 'further and further away into the cold stars'.[27] In thinking about gender and poetry, it is useful to ponder how Shapcott, like many of her contemporaries, expresses her desire to be a 'different kind of writer' – a woman possibly? For her, hesitant about where she belongs, yet wary of alienation, such a writer will be one 'for whom place and language are less certain, and for whom shifting territories are the norm'.[28]

NOTES

1 Quoted in Jack Barbera and William McBrien (eds.), *Me Again: The Uncollected Writings of Stevie Smith* (London: Virago, 1981), p. 6. Subsequently cited in text as *MA*.

2 Peter Orr (ed.), *The Poet Speaks* (London: Routledge, 1966), p. 170.

3 'Context', *London Magazine* 1 (1962), p. 46.

4 Karen V. Kukil (ed.), *The Journals of Sylvia Plath 1950 – 1962* (London: Faber and Faber, 2000), p. 346. Subsequently cited as *J* in text.

5 Jack Barbera and William McBrien, *Stevie: A Biography of Stevie Smith* (London: Heinemann, 1985), p. 242.

6 'Outside History? Stevie Smith, Women Poets and the National Voice', *English* 43 (1993–4), 241.

7 Barbera and McBrien, *Stevie: A Biography*, p. 241.

8 'Stevie Smith's *Collected Poems*' in *Finders Keepers: Selected Prose 1971–2001* (London: Faber and Faber, 2002), pp. 386–7.

9 Orr, *The Poet Speaks*, p. 229.

10 Alison Light, *Forever England: Femininity, Literature and Conservatism Between the Wars* (London: Routledge, 1991), p. 10.

11 Stevie Smith, *Collected Poems*, ed. James MacGibbon (London: Allen Lane, 1975), pp. 410–11. Hereafter *CP* in text.

12 *Over the Frontier* (1938; London: Virago, 1980), p. 264.

13 Romana Huk, *Stevie Smith: Between the Lines* (London: Palgrave, 2005), p. 29.

14 Kay Dick, *Ivy and Stevie* (London: Duckworth 1971), p. 44.

15 The quotation used as the title of this section comes from Orr, *The Poet Speaks*, p. 227.

16 See *Over Her Dead Body: Death, Femininity and the Aesthetic* (Manchester: Manchester University Press, 1992).

17 Frances Spalding, *Stevie Smith* (London: Faber and Faber, 1988), p. 264.

18 Quoted in *ibid.*, p. 267.

19 Aurelia Schober Plath (ed.), *Sylvia Plath: Letters Home* (London: Faber and Faber, 1976), p. 293. Hereafter *LH* in text.

20 Letter to Lynne Lawner, 4 September 1958, quoted in Robin Peel, *Writing Back: Sylvia Plath and Cold War Politics* (London: Associated University Presses, 2002), p. 114.

21 Orr, *The Poet Speaks*, p. 168.

22 Sylvia Plath, *Johnny Panic and the Bible of Dreams* (London: Faber and Faber, 1977), p. 124; p. 120.

23 Sylvia Plath, *Collected Poems*, ed. Ted Hughes (London: Faber and Faber, 1981), p. 211. Hereafter *CP* in text.

24 Orr, *The Poet Speaks*, p. 169.

25 Ted Hughes, 'Foreword', *The Journals of Sylvia Plath*, ed. Francis McCullough (New York: Ballantine, 1982), p. xiv.

26 Deryn Rees-Jones, *Consorting with Angels: Essays on Modern Women Poets* (Tarset: Bloodaxe Books, 2005), pp. 121–2.

27 Jo Shapcott, *Her Book: Poems 1988 – 1998* (London: Faber and Faber, 2000), pp. 65–6 and p. 124.

28 Jo Shapcott, 'Confounding Geography', in Linda Anderson and Jo Shapcott (eds.), *Elizabeth Bishop: Poet of the Periphery* (Tarset: Bloodaxe Books; Newcastle upon Tyne: University of Newcastle, 2002), p. 115.

Further reading

Britzolakis, Christina, *Sylvia Plath and the Theatre of Mourning*, Oxford: Clarendon Press, 1999

Dowson, Jane, and Alice Entwistle, *A History of Twentieth-Century British Women's Poetry*, Cambridge: Cambridge Uinversity Press, 2005

Huk, Romana, *Stevie Smith: Between the Lines*, London: Palgrave, 2005

Peel, Robin, *Writing Back: Sylvia Plath and Cold War Politics*, London: Associated University Presses, 2002

Rees-Jones, Deryn, *Consorting with Angels: Essays on Modern Women Poets*, Tarset: Bloodaxe Books, 2005

Rose, Jacqueline, *The Haunting of Sylvia Plath*, London: Virago, 1992

13

KEVIN HART

Varieties of poetic sequence: Ted Hughes and Geoffrey Hill

The poetic sequence

Chances are that the word 'sequence' when used of English poetry will first conjure the Elizabethan sonnet sequence, beginning with Sidney's *Astrophel and Stella* (1582), and including Spenser's *Amoretti* (1595) and Shakespeare's *Sonnets* (1609). Not all the sequences of the Golden Age are wholly devoted to the sonnet – Sidney's has ten songs in addition to 108 sonnets, and Spenser concludes his eighty-eight sonnets with 'Epithalamion' – but the sonnet is certainly the dominant form. Each sequence is held together by a complex theme, love, and a loose drama or narrative development: unhappiness in an erotic relationship or, with Spenser, eventual marital bliss. Variation in theme notably occurs with Donne's 'Holy Sonnets' (1610–11), while George Herbert's *The Temple* (1633) presents a book-length sequence of religious lyrics only some of which are sonnets, and which is structured as much by reference to church architecture as by a narrative of spiritual development. The lyrical sequence detached itself from the sonnet sequence at an early stage, although it took several centuries to find its characteristic level as a medium-length-to-long poem that links together lyrics in a variety of stanzaic patterns.

Adjustments to the sonnet form by George Meredith in *Modern Love* (1862) opened the way for further (mostly deferred) experiments in the sonnet sequence, not all of which were successful. A century after Meredith, Robert Lowell wrote several volumes of fourteen-liners without rhyme or metre, of which very few individual poems have proved memorable. Ambition was not lacking in Lowell: *History* (1973) presented an idiosyncratic narrative of the West from ancient Greece and Israel to modern America. It is as though the example of Ezra Pound's *The Cantos* (1972), sometimes cited as the longest sequence of the last century and certainly the one with the greatest historical scope, had been followed in another mode, at once less grand, less febrile and more personal. Possibilities of digression, repetition and imaginative variation were embedded in the sonnet sequences of the Golden Age, and the longer cycles realised them from time to time in the larger, and sometimes open, context of a drama or a narrative. With Ted Berrigan's *The Sonnets* (1964), these possibilities are exploited in exuberant fashion, and only literary-historical reference makes the word 'sequence' at all defensible. Of course, it is only barely defensible with Shakespeare's *Sonnets*, which has long challenged readers to find a coherent narrative. Yet with Berrigan, we see something new: individual lyrics relating to one another 'without relation', as Maurice Blanchot would say, that is, without any appeal to unity.[1]

For Meredith and those who came after him, the sonnet sequence was not simply an Elizabethan heritage; it was also a way of writing a long poem in an age in which long poems faced fierce competition from the novel. And it is the quest for medium-length and long poems in which the sequence comes into its own in modern poetry. With Alfred Lord Tennyson's 'In Memoriam' (1851) and Walt Whitman's *Song of Myself* (1855), we find powerful examples of lyrics – not sonnets – joined together to make long poems. W. B. Yeats turned this form to advantage in several medium-length poems, most impressively in 'Meditations in Time of Civil War' (1922), which juxtaposes lyrics with different stanzas, styles and tones, and establishes a model that has been widely imitated. In *Ash-Wednesday* (1930) and *Four Quartets* (1942), T. S. Eliot showed how one could explore possibilities of musical development in the idea of sequence without entirely giving up on narrative. Wallace Stevens grasped in a wholly original way that the sequence offers the opportunity to revive reflective verse with a philosophical tone, if not philosophical substance, in 'Notes Toward a Supreme Fiction' (1942), 'An Ordinary Evening in New Haven' (1949) and the piercingly beautiful 'The Auroras of Autumn' (1950). Whether that final poem is a sequence has been questioned on the ground that 'it is not presentative but ratiocinative in character', but the criticism is misplaced.[2] 'The Auroras of Autumn' is not theoretical discourse but oblique lyrical utterance.

Before Stevens, however, the sequence had become characteristic of poets with high ambition, especially in the United States: Hart Crane's *The Bridge* (1930), Charles Olson's *The Maximus Poems* (1960) and W. C. Williams's *Paterson* (1963). About the same time that Stevens was writing his great sequences, W. H. Auden was composing a remarkable exploration of Shakespeare's *The Tempest*, a sequence that we might now regard as midrashic in impulse. *The Sea and the Mirror* (1942–4) shows just how much flexibility in form, style, tone and voice can be accommodated by the sequence. By contrast, his 'Horæ Canonicæ', written over the period 1949–54, has the air of a unity that has been found for it rather than found by it. Auden modulated from high to low moment in both sequences, and *The Sea and the Mirror* has diverting moments of camp humour ('Good little sunbeams should learn to fly / But it's madly ungay when the goldfish die').[3] Nonetheless, it took John Berryman in his *77 Dream Songs* (1964) to show how popular culture – minstrel show and vaudeville, especially – could be incorporated into the sequence without diluting its emotional intensity. And, like Berrigan's *The Sonnets*, Berryman's songs, especially in their extended, complete version, showed that the age could tolerate the idea of a poetic sequence that was character-driven but that exhibited little if any emotional or narrative development.

One reason for this high degree of toleration is in the ambiguous nature of the word 'sequence.' If the word makes one think first of a continuous and connected series, a second thought will entertain ideas of musical repetition (as in a liturgical 'prose') and a sequence of playing cards, like a flush or a straight. We might think of Stevens's 'An Ordinary Evening in New Haven' as two suits of lyrics played in different games, one involving laying down a sequence of eleven cantos and another comprising an extraordinary flush of thirty-one cantos. Put more philosophically, we might say that a sequence can present greater or fewer profiles of experience, even in different orders, without thereby losing its deep identity. By the time the two poets under consideration, Ted Hughes and Geoffrey Hill, were writing the verse of their respective maturities, the idea of the lyrical sequence had become as accommodating as it would ever be, and both writers availed themselves of its possibilities, early and late.

Ted Hughes

Hughes had established his reputation with *The Hawk in the Rain* (1957), *Lupercal* (1960) and *Wodwo* (1967) before he published his first sequence, 'Scapegoats and Rabies' (1967). The following decade saw him focusing on the form, and writing many of the poems for which he is most likely to be remembered, from *Crow* (1970; expanded edn. 1972) to the several sequences collected in *Moortown* (1979), including 'Prometheus on His Crag', 'Seven Dungeon Songs', a selection of 'Orts', 'Adam and the Sacred Nine', and of course the lyrics that lend their title to the book as a whole. From the end of the decade, Hughes was drawn to writing thematic collections – *Remains of Elmet* (1979) and *River* (1983) – that should be distinguished from the sequence as such. I will focus on *Crow* and its penumbra of associated lyrics and mention other sequences only in so far as they touch on it or are implicated in it in one way or another.

Crow poems were composed over the years 1967 to 1973, and the greater majority was published in the expanded edition of *Crow: From the Life and Songs of the Crow*. The subtitle is highly significant. For what we have is a large fragment, poems and songs detached from an 'epic folk tale' that Hughes presented in part when introducing poems from the sequence but never published as a whole.[4] For most readers of *Crow* it is strange to think that the work, as originally conceived and as represented in interviews and poetry readings, was to have been a prose narrative punctuated by lyrics. Hughes never wrote that narrative, and perhaps its true function was to generate lyrics rather than to become a written text that embeds them. Keith Sagar has given a reprise of it, which I will further condense here.[5]

After Creation, God is trying to sleep when a giant hand seizes him and a voice mocks his Creation, especially human beings, who, it turns out, have sent a representative to heaven to ask for the gift of life to be withdrawn. Exasperated, God dares the voice to do better; and so Crow is born. He undergoes various ordeals in a world in which he can move freely in space and time; he tries to correct Creation, hearing stories and reinterpreting some, learning all the time, singing songs, and telling tales of his adventures and pranks. Throughout, he seeks the one who made him. In time, the ghost of an Eskimo helps him, teaches him powerful spirit songs and leads him to his creator. In the final third of the narrative, we were to have seen Crow cross a river where he encounters a monstrous hag who sits on him and asks him seven questions, and who grows heavier when he strays from the right answer and lighter when he approaches the truth. His answers are poems, only one of which appears in *Crow* ('Lovesong') and others of which were never integrated into the sequence ('The Lovepet' and 'Bride and Groom Lie Hidden for Three Days'). The final poem tells the truth about the relations between man and woman, at which point the hag leaps from Crow's back, reveals herself to be a beautiful maiden and runs towards an oak wood with Crow in pursuit.

So *Crow* is conceived as a quest-romance, and given to us in a doubly truncated form: only as lyrics, and only the lyrics of the first two-thirds of the story. The sheer darkness of the work would have been ameliorated by the intended conclusion. Drawing on Eskimo and Native American stories, the narrative of *Crow* also works with an ancient dualistic cosmology in which there are two creators. The Gnostic syndrome, whenever it breaks out, affirms a creator other than the deity. Here, though, Crow, formed by a malign spirit, must experience the divine creation that has, of course, lost its original goodness and that was not quite right to begin with. The God we see in *Crow* is not the Lord of Abraham, Isaac and Jacob, not the Father of

Jesus, so much as Blake's Nobodaddy, though in the centuries between Blake and Hughes he has become more and more of a cartoon character.[6]

It is one thing to read *Crow* as a satire against the fraying faith and antique cosmology of mainstream Protestantism, and quite another to know what to do with the reading. Epic folk-tales must be deeply embedded in a tradition to have any force. Poets with a mythological imagination draw upon them, vary them, but invent them in the Romantic and Post-Romantic age only at the cost of incredulity. Blake's *Jerusalem* (1804–20) marks a limit of this kind of writing in English. Its power comes more from its vision of regeneration and its pointed social criticism than from any possible assent, even notional, by readers to its cosmology or its theology. Yet Blake remains more firmly rooted in the Judeo-Christian story than Hughes, and the appeal of *Crow* is less in the credibility of its folk-tale than in the grim comedy of its counter-theology, and in its chilling vision of human sexual relations that appeals to a post-Freudian readership for whom Freud has come to supply an intellectual structure that itself has the force of myth.

There are many touchstones of varying power that inform Hughes's mythopoetic imagination. Jung on archetypes, especially the Trickster, is one, and Eliade on shamanism is another. In literature, *Crow*'s roots reach back to Shakespeare and Milton, indeed to Aeschylus and Ovid. At the same time, Hughes learns from his contemporaries: the technique of W. S. Merwin's *The Lice* (1967), for example, though the Vasko Popa of the long sequences is the more important influence. *Earth Erect* (1972), which Hughes had known in part from the mid to late 1960s, probes folk memory more convincingly than is possible in *Crow*. St Sava, the patron saint of Serbia, generates legends that affect people concretely at the level of tribe, religion and nation, in a way that the fiction of a giant hand throttling a weaker version of Nobodaddy cannot for English-speaking readers. Popa's sequence does indeed produce 'a marvelously rich busily-working pattern of associations', as Hughes says, and is 'an organic sequence of dream-visions', 'an alchemical adventure of the soul', 'a psychological adventure, a tribal dream of mythical intensity, and a private commentary on history'.[7]

Yet Hughes learned more, and to greater profit, from individual lyrics by Popa, which he integrated into his native tradition. 'A Grin' and 'The Smile' have gained something at the level of style from the Popa of 'The Yawn of Yawns' ('Once upon a time there was a yawn') and related lyrics in the first part of *Secondary Heaven* (1968). Also folded in the poetic of *Crow* are lyrical insights from Blake, such as 'The Smile', which also detaches and animates an expression from particular faces. Consider 'The Grin'. 'There

was this hidden grin', Crow begins, 'It wanted a permanent home' (213).
And so,

> It tried faces
> In their forgetful moments, the face for instance
> Of a woman pushing a baby out between her legs
> But that didn't last long the face
> Of a man so preoccupied
> With the flying steel in the instant
> Of the car-crash he left his face
> To itself that was even shorter ... (213)

Frustrated, 'The grin / Sank back, temporarily nonplussed, / Into the skull'.
Later in the sequence, a lyric pauses to consider Crow's frown, though a
stronger poem, 'The Smile', is further along. There Crow tells of a smile
that is born in 'the oldest forest', circles the earth, is deflected by people and
settles upon the lips of a dying man whose soul is 'Stripped to its last
shame', where it offers a measure of healing, 'Before it swept out and away
across the earth' (241–2). It reappears, however, in the very next poem,
'Crow Improvises', where we hear that, after being charred to ashes by a
spark, a man smiles momentarily, a smile 'not even Leonardo / Could have
fathomed', that leaves the corpse and flies off 'into the air, the rubbish heap
of laughter / Screams, discretions, indiscretions etcetera' (242). Blake's
'Smile of Love', the only smile that can overcome the 'Frown of Frowns', is
trounced by a smile of Death (or worse) that is stronger than anything the
God of *Crow* can muster.

'A Grin' and 'The Smile' have momentum and remain memorable,
though not for any particular felicities of language or figure. There are few
moments of lyrical intensity in the sequence, 'Dawn's Rose' being a welcome interlude in page after page of approximate language and hammering
repetition. The powerful simplicity of lines such as 'Agony under agony, the
quiet of dust, / And a crow talking to stony skylines' (239) is missed elsewhere in the book. Hughes has spoken of wanting to write in *Crow* 'songs
with no music whatsoever, in a super-simple and a super-ugly language'.[8]
Especially at the start of the sequence, in the pieces that contest the biblical
account of Creation in accounting for Crow's birth, it might be said that the
poems try to efface themselves as poems in order to give the impression of
anonymous legend or myth. The poetic yield is certainly thin. In 'Lineage',
for instance, we hear, presumably at high volume,

> In the beginning was Scream
> Who begat Blood
> Who begat Eye

> Who begat Fear
> Who begat Wing
> Who begat Bone
> Who begat Granite
> Who begat Violet
> Who begat Guitar
> Who begat Sweat (218)

Only the first line has dramatic interest because we expect 'Word' at its end; the counter-lineage is arbitrary and, after several lines, tedious. More generally, we do not hear tuneless songs so much as lines that strain towards a display of rhetorical strength.

The sequences written in the aftermath of *Crow*, 'Prometheus on His Crag' (1973) and *Cave Birds* (1978), mostly confine themselves to stripped-down language with little sensuous interest uttered in a narrow range of tones and with little regard for the pitch of words and phrases. So when Prometheus is said to exult in the fact of his situation, 'That cannot be otherwise / And could not have been otherwise, // And never can be otherwise' (285) the word 'otherwise' is merely insistent, and its repetition is not used to indicate any subtle shift in attitude, feeling, response, or meaning. Only in 'The Knight', the finest piece in *Cave Birds*, does language become specific and memorable, as in the evocation of 'the common wild stones of the earth', 'the small madness of roots', and 'The quaint courtly language / Of wingbones and talons' (426–7). With the sequence 'Moortown Diary', notations of daily life on a farm in North Devon, we are offered *materia poetica* rather than finished poems. The raw immediacy that is desired is more often than not compromised by slapdash technique. One of the best of the group, 'Foxhunt', shows the variety in quality:

> The fox
> Hangs his silver tongue in the world of noise
> Over his splattering paws. Will he run
> Till his muscles suddenly turn to iron,
> Till blood froths his mouth as his lungs tatter,
> Till his feet are raw blood-sticks and his tail
> Trails thin as a rat's? Or will he
> Make a mistake, jump the wrong way, jump right
> Into the hound's mouth? As I write this down
> He runs still fresh, with all his chances before him. (507)

We pass from an image that veers away from cliché at the last moment ('blood froths his mouth' – 'froths *in*' would have ruined the line) to invention ('raw blood-sticks'), yet the energy generated by the two questions is dissipated by the prosaic clause, 'As I write this down'.

Geoffrey Hill

Unlike Hughes, Geoffrey Hill features sequences in his first collection, *For the Unfallen* (1959), and works continuously with the form, pushing it into unexpected places, throughout his writing life. 'Of Commerce and Society' is as strong a sequence as one could find in any first or later book. The use of literary figures as ways of pursuing moral inquiry (here P. B. Shelley and Henry James) is taken further in 'The Songbook of Sebastian Arruruz' in *King Log* (1968). Here Hill disappears into a fictional poet whose songs allow him to probe the relations between life and art, a strong theme of his work, from 'Annunciations' to 'Lachrimæ' and beyond, and one in which he does not spare himself in his criticism of art. *Tenebræ* (1978) contains three sequences, two of which, 'Lachrimæ' and 'An Apology for the Revival of Christian Architecture in England', are wholly composed of sonnets, and of his sequences these are the most likely candidates for long life in literary history.

Hill has written several book-length sequences, the most praised of which is *Mercian Hymns* (1971), which consists of thirty prose versets exploring the animating spirits of the West Midlands. Not all of Hill's book-length sequences are successful: *Speech! Speech!* (2000), 120 twelve-liners, remains clotted and inert, all the more so when compared with the fierce and spiky *The Triumph of Love* (1998), in which Hill's often noticed vituperation and his less often noticed humour are in equal abundance. *The Orchards of Syon* (2002) and *Scenes from Comus* (2005) are partial recoveries of what Hill, following Gerard Manley Hopkins, calls a sense of 'pitch', the peculiar rightness of a word with respect to meaning, sound and rhythm. More impressive are the sequences of *Canaan* (1996), a transitional collection though one of considerable power. 'De Jure Belli Ac Pacis' and 'Psalms of Assize' have a dark, brooding appeal, while 'Mysticism and Democracy' is disseminated throughout the collection; we might call it a discontinuous sequence and see there part of its originality. Hill's most recent collection, *Without Title* (2006), is a more convincing return to form, and the sequence 'Pindarics' sustains several readings, although it is still evident that his most enduring work in the sequence, and elsewhere, is in his *Collected Poems* (1985). The later *Selected Poems* (2006) is a more dilute volume, and selections are made from the better sequences, seriously compromising the unity of the works. I will focus on the 'Lachrimæ' sequence from *Tenebræ*.

'Lachrimæ' is heavily framed, and the framing begins with its subtitle, 'Seven tears figured in seven passionate Pavans', which makes it clear that the sequence will resonate with John Dowland's haunting composition of the same title for five viols, or violins, and lute. It was first heard in 1595, and published in 1604. The second frame follows quickly upon the first. It comes from St Robert Southwell's *St Mary Magdalens Funerall Teares* (1591) and is worth quoting in full: 'Passions I allow, and loves I approve, onely I would wish that men would alter their object and better their intent.' We are placed then in a world in which 'tears poetry' has already featured, not least of all by Southwell himself in 'Saint Peters Complaint' (1595), and in which a moral judgement about passions and love has been passed. Hill's sequence is not a translation (whatever that would mean) of Dowland's music or an illustration of Southwell's moral desire, but a refiguring of both, one that uses translation to its own ends and that explores the vexed relations of art and faith, including the very exploration we are reading. Only four of the seven sonnets take their titles from Dowland, and the order in which they appear differs from that in the musical composition. Southwell's wish is reversed in 'Pavana Dolorosa' so that the sonnet begins, 'Loves I allow and passions I approve'. And the final poem, 'Lachrimæ Amantis', is a free version of a sonnet by Lope de Vega Carpio, while 'The Masque of Blackness' draws heavily from a sonnet by Francisco de Quevedo. Here then is a highly literary sequence, one that uses poetry to analyse devotion and its institutions, rather than directly expressing piety.

The sequence begins with 'Lachrimæ Veræ', and its octave introduces us to the sorts of difficulties we will encounter throughout:

> Crucified Lord, you swim upon your cross
> and never move. Sometimes in dreams of hell
> the body moves but moves to no avail
> and is at one with that eternal loss.
>
> You are the castaway of drowned remorse,
> you are the world's atonement on the hill.
> This is your body twisted by our skill
> into a patience proper for redress.[9]

The directness and simplicity of the phrasing and address belie the density and difficulty of what is being said. Christ is addressed on the cross, and is called 'Lord', implying a relation of faith; and yet it is precisely that relation – its reality and even its possibility – that is put under pressure in the sestet ('You do not dwell in me nor I in you') and later in the sequence ('You are beyond me'). This is not to say that 'Lord' is used merely as a convention; rather, it is a spur to anguished brooding on the relationship between Hill and Christ. It is, as we shall see later, a relationship of dialectical identity, for Hill is himself crucified by Christ's call to believe in Him and follow Him. Another dialectical identity is indicated by way of the sheer physical cruelty of the crucifixion. Christ moves His arms and chest in order to breathe, as though doing breaststroke, but is nailed to the wood. His pain is one with the pains of the damned, which is why his sacrifice is efficacious; and yet, at the same time, people are damned to hell, and experience those pains, precisely because they deny that the crucifixion is a sacrifice and that it is efficacious for salvation.

Continuing the metaphor of swimming, Hill declares Christ to be a castaway, shipwrecked and suffocating on our remorse that has been drowned in tears. Yet there is another shade of meaning to be found if we take the genitive to be objective rather than subjective. Our remorse in trusting Christ only notionally as Savior (a remorse that is perhaps drowned in drink) has turned Him into a castaway in our lives. Christ's sacrifice on Calvary is sufficient to expiate all human sin, we are told, yet the comfortable generality of the statement is conditioned by the phrase 'on the hill', as though Hill admits that Christ suffers personally for him. So when, in the next two lines, Christ is told, in a reversal of the words of institution of the Eucharist, 'This is your body', we are directed once again to the flesh of Christ writhing on the cross and to the artistic representation of that body in the crucifix upon which Hill gazes. Christ was tortured by human skill two thousand years ago, enduring pain beyond all limits and the taunts of those who are inflicting it upon Him ('Father, forgive them . . .') so that reparation may be made for the sins of the world. The crucifix upon which Hill meditates is itself a twisting of Christ, not only in the manipulation of materials but also, unless it is regarded prayerfully, in the reduction of Him by art to an idol. The same is true of the poem we are reading. The patience required properly to write or read a difficult sonnet, a 'religious poem', can almost seem to be fit devotion. Or is it another ruse whereby we deflect what is involved in calling Christ 'Lord'?

The second sonnet in the sequence, 'The Masque of Blackness', continues to probe what we might call the theology of art but does so from a quite different perspective. I quote the opening of the poem:

> Spendour of life so splendidly contained,
> brilliance made bearable. It is the east
> light's embodiment, fit to be caressed,
> the god Amor with his eyes of diamond,
>
> celestial worldliness on which has dawned
> intelligence of angels, Midas' feast,
> the stony hunger of the dispossessed
> locked into Eden by their own demand.   (16)

In keeping with his allusions to Dowland and Southwell, Hill doubly situates the sonnet in the baroque age. The poem cites the title of Ben

Jonson's *The Masque of Blackness* (1605), performed before James I and with his wife, Anne of Denmark, playing the part of Euphoria, an Ethiopian, with blackened face and arms; and it also adapts Francesco de Quevedo's sonnet 'Retrato de Lisi que traia en una sortija'. A brief comment on each is required to bring the lyric into focus.

Jonson's masque concerns the tears of vanity of Ethiopian women, who, having taken the words of poets to heart, have become desirous of perfect beauty, which they believe will be theirs if they travel to England or, rather, the newly named Britain. The River Niger says, 'For were the world with all his wealth a ring, / Britannia, whose new name makes all tongues sing, / Might be a diamond worthy to enchase it' (ll. 221–3). If the black maidens can only bask in the rays of James I, they will turn white and be perfectly lovely. Meanwhile, Quevedo speaks of a portrait of Lisi, with teeth of diamond, imprisoned in a ring. Here too there is an empire, though one of love; here too the ruler, Lisi, is tyrannical. And here too we can find vanity, in the desire to appear a certain way and in the words of the poets who feed this desire. 'Self-love', Hill says, is the 'slavish master of this trade', meaning both the art of court life (including its elaborate masques) and the writing of poems such as the one we have before us. To be sure, Hill offers a sharp critique of the 'little world' of James's court (it is at once earthly and heavenly, touched by 'the intelligence of angels', as Walter Pater renders a phrase by Pico della Mirandola), but he does not exclude himself from the critique.[10]

Everything James touches seems to turn to gold; it is a 'Midas' feast' and anything but nourishing for the soul. James and Anne's is a 'stony hunger', and we think immediately of Luke 4:3 ('command this stone that it be made bread'). King and Queen are locked by their demand – their legal claim and their incessant requests from Parliament for money – into the glittering, superficial life of what B. L. Joseph called 'Shakespeare's Eden' in a book of that title published in 1971. It is readily seen how Hill's sonnets condense history and present a complex relation to it, in a completely different manner than one finds in Lowell's *History*. The sequence diagnoses a corruption at the heart of court life and art, one that has a religious base: the substitution of 'the god Amor' for Christ. 'Self-love' is the demand of court life, and the usual life of the artist: Inigo Jones and Ben Jonson, to be sure, and also Hill himself. As he says in 'Pavana Dolorosa', with Southwell and himself equally in mind, the poet is a 'Self-seeking hunter of forms' and 'there is no end / to such pursuits' (19). The possibility of devotion by art is also the possibility of diverting and corrupting that devotion. 'Beautiful for themselves the icons fade', we hear in 'Lachrimæ Antiquæ Novæ': the Church provides its own version of 'Midas' feast' with the gold on the icons.

We should not take Hill's criticism of 'the god Amor' to be sufficient for him simply to affirm Christ. Of course, it would be disgraceful merely to mouth devotion, to 'pander to your name / or answer to your lords of revenue' (15). A more lukewarm believer might keep himself 'religiously secure' (21), trusting in the rituals and teaching of the Church and not living truly *coram deo*. Yet this desire for religion as a comforter cannot be easily surmounted. 'Lachrimæ Coactæ' puts the matter directly, while also warning us by its title, which means 'crocodile tears', that deception and self-deception in religious matters are possibilities deeply embedded in the psyche and the institution:

> Crucified Lord, however much I burn
> to be enamoured of your paradise,
> knowing what ceases and what will not cease,
> frightened of hell, not knowing where to turn ... (18)

Notice that Hill burns to have faith because he fears burning in hell: he has attrition, not contrition. Later in the poem he feels crucified by the alternatives with which he is faced. There is no 'either–or' here: he would be nailed both by the 'harsh grace' that obliges him to give up a great deal to serve God, and by the 'hurtful scorn' of his secular friends and perhaps even himself.

'Lachrimæ' entertains strongly iconoclastic sentiments while also acknowledging the theology and the allure of the anti-iconoclastic position. The prayers are addressed to the 'Crucified Lord' depicted on the crucifix, and representation of Christ is allowable because of the Incarnation. And yet Hill knows that it is one thing to cross oneself before a crucifix and quite another to be devoted to Christ. To depict Jesus on the cross is an artistic challenge, one that often involves a celebration of the male body, and a sense of artistic fashion (crowns of thorn are worn lower this year). Christians too can miss the prey for the shadow, as Emmanuel Lévinas says in a fierce essay on art.[11] But what is it to get the prey, Christ, or – it is the same thing – to be caught by Him? Hill's fear is that he is not grasped by anything, and grips nothing at all when he searches for Christ. He fastens onto the question 'what does my soul grasp?' while apparently leaving aside the question 'What grips me?' It is answered only, and barely, in the line 'You are beyond me, innermost true light', which can be read in a tone of loving exasperation, and indeed must be if it is to escape the threat of appearing somewhat literary. Or is the question answered indirectly by way of the allusion to the world's 'void embrace' of the dead Jesus on the cross? It is a possibility, to be sure, and only a positive sense of difference between the quiet of Christ and the quiet of the earth would allow us to distinguish the dead body of Jesus from the hope of the resurrected

Christ. That hope can be given only by faith, and 'Lachrimæ' is a sequence that questions faith rather than affirms it.

The final sonnet, 'Lachrimæ Amantis', ends with a sleepy person visited at night by Christ, and who says, 'tomorrow I shall wake to welcome him'. It is possible that he will say exactly the same the next day (which is Lope de Vega's meaning), yet in Hill's free version of the poem it is possible that he will stir himself come morning. Needless to say, the fact that Hill does not decide the matter while not reducing the importance of the question and trying to respond to it from several angles is characteristic of his poetry.

NOTES

1 See Maurice Blanchot, 'The Relation of the Third Kind (Man Without Horizon)', *The Infinite Conversation*, trans. Susan Hanson (Minneapolis: Minnesota University Press, 1993), pp. 66–74.

2 M. L. Rosenthal and Sally M. Gall, *The Modern Poetic Sequence: The Genius of Modern Poetry* (Oxford: Oxford University Press, 1983), p. 355.

3 W. H. Auden, *Collected Poems*, ed. Edward Mendelson (New York: Random House, 1976), p. 320.

4 Ted Hughes, *Collected Poems*, ed. Paul Keegan (London: Faber and Faber, 2003), p. 1254. All quotations from Hughes's poems will be from this edition.

5 See Keith Sagar, 'The Story of Crow', *The Laughter of Foxes: A Study of Ted Hughes* (Liverpool: Liverpool University Press, 2000), pp. 172–80.

6 See Hughes's remarks on the Claddagh Records jacket of *Crow* (1973).

7 Ted Hughes, 'Introduction', *Vasko Popa: Collected Poems, 1943–1976*, trans. Anne Pennington (Manchester: Carcanet Press, 1978), p. 8.

8 I take Hughes's remark from his interview with Ekbert Faas, 'Ted Hughes and Crow', in the former's *Ted Hughes: The Unaccommodated Universe, with Selected Critical Writings by Ted Hughes and Two Interviews* (Santa Barbara: Black Sparrow Press, 1980), p. 208.

9 Geoffrey Hill, *Tenebræ* (London: André Deutsch, 1978), p. 15.

10 See Walter Pater, *The Renaissance: Studies in Art and Poetry* (New York: Macmillan, 1900), p. 42.

11 See Emmanuel Lévinas, 'Art and its Shadow', *Collected Philosophical Papers*, trans. Alphonso Lingis (The Hague: Martinus Nijhoff, 1987), p. 12.

Further reading

Faas, Ekbert, *Ted Hughes: The Unaccommodated Universe, with Selected Critical Writings by Ted Hughes and Two Interviews*, Santa Barbara: Black Sparrow Press, 1980

Rosenthal, M. L., and Sally M. Gall, *The Modern Poetic Sequence: The Genius of Modern Poetry*, Oxford: Oxford University Press, 1983

Sagar, Keith, *The Laughter of Foxes: A Study of Ted Hughes*, Liverpool: Liverpool University Press, 2000

14

JAHAN RAMAZANI

Black British poetry and the translocal

'Wherever I hang me knickers – that's my home', declares the Guyanese-British poet Grace Nichols. Immersed in the sensory present of London and yet vividly remembering her former life in the Caribbean, she gives utterance to a diasporic sensibility, 'divided to de ocean / Divided to de bone'. Her poem enacts these split affinities in code-switching between Guyanese Creole ('me knickers') and Standard English ('my home') and shuttling imagistically between the Caribbean's 'humming-bird splendour' and London's 'misty greyness'.[1] What are the implications of such ocean-splayed, register-shifting poetry for how we understand the relation of poetry to place? In modern and contemporary poetry studies, place is often conceived as either indefinite and abstract, or determinate and highly particularised. Modernist poetry, for example, has normally been understood as arising out of the shocks of modernity, wherever collisions between tradition and modernisation have arisen. At the same time, regionally defined poetries – e.g., the poetry of Northern Ireland or the New York school – are often seen as springing from the soil of a specific location. Yet neither the Aeolian model of poetry as airborne and placeless nor the Antaean model of poetry as drawing strength from a particular earthly plot is adequate to the poetry of geographic and cultural displacement – a poetry of multiple and mobile 'positionings', in Stuart Hall's term.[2] In this chapter, I explore postcolonial and especially black British poetry as translocal – that is, as poetry that reconceives and remaps widely disparate geocultural spaces and histories in relation to one another, particularly in this instance metropolitan Britain as seen by migrants from its former colonies. The poetry of the African diaspora in Britain, I argue, is neither homebound nor homeless, rooted nor rootless, but, in James Clifford's words, both 'rooted and routed in particular landscapes, regional and interregional networks'.[3] Like other postcolonial, diasporic and migrant poetries that mediate between distant yet specific locations across the globe, black British poetry gives expression and shape to a cross-geographic experience, enjambed between the (post)colonies and the Western metropole.

'The Western metropole must confront its postcolonial history', writes Homi Bhabha, 'told by its influx of postwar migrants and refugees.'⁴ Poetry is one means by which that postcolonial history has been told, especially since 21 June, 1948, when the arrival of 492 West Indians aboard the *Empire Windrush* at Tilbury Docks, near London, began large-scale immigration by peoples of African (and later Asian) descent into Britain. These migrant British subjects, most of them in search of economic and educational opportunities, were permitted to enter 'the motherland' as citizens by the 1948 British Nationality Act, many more arriving after 1952, when the McCarran–Walter Act restricted West Indian immigration into the United States. In 1962, the Commonwealth Immigrants Act held immigration from the Commonwealth into England to 30,000 a year, and the 1968 Commonwealth Immigrants Act limited it further to British citizens of British (i.e., white) family origin. Still, by then, the demographic change was substantial and irreversible. By 1970, nearly half a million West Indians had come to Britain, and by 1991, British citizens and subjects of colour made up just under 5.5 percent of the total population.⁵

How has the poetry of African-Caribbean and African migrants and their children represented 'the motherland'? How has it both absorbed and contested colonially disseminated images of an ideal England? And how has it imaginatively mediated between the writers' former or ancestral lands and the English metropolis? These are among the questions that will animate this chapter's readings of a handful of prominent poems and songs written early in the century by the Jamaican Claude McKay, at mid-century by the Jamaican Louise Bennett, the Trinidadian Lord Kitchener and the Nigerian Wole Soyinka, and late in the century and early in the twenty-first century by the Anglo-Jamaican Linton Kwesi Johnson, the Anglo-Guyanese Grace Nichols and the Anglo-Nigerian Bernardine Evaristo. Because poetry lives in its nuances and luminous particulars, this sampling is kept small if heterogeneous for the sake of close analysis, though many of the ideas pursued here also bear on the work of Una Marson, Derek Walcott, Kamau Brathwaite, Edward Markham, John Agard, David Dabydeen, Jean Binta Breeze, Benjamin Zephaniah, Fred D'Aguiar and Jackie Kay, among other prominent poets. The designation 'black British' has often been used to include Asian and other British peoples of non-European origin – usage that would have covered even my Persian grandfather who immigrated into Britain in the 1920s and there met my English grandmother. But this chapter, reflecting the more recent circumscription of the term, focuses on diasporic and black British poets with African-Caribbean and African backgrounds, who have played a crucial role in the early and sustained blackening of British poetry.

I

By disseminating across the colonies the phantasmal space 'England', the British Empire helped legitimise its domination of other, putatively unciv- ilised spaces in the so-called Third World. Poets of non-European back- grounds have had to grapple especially with the glorious 'London' of monuments and palaces as the quintessence of English civilisation.[6] In so doing, they have reconceived the site from which many of the empire's rulers, militaries and missionaries once set sail. Though often 'located' in London, their poems are 'translocal', in that they see the metropolis afresh through the lenses of non-metropolitan history, language and power, and shuttle across and unsettle imperial hierarchies of centre and periphery, motherland and colonial offspring, North and South. In short, they dis- locate the local into translocation. Interleaving European and non-European cultures, histories and topographies, these poems are based on what Stuart Hall calls 'unstable points of identification and suture'; they are defined, as he writes of 'diaspora identities', 'by the recognition of a necessary heterogeneity and diversity; by a conception of "identity" which lives with and through, not despite, difference; by *hybridity*'.[7]

Even before the mass postcolonial migrations to Britain after the Second World War, near the beginning of the twentieth century, a young West Indian poet embarked on an imaginary voyage to the empire's chimerical capital, some years before actually travelling to London. At first blush, Claude McKay's 'Old England' (1912) seems to bow to London's symbolic force as synecdoche for the empire's glorious sights, monuments and history. The speaker professes a yearning to walk London's streets and averts his gaze from the fact that 'de homeland England' has ruled and exploited Jamaica and other Caribbean colonies for hundreds of years.[8] The word 'conquer' in the poem's first line, instead of referring to Jamaica's colonial history, signifies lifelong entrapment within colonial desire: 'I've a longin' in me dept's of heart dat I can conquer not, / 'Tis a wish dat I've been havin' from since I could form a t'o't'. Similarly, the words 'beat' and 'roar' are used to describe not the Middle Passage but ocean waves during the journey to England. Unlike later black British poems more adequate to Paul Gilroy's concept of the 'black Atlantic' – African diasporic culture haunted by the memory of slavery – this lyric seems to whitewash the Atlantic.[9] Imagining himself at Saint Paul's Cathedral listening to the 'massive organ soun', the speaker surrenders to the imperial sublime: 'I would ope me mout' wid wonder'. Stylistically, his light Creole and British ballad metre (alternately rhyming 4s and 3s lineated together) also pay deference to imperial norms.

Yet even this early-twentieth-century imaginative journey affords murmurs of a postcolonial critique, born of cross-geocultural contact and friction. Although the speaker gushes over the 'solemn sacred beauty' of London's tourist sites, what he first sees and mentions are 'de fact'ry chimneys pourin' smoke' and 'matches-children' passing by. Looking upon London from the vantage point of a pre-industrial Jamaica, he notes casualties of industrial modernity, such as the poor match-selling girl who freezes to death on New Year's Eve, in both Hans Christian Andersen's short story 'The Little Match-Seller' and William McGonagall's poem 'The Little Match Girl'. Although planning to visit Saint Paul's and the City Temple, he feels they house but the 'relics of old fait', as spaces 'where de old fait' is a wreck' ('wreck' ironically echoing 'relics'). And although he pays homage to 'Missis Queen, Victoria de Good', under whose reign slaves were freed in the West Indies, his description of royal British power is far from flattering: each monarch passes on 'when all de vanity is done'. While he pays tribute to London's poetic, musical and architectural beauty – above all, poetry by 'de great souls buried' in Poets' Corner of Westminster Abbey – McKay is also alert to the contradictions between the imperial capital's aesthetics and underlying inequities, and he identifies the economic, religious and political underpinnings of British colonialism. When McKay physically travelled to England, from 1919 to 1921, his experience of English racial prejudice against blacks shocked and disenchanted him, as he indicates in A Long Way from Home (1937). Although 'Old England' is far more sanguine, even this early, self-divided poem both idealises London and defamiliarises it from the viewpoint of a British colony, fingering tensions that will emerge ever more clearly in later poets' translocal remappings of metropolitan space.

Nearly half a century later, McKay's foremost Jamaican heir, Louise Bennett, presents not one person's imaginative journey but the post-Second World War mass migration into England that began in 1948. Bennett witnessed Britain's demographic change first hand, having lived there just before and just after the first influx of West Indians, when from 1945 to 1947 she attended the Royal Academy of Dramatic Art in London and from 1950 to 1953 acted in British theatres and worked on a special Caribbean programme for the BBC. In the early 1950s, between 1,000 and 3,000 colonial migrants were entering Britain each year, and by the time she published 'Colonization in Reverse' in 1957, more than 40,000 had arrived in each of several years.[10] Although migrants of African descent had lived in Britain since antiquity, this post-war migration began England's transformation into a more thoroughly multiracial nation, as

West Indians, deflected from the United States, flocked to England to fill the post-war demand for labour:

> By de hundred, by de tousan,
> From country an from town,
> By de ship-load, by de plane-load,
> Jamaica is Englan boun.[11]

Impeded by caesurae in the first and third lines, then released in the second and fourth, the syntax and rhythms of Bennett's ballad stanza enact the onward tumbling rush of this great migration. Relishing the irony that 'Jamaica people colonizin / Englan in reverse', Bennett's poem wryly overlays the northward migration atop centuries of south-bound colonisation, while colonising in reverse Britain's ballad stanza and its language of colonisation. By poetic translocation, Bennett ironically counterpoints discrepant vectors, topographies and histories.

Unlike McKay's awed, if subtly critical, visitor, who opens his 'mout' wid wonder', Bennett's immigrants instead 'box bread / Out a English people mout', as her poem's ebullient tone, Creole diction and wordplay could also be said to snatch poetry 'Out a English people mout'. Instead of travelling to England like McKay's voyager in search of venerable aesthetic glories, these migrants are attracted by the prospect of material gain, though some, such as Bennett's dole-kept couch-potato Jane, merely exploit Britain's largesse. Bennett revealingly excised her unflattering portrait of a welfare cheat when she performed the poem in 1980s London; once a shrewd self-critique, it had come uncomfortably close to racist British depictions of immigrants of Caribbean origin – views stridently espoused and legitimised by politicians such as Enoch Powell in the 1960s and 1970s.[12] Indeed, the first sign of the intensification of such hostilities came the year after the poem's publication, when whites attacked blacks in the 1958 'race riots' in Nottingham and Notting Hill.

2

Among other poetic sites in which criss-crossed imaginings of London – both imperial and subtropical – were negotiated at mid-century was calypso, 'the first popular music transported directly from the West Indies', in Stuart Hall's words, including vocal music recorded in 1950s Britain on the Melodisc label and circulated transatlantically.[13] Derived from Trinidadian Carnival, calypso songs were topical and often satiric, wittily commenting on politics, race, sex and other matters of the moment. In London, the songs proved as responsive to the local as in Trinidad, while also extending to encompass Ghanaian independence, African-American jazz and Jamaican hurricanes. Even without these overtly international, black Atlantic excursions, British calypso is translocal, encountering the metropolis through African-Caribbean deprivations and aspirations, sung in West Indian English to an exuberant duple-metered rhythm.

The most celebrated calypsonian in 1950s Britain, the Trinidadian Lord Kitchener composed 'London Is the Place for Me' on board the *Empire Windrush* en route to England in 1948 and performed it on arrival at Tilbury Docks. The recorded song, book-ended by a rendering of Big Ben's chimes on the piano, idealises London as a most welcoming social space, but even this reverent work translocally reconceives the imperial centre through the aesthetics and viewpoint of the West Indies. Kitchener's utopian song – 'the English people are very much sociable. / They take you here and they take you there' – culturally creolises England by attributing to it a Caribbean hospitality, while also creolising it linguistically (e.g., the West Indian ellipsis in 'you really comfortable') and musically (a buoyantly syncopated sound new to London).[14] Anglocentric but with a destabilising difference, the song exemplifies what Bhabha calls 'the *ambivalence* of mimicry': its vision of an ideal London 'is almost the same, *but not quite*' as through English eyes.[15] Kitchener imagines spaces such as Shaftesbury Avenue as free, open and permeable, as musically intimated by buoyant percussive rhythms and clarinet solos, and as poetically instanced by his use of polysyndeton and long-vowel rhyme: 'There you will laugh and talk and enjoy the breeze, / And admire the beautiful sceneries'. Drawing on calypso's carnivalesque inversion of power structures, Kitchener declares at the end: 'I have every comfort and every sport, / And my residence is at Hampton Court'. These final lines humorously unveil the song's fantastical premise: surely 'life in London is really magnificent', when one ascends to royal status, but of course it was Brixton, not Hampton Court, that black Britons settled. True, some West Indian immigrants prospered in England, including the popular Kitchener, at least until rock and roll sent him back to Trinidad in the early 1960s. But since racial prejudices, social hierarchies and spatial strictures typically limited the prospects of the new black Britons, Kitchener, performing and recording this song in 1950s Britain, sang an egalitarian standard against which to measure these inequities.

In contrast to 'London Is the Place for Me', Kitchener's 'My Landlady's Too Rude' (1956) details the black British scrabble to survive discriminatory housing conditions. Hampton Court is replaced by a cramped, under-furnished, overpriced rental flat, and generous English hosts are supplanted by a mean-spirited, money-grubbing landlady, 'worse than the

landlord from Trinidad'. Threatening and badgering, spying and perse-
cuting, she nosily intrudes at all hours of the night, posts signs restricting
visitors, provides inadequate hot water and bedding, and cares nothing
about her tenant save her weekly demand – the refrain sardonically
intoned by the chorus: 'Mister give me me rent'. Empire and colony seem
to have been relocated and internalised within the metropolis. Hapless,
embattled, querulous, Kitchener's tone, accentuated by the twanging
guitar solos, bears little resemblance to his jubilantly open voice in
'London Is the Place for Me'. Yet both his utopian and dystopian songs
re-envision London translocally, reconsidering the urban ideal circulated
in the West Indies and then reimported by diasporic migrants into the
motherland.

During this period, when for the first time large numbers of African-
Caribbean migrants were bringing their Londons of the mind into direct
contact with Londons of daily life, expressions of reverence for the
motherland often exist in poetry and song alongside, and jostle with, other
impulses. Another calypsonian from Trinidad, Young Tiger gazes 'raptur-
ously' at the sublimely global yet minutely local spectacle of a multinational
procession in 'I Was There (At the Coronation)' – that of Queen Elizabeth II
in 1953. Taking up a position the night before at Marble Arch and ten-
aciously holding it in the cold 'like a young creole', or tough West Indian,
he creolises the heart of the empire by his physical presence. His response to
the Queen ('really divine') and the Duke of Edinburgh ('dignified and neat')
may seem fawning, but his deep-toned refrain casts his relation to them in a
language of symmetry and equivalence: 'She was there. / I was there'; 'He
was there. / I was there'. Syntactic parallelism and deictis horizontally
reconfigure the relation of sovereign to colonial subject. 'Mix Up Matrimony'
by *Windrush*-voyager Lord Beginner, a courageously utopian exaltation of
racial mixture, also uses mirroring poetic devices, such as epanalepsis and
insistent rhyme, to criss-cross the colour line: mixed couples were once a
rarity, but now lovers, realising that a 'race is a race', are choosing partners
of every background and kind; 'Marriage is a fixing / And the races are
mixing', Beginner proclaims, advising in his refrain, as he claims preachers
do, 'Please cooperate / And amalgamate'. Calling for the full miscegenation
of Britain, which would leave it looking ethnically more like the West
Indies, this song, like British calypso more generally, verbally enacts in its
music, diction, intonation and racial politics an aesthetic version of the
hybridisation it gleefully hymns.

As sometimes indicated by these and other songs and poems, many
immigrants to Britain from the late 1940s into the 1960s, crediting the
imperially disseminated ideal of a generous and colourblind motherland

that would receive them as full-fledged British subjects, instead found themselves unwelcome. Because of racial discrimination, most black British immigrants were forced to take jobs below their skill level, and widespread housing discrimination was reflected in signs such as 'Rooms to Let: No dogs, no coloureds'.[16] But if the non-slum spaces of London were often marked off against 'coloured' immigrants, translocal texts, such as the 1960 poem 'Telephone Conversation' by the Nigerian poet and playwright Wole Soyinka, were vehicles by which to question, erode, even overrun these boundaries. Written just a few years after Kitchener's London songs, Soyinka's poem more boldly confronts the racial delimitation of urban English space. From 1954 to 1960, Soyinka had lived in Britain, attending the University of Leeds on an undergraduate scholarship and working as a dramaturge with the Royal Court Theatre in London. In his dramatic poem, an English landlady asks her prospective African tenant about his skin colour: ' "HOW DARK?" ' and ' "ARE YOU LIGHT" / "OR VERY DARK?" '[17] His black body the object of interrogation, the African – trapped, panicked – feels pressed in upon by quintessentially red British sights, including a double-decker bus that suggestively bears down on the black road: 'Red booth. Red pillar-box. Red double-tiered / Omnibus squelching tar. It *was* real!' When his painterly self-description as a man whose skin is ' "West African sepia" ' baffles the landlady, he wittily switches to a hair colour terminology she is more likely to understand. Revealing his skin to display a spectrum of colours, from the 'peroxide blonde' of his palms and foot soles, to his 'brunette' face and 'raven black' bottom, the speaker deconstructs racial binarism, pushing the logic of racialist attention to skin colour so hard that he unmakes it. Ironically, it is his 'sitting down', presumably to nurture an intellect the landlady's views on English racial superiority cannot acknowledge, that blackened his bottom. His final plea to the literally and figuratively unseeing landlady – ' "Wouldn't you rather / "See for yourself?" ' – straddles the line between aggressive taunt (i.e., wouldn't you rather see my black bottom for yourself?) and plaintive humanistic appeal (i.e., wouldn't you rather encounter my full humanity for yourself?). Giving the lie to any such racial gauge of human value, the poem satirically contrasts her befuddled single-mindedness with the African's verbal wit and mental agility, with his metaphorical, syntactic and tonal resourcefulness, and with the poet's deft redeployment of English literary forms, such as blank verse and Jacobean verbal extravagance. Though formally couched, this counter-assault marks a turning point in the poetic relations between migrant and metropole, away from accommodation and toward more active resistance.

3

Whether dreamily utopian or satirically dystopian, musical or literary, Creole or Standard English, African or African-Caribbean, these post-colonial reimaginings of England dislocate it from itself by casting it into translocational conversation with its 'others'. From early to mid-century, the poetic reverse colonisers of England took, as we have seen, an ever more sceptical, if conflicted and often humorous, approach to the empire's cap-ital, where racist, xenophobic and imperialist attitudes frequently greeted migrants of colour. By the 1970s and 1980s, after British politicians and neo-fascists had fomented white racism, and after black Britons had been inspired by decolonisation, the civil rights movement and Black Power to mobilise resistance, poets of African descent in England began to reimagine the colonial metropolis still more assertively. In the 'reggae' or 'dub poetry' of Linton Kwesi Johnson, who arrived from Jamaica at eleven and as a teenager joined a London-based wing of the Black Panthers, the internal colonisation of immigrants and their descendants within Britain meets with fierce resistance. In still sharper contrast with McKay and the calypsonians, Johnson, drawing on recent African-Caribbean oral and musical traditions and on the militancy and musicality of the US Black Arts Movement's poetry, declares, in the title of a 1970s poem, 'Inglan is a Bitch'.[18] Dis-pensing with calypso's more standardised diction and light-hearted rhythms, Johnson drops the grinning mask to assail imperial norms. He often performs to reggae's heavy, four-beat rhythm and transcribes the orality of his Jamaican Creole, or patois, to de-standardise even standard words (e.g., 'fyah' for 'fire'). As John Agard indicates in another poem of the period, 'Listen Mr Oxford Don' (1985), the attack on the empire's literary, grammatical and orthographic norms – 'mugging de Queen's English', 'inciting rhyme to riot', 'assault / on de Oxford dictionary' – is central to black British poetry's effort to reconfigure the politics of race in 1970s and 1980s Britain.[19]

Whereas tourist sites define London in McKay's and Kitchener's verse, Johnson situates his more defiant poetry primarily in African-Caribbean neighbourhoods in and around Brixton. 'New Craas Massakah', for example, commemorates the 1981 death by fire of thirteen young Afro-Britons attending a sixteenth birthday party in New Cross, near Brixton, under circumstances that led many to suspect a racially motivated arson attack, sparking riots in Brixton and other immigrant communities across Britain a few months later.[20] In this poem, London is no longer a place where peoples of African descent expect to be warmly welcomed: they know they may be brutally attacked ('wi did know seh it couda happn').

Even so, the event itself is no less traumatic, and the poem's refrain repeatedly replays the transformation of a dance party – captured in loosely anapaestic cadences and sensual description – into fiery death, as if to make sense of the senseless. To mark the tear in narrative time ('first', 'den'), the poem switches from syncopated rhythms and gerundive feminine rhymes (*dubbin/rubbin, dancin/scankin/swingin*) to abrupt, bottled, monosyllabic masculine rhymes (*bang/trang, smoke/choke*). Because the partygoers are at first doing what the poet is doing – 'di dubbin / an di rubbin / an di rackin to di riddim' – the poem intimately enmeshes the speaker in the African-Caribbean London he describes. It switches back and forth between these songlike refrains – short-lined and intensely rhythmic – and more prosaic, longer-lined, retrospective ruminations on the event's implications and the people's collective response, described in apocalyptic terms: 'how di whole a black Britn did rack wid rage / how di whole a black Britn tun a fiery red'. Britain is not a white space into which migrants of colour struggle to insert themselves: as indicated by Johnson's aggressively anti-traditional style, 'black Britn' is a distinct social sphere, claimed by the poem's audience-and-author connecting 'we' and defined in stark contrast to white Englishness.

Despite the rage and grief firing Johnson's and much poetry of the time, the trajectory of postcolonial and black British poetry cannot be reduced to a linear movement from passive acquiescence to militant defiance. Even in the 1970s and 1980s, some black British poets favour humour as a strategy for creolising the heart of the empire. In *The Fat Black Woman's Poems* (1984), Grace Nichols, who grew up in Guyana and moved to the UK in her twenties, playfully reimagines England's capital with a fat black Caribbean woman translocated to its centre. Celebrated and affirmed, this migrant body inverts metropolitan norms of femininity: 'Beauty / is a fat black woman'.[21] But when the fat black Caribbean woman goes shopping for clothes in London she discovers – amid the cold, thin, white mannequins – that 'the choice is lean // Nothing much beyond size 14', in a characteristically humorous rhyme.[22] Despite these restrictions, a London where a fat black woman has shopped and taken the tube, has loved and cursed, has longed for tropical fruit and danced the limbo, is a changed space, non-hierarchically intermapped with Caribbean spaces once ruled by Britannia.

Stereoscopically conjoining the British metropolis and the West Indian experience, Nichols often uses translocal conjunctures to contrastive effect. A man from a Caribbean island wakes daily 'to the sound of blue surf / in his head', hearing the crash of waves and the clamour of seabirds in his groggy morning state, only to discover that here in London he wakes 'to surge of wheels / to dull North Circular roar'.[23] Although 'Island Man' is built around geocultural difference, its pivot – the phrase 'his small emerald island' – encompasses not only his sun-basking Caribbean island but also the rainy island where he now lives. In another poem of translocal juncture and friction, 'Tropical Death', the fat black woman contrasts Northern European 'quiet', 'polite', abbreviated rites of mourning with the loud 'bawl' and 'sleepless droning' night after night at a tropical wake.[24] Although the fat black woman situates herself within metropolitan England, she decries death 'in some North Europe far/forlorn' – a region that can be described as 'far' only if her psychic attachment to the tropics is so strong that she still imaginatively dwells there. Geography is thus, in this diasporic poem and others in the book, transhemispherically pleated. In Nichols's later poetry, some of these contrasts blur. The speaker of 'Wherever I Hang' misses her sunny Caribbean home amid life in London but is gradually shedding her 'calypso ways' – visits without warning or not waiting in line – a shedding she performs linguistically in shifting from 'me home' in the poem's first line to 'my home' in its last. Nichols's speaker shows herself to be at 'home' in both Creole and Standard English and thus both in the West Indies and England. She is, in Bhabha's phrase, a 'vernacular cosmopolitan', 'moving in-between cultural traditions and revealing hybrid forms of life and art that do not have a prior existence within the discrete world of any single culture or language'.[25] She exists in between cultures that, by virtue of such intercultural negotiation, become 'intricately and intimately interleaved with one another'.[26]

4

Bernardine Evaristo's novel in verse *The Emperor's Babe* (2001) startlingly traces this vernacular cosmopolitanism eighteen centuries back to Roman-occupied Londinium in the year 211. Countering views of Britain as racially homogeneous before 1948, recovering ancient precursors for post-*Windrush* black Britons, Evaristo represents Britain as already richly multicultural in ancient times, as exemplified by her African-born protagonist Zuleika. She and Evaristo's other characters have come to Rome from Africa, Asia and Europe and thus speak a vibrant mixture of languages and dialects, including Latin ('*How nunc brown vacca*' (204)), cockney ('wot 'adn't mastered the lingua Latin proper' (176)), Scots ('Mammy an Faither were chieftens, ye ken' (57)), Jamaican Creole ('likkle') and urban slang ('innit', 'wassup'). Looking backward and forward in time, the poem's hetero-glossia is emblematic of ancient and contemporary creolisation in the British Isles. Unlike the migrant writers discussed so far, Evaristo is London-born, to an English mother and a Nigerian father; like Zadie Smith and other recent black British writers, she takes a cross-racial, polyglot

England to be fundamental and is less interested than some poets of the 1970s and 1980s in championing a separate black experience. Literary classicism is as much hers as jive talk; the third century is as alive to her as the urban present; slave owning is as much her past as enslavement.

Delving backward in time, Evaristo's poem humorously provincialises London, representing it not as the energising hub of empire but, in the Roman scheme of things, as peripheral and marginal, an underdeveloped backwater to the imperial centre. Energetically translocational and transhistorical, Evaristo's verse novel plays on the ironic differences in the layers of its topographical palimpsest. London's past implicitly jangles against its present in descriptions of 'the wheatfields of Hyde Park' (218), 'the wild sloping grassland of Mayfair' (217), 'the jungle of Notting Hill' (158), 'the mud flats of Southwark' (236), 'the forests of Greenwich' (163) and the 'impenetrable swamps of Thamesmead' (169). Fields, grassland, jungle, mud flats, forests, swamps – London oddly comes to resemble the far-off outposts that it later subjugates, defamiliarised through the vocabulary later associated with 'the Third World'. Zuleika's aristocratic husband talks of making London 'my far-western base' (15), and her Sudanese immigrant parents had 'heard / of Londinium, way out in the wild west' (26). Instead of being the centre against which east and west are measured, London is a far-off, north-western fringe. Evaristo puts flesh on Walcott's declaration in 'Ruins of a Great House' 'That Albion too was once / A colony like ours'.[27] In so doing, she destabilises the relations between coloniser and colonised, centre and periphery, showing them to be temporary, historically contingent and so subject to strange and unexpected reversals.

If London is paradoxically made to seem akin to territories conquered by Britain, then the colonisation of Britain has two antithetical resonances in *The Emperor's Babe*, as indicated by the emperor Septimius Severus's imperial plans. According to various orators, the emperor 'would surely one day visit Britannia, / this far-flung northern outpost of empire' (41), and violently quell all resisters, 'colonize their terra firma, make them speak // our lingo, impose taxes, yay! And thus / bring Pax Romana to this our blessed island' (42). Indeed, the historical Severus died at York trying to subdue Britain. In Evaristo's book, the language of forcible occupation, linguistic imposition and economic exploitation is eerily made to anticipate Britain's subsequent colonisation of much of the world in its supposed quest of a Pax Britannia. Yet because the emperor is African-born and speaks with a strong '*Leeebyan*' (i.e., African) accent (53), this colonisation of Britain is also oddly made to look ahead to the reverse colonisation of Britain by its former empire. When Zuleika's parents decide to migrate to Londinium, this migration sounds uncannily like that of many later colonial subjects to London: 'a sea to cross, a man / could make millions of denarii' (26). By making the Roman subjugation of Britain parallel both Britain's colonisation of far-flung territories and the colonies' reverse 'colonisation' of Britain, *The Emperor's Babe* casts doubt on sharply drawn moral and political boundaries between centres and peripheries – positionalities that unpredictably reverse, blur or merge over time. In contrast to the identity-founding gestures of Johnson's and other 1970s and 1980s poems, identity in this and many later black British poems, as cultural theorist Paul Gilroy writes more generally, 'becomes a noun of process. Its openness provides a timely alternative to the clockwork solidarity based on outmoded notions of "race" and disputed ideas of national belonging.'[28] Evaristo makes use of the social fabric knotted into the form of the verse novel to contextualise identities and historicise experiences. In her book's complex racial-power-gender nexus, Zuleika lives in luxury as a slave-owner and treats her slaves like chained animals, and she also has some things in common with her powerless slaves, as a woman trapped and ultimately poisoned within her husband's house. After watching a grand-guignol spectacle of killing at an amphitheatre in Greenwich, Zuleika concludes, 'None of us is guilty / each of us took part', in an aphorism that blurs the hard-and-fast lines that in some black British poetry once separated victimiser from victimised, col-oniser from colonised (184). 'What had I become? But a composite' (204), affirms Zuleika, her character's complicities and ambiguities complicating the racial and power divide that may have once seemed intractable.

Just as British imperialism reversed the Londinium-era migration of Africans and other peoples into Britain, so too the mass displacement of post-Second World War non-Europeans into England turned around cen-turies of human movement from the British Isles into the colonies. These demographic flows brought cultural flows. If the empire once transplanted Wordsworth's lyric daffodils and anglocentric representations of London from England into the tropics, where no real daffodils grew, poets of the African diaspora in Britain have borne black bodies and creoles, calypso and reggae to London, along with idealistic, sceptical and humorous atti-tudes towards the imperial centre. At different times, their emphasis has been more accommodating or resistant, but poetry – whether angry or idealistic or both, whether in the form of lyric, calypso, dramatic verse, reggae performance or novel in verse – has been a flexible and multifaceted resource by which migrants to Britain and their children have given expression to, and enacted, their creolisation of Britain and Britain's creolisation of themselves. '[C]onstantly producing and reproducing themselves anew, through transformation and difference', as Hall writes of 'diaspora identities',[29] black British and postcolonial writers have used the musical, tonal and imagistic richness of poetry to help produce and reproduce, re-imagine and re-envision themselves as both 'rooted and routed' in and through London to Africa and the Caribbean – living and writing between styles, between histories, between hemispheres.

NOTES

1 Grace Nichols, 'Wherever I Hang', *Lazy Thoughts of a Lazy Woman* (London: Virago, 1989), p. 10.

2 Stuart Hall, 'Cultural Identity and Diaspora', in Jonathan Rutherford (ed.), *Identity, Community, Culture, Difference* (London: Lawrence and Wishart, 1990), pp. 222, 226.

3 James Clifford, *Routes: Travel and Translation in the Late Twentieth Century* (Cambridge, Mass.: Harvard University Press, 1997), p. 254.

4 Homi K. Bhabha, *The Location of Culture* (London: Routledge, 1994), p. 6.

5 This historical information is drawn from Peter Fryer, *Staying Power: The History of Black People in Britain* (London: Pluto Press, 1984), pp. 373–99; Paul Gilroy, *'There Ain't No Black in the Union Jack': The Cultural Politics of Race and Nation* (Chicago: University of Chicago Press, 1987); and Kathleen Paul, *Whitewashing Britain: Race and Citizenship in the Postwar Era* (Ithaca: Cornell University Press, 1997).

6 On postcolonial representations of London, see John McLeod, *Postcolonial London: Rewriting the Metropolis* (London: Routledge, 2004).

7 Hall, 'Cultural Identity', pp. 226, 235.

8 Claude McKay, 'Old England', *Complete Poems*, ed. William J. Maxwell (Urbana: University of Illinois Press, 2004), pp. 45–6.

9 Paul Gilroy, *The Black Atlantic* (Cambridge, Mass.: Harvard University Press, 1993).

10 Paul, *Whitewashing Britain*, p. 132.

11 Louise Bennett, 'Colonization in Reverse', in Mervyn Morris (ed.), *Selected Poems* (Kingston: Sangster's Book Stores Ltd, 1983), pp. 106–7.

12 Louise Bennett, 'Yes M'Dear: Miss Lou Live' (Island Records, 1983).

13 Stuart Hall, 'Calypso Kings', *Guardian*, 28 June, 2002.

14 The following calypso transcriptions are mine, from 'London Is the Place for Me: Trinidadian Calypso in London, 1950–56' (Honest Jons Records, 2002).

15 Bhabha, *Location of Culture*, p. 86.

16 The National Archives, 'Bound for Britain: Experiences of Migration to the UK', 11 April, 2006. Available at www.learningcurve.gov.uk/snapshots/snapshot11/snapshot11.htm 2000. These signs often also excluded the Irish.

17 Wole Soyinka, 'Telephone Conversation', *Times Literary Supplement* 10 August, 1962, p. 569.

18 Linton Kwesi Johnson, 'Inglan Is a Bitch', *Mi Revalueshanary Fren: Selected Poems* (London: Penguin Books, 2002), pp. 39–41. Ensuing references to 'New Craas Massakah' are to the same collection (54–9).

19 John Agard, *Mangoes and Bullets: Selected and New Poems, 1972–84* (London: Pluto Press, 1985), p. 44.
20 Fryer, *Staying Power*, pp. 398–9.
21 Grace Nichols, 'Beauty', *The Fat Black Woman's Poems* (London: Virago, 1984), p. 7.
22 Nichols, 'The Fat Black Woman Goes Shopping', *ibid.*, p. 11.
23 Nichols, 'Island Man', *ibid.*, p. 29.
24 Nichols, 'Tropical Death', *ibid.*, p. 19.
25 Homi K. Bhabha, 'The Vernacular Cosmopolitan', in Ferdinand Dennis and Naseem Khan (eds.), *Voices of the Crossing* (London: Serpent's Tail, 2000), p. 141.
26 *Ibid.*, p. 140.
27 Derek Walcott, 'Ruins of a Great House', *Collected Poems, 1948–1984* (New York: Farrar, Straus and Giroux, 1986), p. 20.
28 Paul Gilroy, *Against Race* (Cambridge, Mass.: Harvard University Press, 2000), p. 252.
29 Hall, 'Cultural Identity', p. 235.

Further reading

D'Aguiar, Fred, 'Have You Been Here Long? Black Poetry in Britain', in Robert Hampson and Peter Barry (eds.), *New British Poetries*, Manchester: Manchester University Press, 1993, pp. 51–71
Huk, Romana, 'In AnOther's Pocket: The Address of the "Pocket Epic" in Postmodern Black British Poetry', *Yale Journal of Criticism* 13, 1 (2000), 23–47
King, Bruce, *The Internationalization of English Literature*, Vol. 13 of the Oxford English Literary History, Oxford: Oxford University Press, 2004
McLeod, John, *Postcolonial London: Rewriting the Metropolis*, New York: Routledge, 2004
Marsh, Nicky, '"Peddlin Noh Puerile Parchment of Etnicity": Questioning Performance in New Black British Poetry', *Wasafiri*, 45 (2005), 46–51
Ramazani, Jahan, *The Hybrid Muse: Postcolonial Poetry in English*, Chicago: University of Chicago Press, 2001
Sesay, Kadija (ed.). *Write Black, Write British: From Post Colonial to Black British Literature*, Hertford: Hansib Publications Ltd, 2005

15

NEIL ROBERTS

Poetry and class: Tony Harrison, Peter Reading, Ken Smith, Sean O'Brien

Where better to start than with Charles Tomlinson's poem, 'Class', whose speaker confesses, 'Those midland *a*'s / once cost me a job'? He had been employed as secretary to the author of *The Craft of Fiction*, a title that is 'full of class', but 'the job couldn't last' because his accent 'visibly shredded' the upper-class writer's 'fineness'. Still, the speaker reflects, 'I'd always thought him an ass / which he pronounced "arse"'. There's no accounting for taste.'[1]

Tomlinson's anecdotal poem prompts a number of reflections about poetry and class. One is that class, at least as it is manifested in poetry, is apparently inseparable from region. When I recently tried to get students to talk about class in Tony Harrison's poetry, what I actually provoked was a heated discussion of the cultural divisions between the north and south of England. Another is that it becomes visible in poetry only when a working-class point of view is being articulated. 'Middle-classness' tends to be invisible in poetry. This is what Harrison means when, addressing the bourgeoisie, he calls poetry 'your lousy leasehold' ('Them & [uz]'). A third reflection is that 'class' and the associated region are inscribed on the body of the language of poetry, and this is at least as important as overt thematic treatment. Tomlinson plays on this explicitly in his poem (when I heard him read it he pronounced 'class' with a short 'a' and 'craft' with a long 'a'). Harrison does so less explicitly in 'Book-Ends' where he rhymes 'gas' with 'pass', forcing a northern pronunciation, and most explicitly of all in 'Them & [uz]' where he distinguishes a working-class Leeds accent from Received Pronunciation by using the phonetic alphabet. The importance of class and region in poetry can be as well illustrated by Ted Hughes's 'View of a Pig' as by any lines more obviously thematically motivated:

> The pig lay on a barrow dead.
> It weighed, they said, as much as three men.
> Its eyes closed, pink white eyelashes.
> Its trotters stuck straight out.

NEIL ROBERTS

> Such weight and thick pink bulk
> Set in death seemed not just dead.
> It was less than lifeless, further off.
> It was like a sack of wheat.[2]

The effect is one of dour plain speaking, achieved by the predominantly Anglo-Saxon/Norse lexis, emphatic monosyllabic internal rhyming, consonantal clusters that resist euphony and the solitary, colloquial, unliterary simile. These lines illustrate Hughes's claim that 'Whatever other speech you grow into ... your dialect stays alive in a sort of inner freedom' and that his own West Yorkshire dialect 'connects you ... to middle English poetry'[3] – an observation that is paralleled by Ken Smith's statement that he was drawn to Anglo-Saxon poetry 'because it's akin to the dialect of North Yorkshire ... the dialect of my childhood ... I suddenly thought it sounds like, *"Here lad. Go get yon bucket a' water."* It has that clipped, guttural sound.'[4]

Yet another reflection prompted by Tomlinson's poem is that the language of the people has, to use Harrison's metaphor in 'Them & [uz]', 'occupied' poetry very successfully in the decades since the Second World War. Tomlinson concludes his poem with a jibe against Percy Lubbock's accent that he is confident will be shared by his audience, and which is echoed in Harrison's battle-cry, 'RIP RP'. Hughes's protest in 1959 against 'the English gentleman with the stereotype English voice ... & the tabu on dialect as a language proper for literate men'[5] was soon to become anachronistic, as one can tell by listening to readings by Hughes himself, Harrison, Smith, Sean O'Brien, Carol Ann Duffy and Simon Armitage for example.

Tony Harrison

Nevertheless class has continued to be a ground of contention in contemporary English poetry, and the most significant protagonist has been Tony Harrison. The strength of Harrison's best poetry, and also the source of some of its problematic aspects, is his overt identification of himself as both poet and working-class boy. In 'Them & [uz]'[6] the consequence is a discursive tour de force that is radical on a number of levels. It opens by juxtaposing the same phonemes, 'Ay ay', in Greek and Roman alphabets, evoking a tragic chorus and a northern comedian, followed by a reference to Demosthenes as a 'stutterer', curing himself by 'outshouting seas' with a 'gobful of pebbles'. The stutterer is a foundational figure in *The School of Eloquence* sequence to which this poem belongs: 'Heredity', 'Study' and 'Clearing' all cite a stuttering uncle who represents the historical silencing of the working class. In the very first line, then, two devices claim kinship between ancient Greek culture and the speaker's northern working-class roots.

The clash of discourse in this poem is not merely a matter of juxtaposition: a literal struggle is enacted. As a schoolboy (explicitly, the young Harrison himself, a scholarship boy at the independent Leeds Grammar School) the speaker attempts to recite Keats – '*mi*' *art aches*' – but is silenced as a 'barbarian' by a teacher: 'Poetry's the speech of kings. You're one of those / Shakespeare gives the comic bits to: prose!' Consequently the boy plays 'the Drunken Porter in *Macbeth*'. The poem evokes a large and complex swathe of cultural history. There is indeed a strong influence of what Erich Auerbach calls 'separation of styles' in Shakespeare's plays, whereby 'the sublime and the realm of everyday realities' are represented by 'high and low expressions' that are mapped on to class distinctions. But, as Auerbach argues and demonstrates in *Mimesis*, Shakespeare is far more distinctively characterised by a challenge to such separation, by 'the mixture of classes involving persons of high and low rank' and 'a marked mixture of high and low expressions in the diction'.[7] Harrison does not make this latter point, nor cite the fact that Shakespeare's speech would certainly not have resembled the teacher's Received Pronunciation – though he does refer pointedly to 'Cockney Keats' and Wordsworth's Cumbrian accent.

Grammar schools were founded to give education to the children of the poor. By the middle of the twentieth century, however, they were dependent on fees affordable only by the rich. To compound this historical irony, the minority of pupils, funded by scholarships, who represented the schools' original purpose, could be humiliated and made to feel out of place. Harrison's poem is not the only literary testimony to this: in the Yorkshire writer David Storey's novel *Saville* (1976) the hero, a miner's son, is subjected to a prolonged and sadistic humiliation because of his accent by a teacher at a similar school (Storey, four years older than Harrison and himself a miner's son, was educated at Queen Elizabeth Grammar School in Wakefield).[8] The boy's ordeal in Harrison's poem exemplifies in an extreme form the *rite de passage* by which working-class children were prepared for professional careers: a process that became more widespread, though also less crassly class-ridden, as a result of the 1944 Education Act. The key twist in Harrison's poem, however, is that it is also the *rite de passage* by which he becomes the scholar-poet able to quote Greek, represent accents by using the phonetic alphabet, correct old snobs about the way canonical poets spoke and 'occupy / your lousy leasehold Poetry' by a dazzlingly original manipulation of the iambic pentameter.

Harrison's choice of verse form is a crucial element in this ideological project. *The School of Eloquence* is a sequence of poems, all of sixteen lines, in varying but always regular rhyme schemes, and iambic pentameter. The form derives directly from Meredith's *Modern Love* (1864) and has come to be known as the 'Meredithian sonnet'. The allusion, however, is not specifically to Meredith but to the tradition of the sonnet sequence and, through that, canonical English poetry in general.

Antony Easthope has argued that iambic pentameter is not neutral in terms of class and ideology: that it is a 'hegemonic form' that 'includes and excludes, ... discriminates the "properly" poetic from the "improperly" poetic', the latter represented by the forms of accentual metre found in nursery rhymes, industrial folk-songs and football chants.[9] Harrison seems both to assent to and to demur from this argument.

> Originally I was drawn to metrical verse because I wanted to 'occupy' literature, as I said in 'Them & [uz]'. Now that I've occupied it in the sense that I can do it – I learned it as skilfully as I could in order that people would have to pay attention – I still instinctively feel that it's associated with the heart beat, with the sexual instinct, with all those physical rhythms.[10]

The word 'occupy' suggests an ideological structure that belongs to, or has at least been appropriated by, the ruling class. The choice of a metrical pattern that has some, albeit virtual, existence independent of the words that fill it gives this trope a particular rhetorical force. Harrison's 'occupation' is both brilliant and subversive. The tendency of the iambic pentameter to smooth the surface of language, the unique balance that it holds between the rhythms of song and speech, is constantly disrupted by typography, quoted speech, abbreviations and so on. 'RIP RP, RIP T.W.' must be the only line of (albeit irregular) iambic pentameter that consists entirely of initial letters. On the one hand the poem is strikingly visual: a lot of its effect comes from its untidy appearance on the page. On the other hand it is fundamentally aural: its central trope is the conflicting pronunciations of the word 'us'. It exhausts itself neither in writing nor in speech, challenging the adequacy, and commonality, of both forms of language.

But, as we see in the second half of my quotation, Harrison is also wedded to the idea that metre has a *natural* aspect. He insists, in 'Confessional Poetry', that his father's words really did scan (128), as he represents them doing in, for example, 'Book-Ends', where father and son quarrel after the mother's death:

> The stone's too full. The wording must be terse.
> There's scarcely room to carve the FLORENCE on it –
>
> *Come on, it's not as if we're wanting verse.*
> *It's not as if we're wanting a whole sonnet.*   (127)

Unlike much of Harrison's poetry – certainly unlike 'Them & [uz]' – the father's lines serve the traditional purpose of iambic pentameter, reconciling regularity of rhythm with the illusion of natural speech. Moreover, he completes the quatrain with full rhymes: at the level of poetic discourse, father and son could not be more harmonious.

However, *The School of Eloquence* is shot through with expressions of guilt – towards his father and other working-class victims – about Harrison's practice of the very art that he has sought to 'occupy' on their behalf. Patience Kershaw, the young woman condemned to pull coal-trucks underground in 'Working', is 'lost in this sonnet for the bourgeoisie' (124). In 'A Good Read' he tells his father that he has come round to his position on 'the arts' but apologises for saying so in poetry (141). In 'Turns' he reverses his usual insistence that 'articulation is the tongue-tied's fighting' ('On Not Being Milton', 112) by dignifying his father's silence – 'He never begged. For nowt! Death's reticence / crowns his life's' – and devaluing his own verse as 'busk[ing] the class that broke him' (149). Such protestations do not ring entirely true, from a writer who unironically calls himself 'bard' and pioneered television programmes in which the commentary is entirely in verse.

A similar pattern, though more harshly articulated, is evident in *v*. In this poem there is an identifiable single precursor: Thomas Gray's 'Elegy Written in a Country Churchyard' (1751). There are lines that seem directly, and unironically, haunted by Gray's poem, such as 'a blackened dynasty of unclaimed stone' and 'the hymnal fragments and the gilded prayer' (237), whose diction and balanced rhythm could easily be mistaken for Augustan. (Compare Gray's 'the long-drawn aisle and fretted vault' and 'storied urn or animated bust'.) More characteristically, however, the pentameters of *v*. are so energetically counterpointed as to be almost unrecognisable: Luke Spencer has commented of the third line, 'butcher, publican, and baker, now me, bard' (237), that it is 'irregular to the point of a quantum difference from anything Gray would have countenanced'.[11]

In *v*. the poet has an abrasive encounter with a 'skinhead' who materialises out of the poet's outraged reflections on the desecration of his parents' and others' graves. The skinhead turns out to have the poet's name, in other words to be an alter ego, suggesting that the 'poet' portrayed in the text does not wholly represent the poet who wrote it. This might account for the feebleness of some of the poet's utterances, such as the one that immediately precedes the skinhead's appearance:

> What is it that these crude words are revealing?
> What is it that this aggro act implies?
> Giving the dead their xenophobic feeling
> or just a *cri-de-coeur* because man dies? (241)

It almost certainly accounts for the vigour of the skinhead's utterance, and the ease with which he, like Harrison's father, fits into the verse form. In this stanza he sarcastically picks up and flings back a word used by the 'poet':

> *Aspirations, cunt! Folk on t'fucking dole*
> *'ave got about as much scope to aspire*
> *above the shit they're dumped in, cunt, as coal*
> *aspires to be chucked on t'fucking fire.*　　(241)

These lines are more memorable than the 'poet's' not just because of the expletives, but because of the wit and literacy with which the supposed skinhead appropriates the poet's word, the forceful alliteration and the apposite analogy (the poem is set at the time of the miners' strike in a graveyard over a worked-out pit). However, the skinhead is not really the ideological enemy that he might seem to be, conjured out of the often racist graffiti in the graveyard. His explanation of vandalism suits the poet's ideology, as does his use of the phrase 'class war'. His lines are noticeably free from the racism evident in the graffiti. As Luke Spencer remarks, he is not as one might expect 'a lumpenproletarian racist but ... a tough-minded class warrior'.[12]

The language of the skinhead is undoubtedly the main artistic triumph of *v*. It is therefore disconcerting that, after the skinhead disappears two-thirds through the poem, the poet smugly intones, 'Home, home to my woman' (246–7) and retreats to an evening spent listening to Alban Berg with his opera singer wife. If this is, as I have suggested his earlier feeble utterances might be, a dramatisation of the 'bourgeois' poet from whom the 'class warrior' has been excised, the implication is that he has learned little from the encounter.

Peter Reading

The Harrison skinhead's jibes, '*it's not poetry we want in this class war*' (244) and '*ah bet yer wrote a poem, yer wanker you*' (242), would probably be applauded by Peter Reading, who wrote in his sequence *C*, 'Verse is for healthy / arty-farties. The dying / and surgeons use prose.'[13] The fact that this is a haiku is typical of Reading's self-reflexiveness. Like Harrison's *v.*, Reading's *Ukulele Music* constructs an image of the poet as a bourgeois 'wanker', who is set in dialogue, of a kind, with a working-class voice.

Class is not central to Reading's work in the way it is to Harrison's, and although his poet is 'Peter Reading', he is not in any substantial sense autobiographical: he is not weighted with the intimate and painful family background that afflicts Harrison's poetic persona. Class warfare is merely one among many grim aspects of the contemporary world (in *Ukulele Music*, the 1980s), about which the poet composes vehement and obsessive jeremiads:

> 'Life is too black as he paints it' and 'Reading's nastiness sometimes seems a bit over the top' thinks a review – so does *he*.

> Too black and over the top, though, is what the Actual often happens to be, I'm afraid. He don't *invent* it, you know.

> Take, for example, some snippets from last week's dailies before they're screwed up to light the Parkray: Birmingham, March '83,

> on her allotment in King's Heath, picking daffodils, Dr Dorris McCutcheon (retired) pauses to look at her veg.

> Dr McCutcheon (aged 81) does not know that behind her, Dennis (aged 36) lurks, clutching an old iron bar.

> Unemployed labourer Dennis Bowering sneaks up behind her, bashes her over the head – jaw, nose and cheek are smashed-in.[14]

There is a great deal of this kind of writing in Reading, especially in *Ukulele Music*. In contrast to the overtly left-liberal stance of Harrison (who writes of the vandal in *v.*, 'It isn't all his fault though. Much is ours') the sentiment is reminiscent of a latter-day *Daily Mail*. Reading cannot, in fact, be so easily politically pigeonholed: this is, rather, a rhetorical device for presenting social realities in a stark, two-dimensional way. However, both those last two phrases need to be qualified. I have no doubt that part of Reading's motivation is to confront his readers with the ugliness of the world they live in; yet he does so in a way that transparently exposes his own distance from those 'realities'. It is typical that, in answering his critics, he appeals not to personal experience but to the newspaper. These realities are already mediated. He also gratuitously draws attention to the transitoriness of his attention to them by telling us that they are on their way to be burned on his domestic fire. This is a poetic voice that undermines its own authority even as it asserts it.

Another complicating factor in the overall effect of this writing is the verse form. Reading writes in a variety of imitations of classical metres: in this case, elegiac distich (hexameter and pentameter alternating). The effect of this is double-edged. It seems to evoke the most authoritative poetic discourse in Western literature, but in reality few of Reading's readers will have read Latin and Greek poetry in the original, and the translations they have read are unlikely to have used classical metre. Reading himself does not read classical languages and, although there is a brief imitation of Homer in *Ukulele Music*, the classical world is rarely evoked. Unlike Harrison's English metres, Reading's are not freighted with canonical reference. The effect of his metres is rather, in his own word, ludic:

> Bit of a habit, the feigned indignation,
> various metres, Alcmanics and so forth.
> ludic responses to global débâcles.   (76)

The effects I have discussed so far would be rather thin fare, if this were the only voice in the poem. But *Ukulele Music* is a multi-voiced text, in which the various voices comment on and interpenetrate each other. From my present point of view, the most important voice is that of the poet's cleaner, Viv.

> *dear Sir,*
>
> *well I have hooverd and wax pollish the desk so I will collect money tomorrow. There is trouble on our block since my Tom plays the bones to tunes of George Formby and was due to give a TURN at the club tonight but was paralitic last night and WOULD try to practise and of course one of them. the bones. went over next door and the woman there that has the bitch that MARLD the child well her bitch grabs the bone but my Tom shouts abuse and. of course the outcome is there is a window broke. Which the man next door have only just mended after the last trouble. so we will see how it goes tonight at the Club he does that one he played his Youkerlaylie as the Ship Went down. and I know how He felt, because it is the same with my eldest Trevor who is REPRIMANDED IN CUSTARDY as the policeman put it who is a nice man but I know my lad is innerscent of that awful thing they say he done. But these things are sent to TRY Us as my Man says and I hope he plays his bones well tonight.   (20)*

The most obvious feature of this voice is that it is 'on display'[15] in Bakhtin's phrase: reduced to an object, without any expressive power beyond the intentions of the parodying author: the misspellings, grammatical errors and malapropisms all signal a literary intention that is not shared by the supposed writer. A natural first reaction is that this is an offensively superior representation of working-class discourse. This would be an over-simplified response, however. The cleaner, 'Viv', supplies the motif that gives the sequence its title, and the irritating 'plink-a-plink' of the ukulele (playing 'as the ship went down' – 'Ludic responses to global débâcles') takes over the poet's elegiac distiches in the final lines of the poem. Viv also *lives* the events about which the poet reads in the newspaper, and he cannibalises her notes for his writing. She is a character of Dickensian vitality whose ostensibly practical requests to her employer burgeon into comic and horrific anecdotes of working-class life. Throughout she maintains a stoicism epitomised by phrases such as *'we can only carry on the best we can manage'* (20) and *'worse things happen at SEA'* (18), supplying the title also for Reading's companion sequence, 'Going On' (70). Perhaps most notably, she engages constantly in one-sided dialogue with the poet, humanly addressing him, to which we don't see him responding till the very end, when they are together in a nuclear fall-out shelter, and he tells her that *'Viv ... MEANS life'* (46).

The structure of *Ukulele Music* is based on four voices: the poet, Viv, a demented sea captain and an inane ukulele manual. These voices are first presented separately, and in the final section dialogically combined. For our present purpose, the most important combination occurs when Viv begins to write in the elegiac couplets of the poet:

> *Who would have thought it Sir, actually putting ME in a WRITING!*
> *me and the Capting and ALL. What a turn up for the books.*
> *Only, I must say I do not know HOW them people in poems*
> *manage to say what they want – you know, in funny short lines.* (34)

It would be rash to assert that this is an example exactly of what Harrison meant by 'occupying' poetry, or that it corresponds to Harrison's father and skinhead speaking in iambic quatrains. Harrison's verse form represents the history of English poetry, a culturally valorised territory that is, in his work, the site of 'class war'. Reading's metres, as I have argued, do not carry this freight. They are, however, a sign of educated, literary discourse, and especially of the poet's control of the text. Viv speaking in these metres erodes the boundary between literary and non-literary, educated and uneducated. Moreover, when she returns to prose, protesting that *'Allergic / Dis Talk'* isn't *'natural-like'* (43), we read on with an enhanced awareness of the 'literary' qualities that were always present in her writing.

Ken Smith

Ken Smith's two compendium collections, *The Poet Reclining* and *Shed*, covering his work from 1962 to 2001, begin and end with poems about his father, an angry itinerant agricultural labourer who later became a dissatisfied shopkeeper. It is therefore at first surprising that Smith should have written about Harrison, 'I'm bored with Tony's poems about his dead father.'[16] Smith goes on to say that in Harrison's poems 'the particulars don't include but exclude, and what I'm after is (I hope) more universal'.

We might conclude that 'class' is not relevant to Smith's work. However, the bleak landscape of Smith's childhood, and especially the image of his father, 'bent through the frozen turnips'[17] and 'knee deep in the landscape'[18] haunts his poetry. If class, in the sense of culturally marked social status, is not relevant, poverty certainly is.

Smith may have had in mind lines of Harrison's such as 'The Baker's Man that no one will see rise / and England made to feel like some dull oaf' ('Marked with D.', 155). Although Harrison's writing about his father is often intensely moving, these lines, by representing him as a passive victim of social and cultural forces larger than himself, explain him in a finalising way. Smith's father, like Harrison's, was uncommunicative – even about his family origins, which Smith learned only after his death were Irish. He is represented in the poetry not as a victim but as a mystery:

> His silence was absolute, nothing again nothing,
> maybe he knew nothing, shuddered in sleep
> ... though whether in his sleep
> or my own I don't know, never will now ...

This poem ends by describing the father as 'Unfinished, as everything is.'[19] He figures as a provocative and unresolved memory, whose anger is not, like Harrison's father's passivity, subordinated to an external and superior agency such as 'England'.

This rural and itinerant childhood perhaps accounts for the strong presence less of 'working class' figures than of vagrants such as the wanderer Yacob (*Shed*, 105–9), the rootless Americans of 'Eddie's other lives' (*Shed*, 212–63) and above all the protagonist of his masterpiece 'Fox Running' (*Poet Reclining*, 130–70), in which the natural outlaw, 'scavenger of skips parks / and desirable period residences', is unforgettably superimposed on the urban freefall of the man who has 'not paid the mortgage ... not paid the bank' and is 'never going home'. Smith's childhood provides the groundwork of his poetry. As he writes in 'Roads in the north between two seas', 'I am again in my own true country ... a place it has always just stopped raining' (*Shed*, 52). This 'country' exerts a constant pull in Smith's poetry. It would not be accurate to call this nostalgia, because the childhood memories, and the landscape associated with them, are comfortless. Rather, it is an aesthetic point of reference, taken for granted in the poetry because it is grounded in the poet's primal experience. The same poem continues:

> So much childhood: the sun's raw eye,
> the northern sea grey and unloveable,
> the swift constellations of birds
> over the bayline, like silk's shine.

The harshness is not a matter of victimisation, and there is no self-pity in Smith's reminiscences. They are rather, in Hughes's words, 'the revelations of necessity'.[20] The 'raw' sun and 'grey and unloveable' sea give us the natural world stripped of pastoral illusion, but it is a perspective that allows a momentary vision. Such moments occur frequently in Smith's poetry, their own swiftness matching that of their subject, gone 'over the bayline' almost before the reader has registered, in a few strokes like a Japanese artist.

This quality of Smith's imagination gives him access to traditional modes such as ballad, which he can write without the effect of pastiche. This is most striking in his first major work, 'The Eli Poems' (*Poet Reclining*, 57–68). This sequence was based on a series of dreams about the obsessive love of a married lodging-house keeper for an Irish mill girl who lives in his house. She becomes pregnant, he deserts her and she dies in childbirth. It is set in the late eighteenth century, at the beginning of the industrial revolution, hence the combination of an industrial setting with a characteristic Smith landscape of 'marshland, hills one way, the tidal estuary of rising birds another' (66). The final poem, 'Half Songs, 1790', begins,

> I saw you come down the shale, love,
> the stones black in the rain.
> In your hand a kerchief,
> in that plain bread.
>
> Your frock's all frayed,
> your face white as thistle hair.
> And the wildness in your face, love,
> and the cold stood there.   (69)

The last two lines, in isolation, could be taken for pastiche. But the preceding lines combine hints of ballad metre with diction and imagery plausibly derived from Smith's childhood. The first line seems very ballad-like, but 'shale', suggestive of difficult, unstable terrain, adds a grim note of realism, developed in the second line. The fourth line refuses the rhyme, tucking it inside the line and preferring dour speech. The 'clipped, guttural sound' of the fifth line exemplifies what Smith said about Anglo-Saxon poetry and his native dialect. The alliteration doesn't make it any less the vernacular reproach of mother to daughter. The one metaphor, 'thistle hair', has an equally fitting plainness, poverty and harshness.

Sean O'Brien

We have seen that Harrison tackles the problem of poetry and class by 'occupying' the most canonical metre; Reading appropriates a metre from outside the English canon (and therefore, perhaps, outside the nexus of poetry and class); Smith's imaginative immersion in the landscape of his childhood is strong enough for him to sidestep the problem of the 'lousy leasehold'.

Sean O'Brien has a different strategy still. In some ways a formally conservative poet, he has developed a metre that endows his lines with a powerful rhythmical signature but maintains a distance from the canonical pull of the iambic. This rhythm is basically anapaestic, but O'Brien uses it to a very different effect from the most celebrated instance of this metre, Byron's 'The Destruction of Sennacherib':

> The Assyrian came down like the wolf on the fold,
> And his cohorts were gleaming in purple and gold.

Byron's metre imposes itself tyrannically on speech-rhythm and identifies the poetic speaker with the power and energy of his subject. O'Brien subdues the bounding anapaest to something much closer to spoken English:

> Here is the stuff that gets left in the gaps
> Between houses – ambitious settees in black frogskin
>
> And minibars missing their castors, the catalogues
> Turning to mush, the unnameable objects
> That used to be something with knobs on ...   ('After Laforgue')[21]

The difference is accounted for by the much more everyday lexis, the absence of rhyme, the variation of line length, and feminine endings. O'Brien's characteristic rhythm has to do with class in two ways. The driving, insistent voice, verging on monotony but always rescued from it by the wealth of detail revealing the grotesque in the mundane, is, like Smith's, for all its English graduate's knowledge of Laforgue, that of a northerner revelling in dourness just leavened by humour: 'I imagine the north in its drizzle' (53); 'I am again in my own true country ... a place it has always just stopped raining' (Smith, Shed, 52). O'Brien's poetic voice is very unlike Smith's, but both are steeped in their material. I also think that there is a class significance in O'Brien's residual attachment to metre. The metres that Harrison chooses may be the 'lousy leasehold' of the bourgeoisie, but there is such a thing as working-class poetry, and it is invariably metrical. O'Brien's rhythms carry an echo of Easthope's 'nursery rhymes, industrial folk songs and football chants'.

O'Brien was born to working-class parents but grew up feeling that he had 'a foot in both camps, working class and middle class', without belonging 'precisely to either'.[22] His is not poetry of working-class testimony as Harrison's and, more marginally, Smith's is. It is notable that he writes as often in the first-person plural as singular: 'people like us are a gleam of prolepsis' (49). In his poetry, as that line hints, class is closely tied to temporality and history, in a very original way. One might think of him as speaking for a generation, except that his poetry is extraordinarily obsessed with the Fifties – a decade at the end of which O'Brien was only eight – in a way that would seem characteristic of someone older. This is the most notable sign of what he has called 'a feeling of belatedness ... [a] feeling that you have missed the time when you might have lived most fully'. This might be a personal psychological characteristic, but it has a historical significance, being tied to his sense of 'the great unfinished project' of democratic socialism launched in 1945 (Lewis interview). He insists that it is a matter not of 'nostalgia', but of 'the road not taken'. His 'we' is less that of a generation than of a shared consciousness, haunted by that 'unfinished project'.

O'Brien's 'country' is the period of his childhood, and the years immediately preceding, represented as always already past. The passage quoted above is a humorous example of this: a catalogue of items that seem always to have been derelict. But things do not need to be derelict to bear this apparently essential pastness:

> The carriages smelled of when everyone smoked.
> In the corridors nurses and servicemen flirted,
> Incurring the mass disapproval of character-actors
> Distracted from *Penguin New Writing*.   ('Special Train')[23]

The effect I am discussing is not just a matter of period detail but the way one temporal perspective is superimposed on another: the way, for example, the smell of the carriages *then* is described in a way only possible *now*, when things are no longer like that. This effect is perhaps most haunting in 'Revenants' (3), in which the young people of the post-war period, 'In the young middle-age of their times, / Demob suits and made-over dresses', are literally ghosts. These are the 'nurses and servicemen' of 'Special Train', the hopeful generation of the Attlee government (or, more accurately, the bearers of the speaker's retrospectively disappointed hope), the 'defeated majority' who return to behold the later generation. In a subtle twist on the 'revenant' motif it is this new generation that is 'Haunting your deaths with the England / We speak for'. This reversed haunting is another device for imprinting on the past its supersession and defeat. 'We [the generation that inherits this defeat] are the masters now', the speaker announces: the boast supposedly made by Hartley Shawcross when debating the repeal of anti-union laws in 1946 rings with a bitter irony in the wake of the Thatcher government's triumph over the unions.

As indicated by the titles of his books, the park and the train are resonant scenes for O'Brien. We can be sure it is a municipal park and a nationalised train. O'Brien is the 'belated' laureate of the classless England they promised, 'the road not taken'.

NOTES

1 Charles Tomlinson, 'Class', *The Way In* (London: Oxford University Press, 1974), p. 11.

2 Ted Hughes, 'View of a Pig', *Lupercal* (London: Faber, 1960).

3 'Ted Hughes and *Crow*', interview with Ted Hughes, in Ekbert Faas, *Ted Hughes: The Unaccommodated Universe* (Santa Barbara: Black Sparrow Press, 1980), p. 202.

4 Ken Smith, 'The Godfather of the New Poetry', interview with Colin Raw, in *You Again: Last Poems & Other Words* (Tarset: Bloodaxe, 2004), p. 140.

5 Ted Hughes, letter to Lucas Myers, 9 June 1959, Manuscript, Archive and Rare Books Library, Emory University, MSS 865, ff5.

6 Tony Harrison, *Selected Poems* (Harmondsworth: Penguin, 1984), pp. 122–3. All later references to Harrison's poetry are to this text.

7 Erich Auerbach, *Mimesis: The Representation of Reality in Western Literature*, trans. Willard R. Trask (Princeton: Princeton University Press, 1968), pp. 312–13.

8 David Storey, *Saville* (London: Jonathan Cape, 1976), pp. 137–40.

9 Antony Easthope, *Poetry as Discourse* (London: Methuen, 1983), p. 65.

10 John Haffenden, 'Interview with Tony Harrison', in Neil Astley (ed.), *Bloodaxe Critical Anthologies 1: Tony Harrison* (Newcastle upon Tyne: Bloodaxe, 1991), p. 236.

11 Luke Spencer, *The Poetry of Tony Harrison* (Hemel Hempstead: Harvester/Wheatsheaf, 1994), p. 92.

12 Spencer, *The Poetry of Tony Harrison*, p. 95.

13 Peter Reading, *Collected Poems 1: Poems 1970–1984* (Newcastle upon Tyne: Bloodaxe, 1995).

14 Peter Reading, *Collected Poems 2: Poems 1985–1996* (Newcastle upon Tyne: Bloodaxe, 1996) p. 19. All later references to Peter Reading's poetry are to this text.

15 M. M. Bakhtin, *The Dialogic Imagination*, trans. Caryl Emerson and Michael Holquist (Austin: University of Texas Press, 1981), p. 322.

16 Ken Smith, letter to Colin Raw, *You Again*, p. 129.

17 Ken Smith, 'My Father Fading Out', *The Poet Reclining: Selected Poems 1962–1980* (Newcastle upon Tyne: Bloodaxe, 1982), p. 76.

18 Ken Smith, 'For the boys on the wing', *Shed: Poems 1980–2001* (Tarset: Bloodaxe, 2002), p. 122.

19 Smith, 'The Donegal Liar', *Shed*, p. 332.

20 Ted Hughes, 'Vasco Popa', *Winter Pollen* (London: Faber, 1994), p. 222.

21 Sean O'Brien, 'After Laforgue', *H.M.S Glasshouse* (Oxford: Oxford University Press, 1991), p. 54.

22 Sean O'Brien, interview with Steven Lewis, 2005, unpublished.

23 Sean O'Brien, 'Special Train', *Ghost Train* (Oxford: Oxford University Press, 1995), p. 6.

Further reading

Astley, Neil (ed)., *Bloodaxe Critical Anthologies 1: Tony Harrison*, Newcastle upon Tyne: Bloodaxe, 1991

Byrne, Sandie, H, *v & O: The Poetry of Tony Harrison*, Manchester: Manchester University Press, 1998

Byrne, Sandie (ed.), *Tony Harrison: Loiner*, Oxford: Clarendon Press, 1997

Easthope, Antony, *Poetry as Discourse*, London: Methuen, 1983

Kennedy, David, *New Relations: The Refashioning of British Poetry 1980–94*, Bridgend: Seren, 1996

Martin, Isabel, *Reading Peter Reading*, Newcastle upon Tyne: Bloodaxe, 2000

O'Brien, Sean, *The Deregulated Muse: Essays on Contemporary British and Irish Poetry*, Newcastle upon Tyne: Bloodaxe, 1998

Roberts, Neil, *Narrative and Voice in Postwar Poetry*, Harlow: Longman, 1999

Rowland, Antony, *Tony Harrison and the Holocaust*, Liverpool: Liverpool University Press, 2001

Smith, Ken, *You Again: Last Poems and Other Words*, Tarset: Bloodaxe, 2004

Spencer, Luke, *The Poetry of Tony Harrison*, Hemel Hempstead: Harvester/ Wheatsheaf, 1994

16

FIONA STAFFORD

A Scottish Renaissance: Edwin Morgan, Douglas Dunn, Liz Lochhead, Robert Crawford, Don Paterson, Kathleen Jamie

Let us begin at the end: contemporary poetry ceased to be 'twentieth-century' in December 1999. Throughout the world, the Millennium was a moment for reflection on the expiring century, but in Scotland, especially, it also meant rebirth. In the previous July, the Scottish Parliament had opened in Edinburgh after a recess lasting two hundred and ninety-two years, and its re-establishment confirmed the confidence in Scotland's culture and independent identity that had been growing, albeit fitfully, since the 1960s. The time was right for a new anthology of Scottish poetry, which could present the country 'hale and whole' and provide a literary context for poets working in Scotland at the beginning of the twenty-first century.[1] *The New Penguin Book of Scottish Verse*, edited by Robert Crawford and Mick Imlah, opens with St Columba's 'Altus Prosatur' ('The Maker on High'). The sixth-century Latin may seem startlingly remote from the experience of modern readers, but on the facing page is the English translation by Edwin Morgan, through whose powerful rhythms the traditional faith in eternal creative energy comes pouring through, breaking down linguistic barriers and opening poetic channels through the centuries. As Morgan has observed in a recent sonnet on Scottish literary tradition,

> did you expect woad and spears?
> In *Altus Prosator* the bristly blustery land
> Bursts in buzz and fouth within a grand
> Music of metrical thought.[2]

The translation is a tribute to St Columba's hymnody, but it is also the perfect opening for the new book of Scottish verse. Columba is a founding figure in Scottish history, the bringer of Celtic Christianity to Iona, the tiny island that nevertheless became a world-renowned centre of spirituality, art and civilisation. His words are a hymn to an omnipotent, creative energy, which 'is and will be in all places in all time and all ages'.[3] Succeeding centuries of Scottish verse unfold from this exciting, all-embracing moment, and the anthology is a testament to Scotland's centrality, longevity and openness to external influences.

The parallel text chosen to mark the beginning of Scottish literary tradition is also an image of doubleness and dialogue. Duality has long been seen as characteristic of Scottish identity, often associated with feelings of anxiety, Calvinist guilt, linguistic inadequacy or political impotence, and manifest in fragmentation, uncanny narratives, doubleness and self-division. The Janus-turn of the new century, however, helped to transform old doubts into new strengths. Viewed from the freshly devolved perspective of 2000, the multiple tendencies in Scottish identity could at last be seen as a boon rather than a handicap for creative writers. Translation and imitation are no longer to be regarded as signs of national under-confidence, ostentatious erudition or wavering originality, but rather as opportunities for innovation, wordplay and technical virtuosity. The parallel text can be read as a sign of receptiveness to other cultures, as well as of the multivocal audiences at home. Scotland's literature has never been monolingual – English, Gaelic, Scots and Latin have each furnished Scottish poets with creative resources, while their readers have often been accustomed to more than one mode of speech. The sense of Scottish plurality is well expressed in the Bakhtinian epigraph chosen by Robert Crawford for his 1992 collection, *Talkies*: 'one's own language is never a single language'.[4] Once dualism and its discontents became dialogism, 'Scotland' was free to be 'Scotlands', its literary and linguistic heritage a rich resource to be celebrated and extended.

This is not the place to attempt a detailed history of Scottish poetry in the later twentieth century, which would demand discussion of numerous writers as well as complicated political and social developments. What may be valuable, nonetheless, is to approach the new mood of poetic confidence through the work of six prominent contemporary poets, whose highly distinctive voices share certain characteristics and preoccupations. Some are well known for their devolutionary enthusiasm; some have composed poetry in Scots as well as English; all have engaged in different ways with local, national and international issues. To read their poetry primarily in terms of Scotland's place in the United Kingdom is, however, to risk missing the literary pleasures, emotional charges and aural satisfactions that have defined the latest Scottish Renaissance. Although this discussion is alert to the importance of the nationalist movement for Scottish poetry of the late twentieth century, its focus is not so much on the enabling – or disabling – contexts, as on the poems themselves.

Edwin Morgan's presence at the start of *The New Penguin Book of Scottish Verse* is entirely apt, since he is a foundational figure for contemporary Scottish poets. Those who come at the end of the anthology look back not only through centuries of diverse and evolving Scottish tradition, but also to Morgan's example. Kathleen Jamie has expressed her gratitude to Morgan for giving his younger contemporaries 'The kit and caboodle, the full fig, the / Hale / Clamjamfrie / The kitchen sink';[5] while Morgan's skills as a performance poet are vividly caught by Liz Lochhead in 'The People's Poet', with its acoustic portrayal of 'his quick light voice not tripping ever / over his own peppery rhythms'.[6] It is in 'Five Berlin Poems', however, that her deeper sense of indebtedness emerges, as she describes the reassurance embodied in a 'signed copy of *Sonnets from Scotland*' during a bewildering visit to Germany after the fall of the Berlin Wall.[7] Her own poem, with its broken images of the city, records the struggle to comprehend her experience and acknowledges her literary lifeline:

> I think who could make sense of it?
> Morgan could, yes Eddie could, he would.
> And that makes me want to try.

Contemporary poets turn to Morgan for inspiration, repaying their debts in poems, allusions and critical essays. The confident tone of modern Scottish poetry may be consequent on increasing national prosperity and independence, but its playfulness, linguistic innovation and underlying sense of what matters owes much to the poet who was perhaps the most forward-looking of those who began publishing in the 1950s.

Although Morgan's early work attracted some attention, the current Scottish Renaissance really began with the publication of *The Second Life* in 1968, which together with Douglas Dunn's *Terry Street* in 1969 demonstrated the arrival of a new, Scottish, urban presence in British poetry. Morgan and Dunn continued to develop their reputations in the following decade, which also saw the emergence in Glasgow of Liz Lochhead as a lively performance poet, whose work challenged a still largely male-dominated literary scene. All three have been energetic proponents of poetry, determined to bring their work to younger audiences, and keen to experiment with new media and to establish creative writing in Scottish universities. Robert Crawford, Kathleen Jamie and Don Paterson belong to a younger generation of writers, whose early adulthood in the 1980s coincided with acute economic depression and widespread disaffection with Margaret Thatcher's policies in Scotland, but whose creative work, benefiting from the efforts of the more established generation of poets, flourished in the 1990s and has now been recognised internationally. The work of all six shows a strong awareness of time and place, but many of their poems also reach beyond the immediate to distant pasts, personalities and even planets. Expression of the present, though sometimes almost painfully direct, can often be mirrored obliquely through the ancient or futuristic.

When Edwin Morgan returned to Glasgow after serving in the Royal Medical Corps during the Second World War, he began a translation of the Old English epic *Beowulf*. Temporarily silenced by his experiences in the Middle East, Morgan turned to the ancient text to produce his 'unwritten war poem', a literary task of heroic dimensions.[8] In the preface, Morgan revealed a whole-hearted commitment to his art, as he set out the translator's manifesto: 'Communication must take place; the nerves must sometimes tingle and the skin flush, as with original poetry.' The task was to reach across the boundaries of time, in order to realise 'a secret and passionate sympathy with the alien poet', and to bring the unfamiliar into exciting contact with the present. The seriousness with which Morgan rejected archaic diction and syllabic metres showed a deep understanding of both modern poetry and Old English, but equally important in his engagement with the ancient battle of good and evil was the realisation of a means to express his own moral conviction. His assessment of *Beowulf* as 'something traditional, strong, and severe, which must return' sounds very unlike the playfulness so often singled out for admiration in his own poetry, but it is an ideal that underlies much of his subsequent effervescent and apparently mercurial output. Morgan's profoundly moral attitude has continued to emerge in non-judgemental representations of street violence, in humane exchanges with extraterrestrial life and in his capacity to give voice to the most unlikely subjects – from the Loch Ness monster to the mummified Rameses II. The 'secret and passionate sympathy with the alien' first acknowledged in response to *Beowulf* pervades Morgan's work and helps to explain both his persistent labours as a translator and his appeal to other writers.

Cultural Renaissance is often interpreted in terms of discovery of the unknown and recovery of the forgotten. Morgan's preoccupation with texts from Russia, Hungary, Germany, France, Spain, Armenia, Renaissance Italy, Anglo-Saxon England or Ancient Greece, and his openness to American influences, suggests a remarkable determination to widen Scotland's circle of international and temporal connections. His example challenges contemporary Scottish poets to look outwards for their own work, to hone their individual styles through reference to other languages and to engage with both the great and the unfamiliar in different cultures.

Don Paterson's collection *Landing Light* (2003) includes poems after Rilke and Cavafy, a Zen song in Scots, an epigraph from Plutarch and a disconcerting version of part of Dante's *Inferno*. 'The Forest of Suicides' is a carefully crafted translation of Canto xiii, with startling variations that allow Dante's blood-black tree to break open and release the voice of Sylvia Plath. In this bold image, Paterson finds a metaphor for creative translation, a process which opens up classic texts and reveals new meanings for contemporary readers. His fascination with the *Inferno* also emerges in 'Waking with Russell', a sonnet on the birth of his son, but here the response takes the form of a disembodied quotation rather than a creative rendering from Italian to English: 'Dear son, I was *mezzo del cammin*'. The personal engagement with Dante connects Paterson not only to the Italian Renaissance, but also to English Romantic and contemporary Irish poets, who have responded imaginatively to the *Divine Comedy* and whose work forms a complicated and cumulative literary context.

Dante's presence also haunts the more recent work of Douglas Dunn, whose tongue is firmly in his cheek when describing his own adaptations of *terza rima*:

> Post-this, post-that – pre-*what*? The obsolete's
> Established as a form (like this), parodic
> Purloining of a thirteenth-century beat,
>
> Dante's drum-kit, a metronomic tick.

In its irreverence and self-consciousness, Dunn's 'Disenchantments' in *Dante's Drum-kit* (1993) is reminiscent not so much of Romantic responses to Dante, as of Byron's memorable use of Italian tradition for *Don Juan*, where playful adaptations of *ottava rima* provide a form for wry meditation on the contemporary world. The creative appropriation of earlier texts is an enduring element in Anglo-Scottish literary tradition.

Paterson and Dunn both demonstrate rich European, American and classical influences in their work, but it is Robert Crawford who has been most concerned with the cultural significance of translation, writing eloquently in his critical prose of Scotland's multilingual traditions and adapting poems from Vietnamese, Italian, French and German. He has recently published his own 'versions' of Scotland's pre-eminent Latin poets Johnston and Buchanan, and has also promoted interest in Celtic tradition by devoting a substantial part of the Penguin anthology to Gaelic poetry.[9] A more urgent concern in his early collections, however, was the question of Scots – the traditional language of Lowland Scotland – which became such a crucial issue for writers of the earlier twentieth-century Scottish Renaissance, following MacDiarmid's *A Drunk Man Looks at the Thistle*. Among Crawford's early collections was the exuberant *Sharawaggi*, self-conscious in its Scottish doubleness, being co-authored by W. N. Herbert. *Sharawaggi* includes numerous original poems in Scots, translations into Scots and distinctly Scottish kinds such as 'The Flyting of Crawford and Herbert' – a battle of words in the tradition of Scottish poets from Dunbar to MacDiarmid. *Sharawaggi* and *A Scottish Assembly*, both published in 1990, made clear statements about Crawford's commitment to Scotland, but his use of Scots as a literary language was facilitated by his obvious proficiency in other languages and literatures. The writer who offers Scots versions of Vietnamese poetry is not one who feels limited by his educational background: for Crawford, the use of Scots is a literary and political decision.

It is not everyone's medium of choice, however. For Dunn, Scots represents a 'dead language', unusable for his own literary purposes.[10] Even those most committed to its continuing vitality tend to annotate their own verse with glosses, which can give a rather studied appearance to what is often meant to seem closer to the oral discourse of Scotland. In *Sharawaggi*, Crawford offered extensive glosses and translations, which seemed to emphasise the prosaic quality of the English language; this very playfulness, however, has the additional effect of emphasising English as the norm, and thus reviving memories of less ebullient attitudes to Scots and English. Nevertheless, the determination to translate texts from foreign languages into Scots has been an important feature of twentieth-century Scottish poetry, and Morgan's lively renderings of the Russian poet Mayakovsky have been an inspiration to subsequent poets.[11] Lochhead, with typical energy and theatrical enthusiasm, translated Molière's *Tartuffe* into Scots in 1976, while more recently Jamie has published lyrics 'efter Hölderlin'.

The growing popularity of poetry readings in recent decades has placed great emphasis on pronunciation, and so contemporary poets have developed ways of suggesting Scottish speech even though their written language is English. Reading their work can thus involve a kind of mental translation, as a printed word is transformed in the acoustic imagination to conjure up a voice from Fife, Glasgow or Dundee. Often Scots is used only very sparingly to create a Scottish speaker or perspective, and then it may be a syntactical or idiomatic technique, rather than a question of vocabulary. Lochhead's 'The Complete Alternative History of the World. Part One' in *Bagpipe Muzack* underlines its fresh perspective on the Eden myth by giving Adam a distinctly Glaswegian turn of speech: 'He couldny put his finger on it, / He was in a right tizz'. While this is hardly a literal translation of the Bible into Scots, its demonstration of the possibilities opened up by linguistic choices is representative of the late-twentieth-century impulse to challenge convention through cultural exchanges.

Lochhead's poem is 'alternative' not only in the sense of rendering Adam's confusions in colloquial language, but also because of its overtly feminist stance. The second half muses humorously on what Eve might have usefully pointed out:

> I'm not Jezebel
> And I'm not Delilah
> I'm not Mary Magdalen
> Or the Virgin Mary either.

The list runs on, reiterating its point with increasingly modern examples. Revisiting traditional myths and narratives has been a major concern for women writers since the 1970s, and several of Lochhead's poems such as 'The Ariadne Version', 'Song of Solomon', or 'Three Twists' can fruitfully be seen in the context of international feminism. In many of her poems, however, familiar situations are being translated not just into a new world of gender-conscious literature, but into a specifically Scottish one. 'Almost Miss Scotland' takes the common feminist objection to beauty contests and offers an ironic alternative to the high-profile bra-burnings and protests against the Miss World competition: 'I / Just stuck on my headsquerr and snuck away oot o therr –'. Lochhead's deft comedy may divert attention from the seriousness of her contribution, for her rewriting of myth and redefinition of legendary figures has become a key element in contemporary Scottish poetry by both men and women.

Kathleen Jamie has given an explicitly Scottish angle to her lively emancipatory poem, 'The Queen of Sheba', which begins:

> Scotland, you have invoked her name
> just once too often
> in your Presbyterian living rooms.[12]

Unlike Lochhead's Eve, who announces at some length what she is not, Jamie's fantastic Queen sweeps through Scotland, leading her 'great soft camels / widdershins round the kirk-yaird', and gathering followers on her way to face the overwhelming question:

> *whae do you think y'ur?*

The answer forms the thrilling climax to the poem:

> and a thousand laughing girls and she
> draw our hot breath
> and shout:
> THE QUEEN OF SHEBA!

Although Jamie's work frequently demonstrates a recognisably female perspective on her subject, 'The Queen of Sheba' is also indicative of a more general desire to encounter the marvellous at home – 'Yes, we'd like to / clap the camels, / to smell the spice'. Unlike the work of Paterson and Crawford, which often discovers the mythic in contemporary Scotland, however, Jamie's poetry is charged with a more spiritual dimension. In 'A dream of the Dalai Lama on Skye', she brings the fascination with Tibet that inspired her collection of travel poems, *The Autonomous Region*, into the Western Isles, to reanimate the landscape: when the Lama appears on Soay

> airborne seeds
> of saxifrage, settled
>   on the barren Cuillin
> waken into countless tiny stars.[13]

The capacity of the barren Scottish hills to waken into new life is a kind of metamorphosis enabled by the experience of other cultures. In *The Autonomous Region* Jamie described how she 'began to see ghosts, lines of energy and wanderings, criss-crossed routes of travel', while the poems suggest that the mythic dimensions of her journey across China were also criss-crossing with her home, since several use Scots and feature images such as 'a lassie in a red scarf', 'a loch called Qinghai'.[14]

The discovery that though her steed may not be celestial, it is nevertheless possible to ride on 'astonished and glad' is perhaps the most important legacy of Jamie's experience in the East, and one which has strengthened her capacity to reveal aspects of the divine in her immediate surroundings.[15] 'The Buddleia' describes the attempt to evoke 'the divine / in the lupins, or foxgloves, or self- / seeded buddleia', while 'The Puddle' in *The Tree House* (2004) seeks spiritual illumination from the winter landscape, asking, 'how should we live?' The humility inspired by the natural world, and the sense of what man has made of it, suggests a kind of contemporary devotional poetry. In 'Flight of Birds', old ideas of the earth ruined by man become urgent, personal concerns:

> From our gardens the mavis is melted away,
> she is gravel; waders veer overhead
> crying *whither? whither?*

But if nature is vulnerable, it is also brimming with hope; in 'Landfall', the sight of a single swallow 'veering towards the earth- / and blossom-scented breeze' provokes the self-bracing thought, 'can we allow ourselves to fail'. The openness to alternative perspectives on the world, nurtured by her experience of China and Northern Pakistan, has helped Jamie to create perfectly balanced lyrics in which large, human questions are addressed with deceptive simplicity.

The creative benefits of experiencing unfamiliar cultures are not necessarily dependent on travelling thousands of miles, however. Dunn, whose work has been such a significant part of the current Renaissance, found inspiration for his first collection in Hull. Ordinary life in the East Yorkshire city forms the basis of *Terry Street* (1969). The voice of the young Scot in the south often conveys perplexity in the face of the mundane not unlike that of the later 'Martian' school of Craig Raine, although Dunn's insistently urban images can also be seen in relation to Larkin, Baudelaire and Laforgue. The visual detail creates a vivid sense of the street, with its small backyards and clothes-lines sagging with 'old men's long underwear', its pavements strewn with 'Saturday night's fag-packets' and 'dog-shit under frost'. Everything is thrust sharply at the reader, except the nameless people – the 'chatty women', 'the children', 'the drunks', 'the dustmen', the 'trawlermen' – who seem at once too close for comfort and yet oddly remote.

A certain pessimism emerges through unambiguous assessments of 'the street tarts and their celebrating trawlermen' as 'agents of rot' or of the Terry Street children, 'grown too old to cry out for change'. Despite such negative moments, the carefully crafted lines, which turn blank verse into unrhymed couplets, triplets or quatrains, demonstrate the power of art to transfigure the least promising things. In *Terry Street*, Dunn develops a self-consciously urban mode, where traditional lyric forms and metres are just visible enough to be missed:

> It is urban silence, it is not true silence.
> The main road, growling in the distance,
> Continuous, is absorbed into it;
> The birds, their noises become lost in it;
> Faint, civilised music decorates it.

Birdsong, traditionally a symbol of lyric poetry, can only turn to noise, before disappearing into 'urban silence' where everything is reduced to 'it'. The skill with which the half rhymes are deployed and the impersonal pronoun repeated nevertheless works to counter the threat of silence. The poet's obvious care may accentuate the hopelessness of the community under scrutiny, but it also renders them oddly marvellous.

Dunn's creation of art from the everyday does not involve a revelation of the divine, remaining closer to Morgan's humanism: 'Cosmic circumstance / Hides in nearest, most ordinary things' ('Retrieving and Reviewing'). Both poets are pioneers of a photographic poetry that captures the details of life in a modern city with provocative clarity. The snapshots of *Terry Street* find a counterpart in Morgan's apparently unmediated records of contemporary Glasgow:

> With a ragged diamond
> of shattered plate-glass
> a young man and his girl
> are falling backwards into a shop-window.[16]

In *Terry Street*, Dunn was aiming for a new 'objective realism' in poetry, and a similar emphasis is evident in 'Glasgow Green', one of Morgan's most graphic depictions of the city, in which 'the dirty starless river / is the real Clyde'.[17] As the poem develops, the documentary tone gives way to universal comment on the human condition, adopting quasi-biblical cadences, 'Man take in that harvest! / Help that tree to bear its fruit!' In *Instamatic Poems* (1972), Morgan was less inclined to underline his indignation over suffering, allowing moral comment to emerge more quietly, through observations of human behaviour. 'Glasgow 5 March 1971' begins with the couple falling through the plate-glass window, moves on to describe 'the two youths who have pushed them', before concluding:

> It is a sharp clear night
> In Sauchiehall Street.
> In the background two drivers
> Keep their eyes on the road.

The commonplace description of the night, however, is charged with thoughts of the shattered glass embedded in the young man's face, while the image of the drivers turns the familiar phrase about keeping your eye on the road into a chilling mantra issuing from fear – or indifference. 'Glasgow Green' grapples explicitly with the baffling reality of a place which welcomes mothers and children by day, and at night becomes the setting for homosexual rape. 'Glasgow 5 March 1971' is just as concerned with the horrifyingly casual juxtapositions of human experience but leaves readers to engage imaginatively with the scene and respond accordingly.

For both Morgan and Dunn, the metaphor of photography is important. The urban realism that attracted readers in the 1960s was not just a matter of conveying the lives of ordinary people in sharp, focused poems. The camera also offered opportunities for exploring the poet's role and his relationship to his 'material'. In 'I Am a Cameraman' in *Love or Nothing* (1974), Dunn plays on Christopher Isherwood's well-known line to reflect on the limitations of art in the face of suffering. On one level, the poem is a dramatic monologue in which the cameraman exposes the shortcomings of his medium ('Film has no words of its own') but it is also questioning the validity of any realism achieved by fleeting visual images of ordinary life:

> They suffer, and I catch only the surface.
> The rest is inexpressible, beyond
> What can be recorded. You can't be them.

Truth is beyond the power of the lens, real life 'the film that always comes out blank'. As in *Terry Street*, the pessimism of the sentiment is conveyed in the most satisfying language.

The elusiveness of things apparently caught for posterity is also explored in 'St Kilda's Parliament: 1879–1979' in *St Kilda's Parliament* (1981), with its subtitle, 'The photographer revisits his picture'. In this more elaborate monologue, the Victorian photographer of the tiny island, which was finally evacuated in 1930, revisits his pictures a century later. The difference between Scotland in 1979, when the referendum had decided against devolution, and St Kilda in 1879, with a micro-democracy that gave everyone a say in the island's affairs, provides the frame for a self-punishing meditation on the nature of art in modern society. Throughout, the camera is a mark of the inept outsider, regarded with contempt by those it has come to capture. The islanders have a completeness and directness unavailable to the modern photographer, who is always 'looking through' his 'apparatus'. Their gaze is uninhibited and unhindered, their poetry that of people 'who never were contorted by / Hierarchies of cuisine and literacy'. Rather than serving as the instrument of objective realism, photography emerges as the means to glimpse, but not understand, a people whose life is in every way superior to that of the modern artist.

Like Dunn, Morgan is preoccupied with problems of realism and reality, though his approach to the question has taken different paths. In the 1960s he began to experiment with both concrete poetry and computation, struck by their creative possibilities and associated challenges to literary convention. In 'The Computer's First Christmas Card', he explored the nature of language and creativity, by playing with the illusion of letters spewing from an inanimate machine:

> j o l l y m e r r y
> h o l l y b e r r y
> j o l l y b e r r y
> m e r r y h o l l y
> h a p p y j o l l y

The reader struggles to turn the letters into meaningful sentences, and in the process the computer itself begins to seem engaged with a heroic struggle to make sense and get things right. Morgan explores the comic potential of language in numerous poems whose meaning emerges in several dimensions, with careful page layout to convey additional ideas. 'Construction for I. K. Brunel', with its vertical word columns and intervening longer lines resembles the Clifton Suspension Bridge, while the wordplay within the poem, 'I AM BARD', points to the parallels between the poet and the engineer. It is a kind of poetry that confronts reality by addressing the illusions of language, but in doing so wittily affirms human intelligence and celebrates the endless possibilities of the universe, whether virtual or otherwise.

Scottish poetry has always been drawn to scientific discovery. Morgan's work, especially, displays the different impulses observed by Crawford in 'Sir David Brewster Invents the Kaleidoscope' in *A Scottish Assembly*: on the one hand, fascinated by 'how the real will open up', spilling stars 'Light years from Scotland', while on the other, remaining insistently 'local' and factual. If Morgan's computer poems heralded the electronic revolution, his recent work has continued to address *Virtual and Other Realities* (1997). This impressive collection examines fax machines, tape recordings, parallel universes and chaos theory but is always most concerned with the human dimensions of reality. In 'The Race', the spectacle of square-riggers – 'dead and gone', but actually racing through the sea before a huge crowd – challenges straightforward assumptions and leads to the conclusion that

> here the virtual and the real
> Are married, and such human scenes reveal
> Our longing for the plenum of the weal.

The nature of traditional language, dreams, imagination and memory are all part of Morgan's explorations, which eventually confront the eternal questions of love, death and suffering. The final poem, 'Day's End', leaves readers with another version of reality that marries traditional realism with multidimensional semantic meaning, in the words 'still real':

> The homeless in their doorways clutch the cold,
> Still real, still waiting for the story to be told.

What is most powerful here, though, is not the cleverness of the still real/ still reel, but the quiet affirmation of the tenacity of hope and imagination. As in Morgan's earlier photographic poems, there is no sentimental air-brushing out of human suffering, but the sense of what *is* real has been magnified by the discoveries of the intervening years: 'What is more real than love?'

The reality of love is one of the abiding concerns of the new Scottish Renaissance, just as it has been in earlier periods of cultural rebirth. But, as in traditional Scottish poetry, love often emerges most powerfully through loss, concentrated in Morgan's work into 'One Cigarette', or a single glass. Lochhead's poetry is similarly moving when dealing with aftermaths, as in the painfully empty details of 'Inventory', or in 'Morning After' in *Dreaming Frankenstein* (1984) with its all too human recognition of

> how
> Sunday morning finds us
> separate after all,
> side by side with nothing between us
> but the Sunday papers.

Dunn's finest volume is *Elegies* (1985), published after the death of his first wife, through cancer. The experience transformed both his life and his poetry, which suddenly found an intense vividness different in kind from the earlier photographic or meditative poems. The personal torment of 'Empty Wardrobes' is quite unlike the thoughtful self-punishment of the St Kilda photographer, as the speaker, remembering his wife's delight in clothes, is troubled by 'that day in Paris, that I regret / When I said No, franc-less and husbandly'. Photography is now transfigured into his late wife's 'Writing with Light', a redemptive art that shines on the poet's grief. The entire volume is a homage to Lesley Balfour Dunn and seems to fulfil the advice she herself gives in 'Tursac': 'Write out of me, not out of what you read.' In writing out of his wife, however, Dunn is also adopting a highly literary and self-conscious poetic form, and demonstrating its validity in the modern world.

Although the distinction between lived and literary experience has provided a creative tension in Dunn's work, for others human relations are often best expressed in poems heavy with allusion. Paterson's paired poems on parting, 'A Private Bottling' and 'To Cut it Short' in *God's Gift to Women* (1997), begin with an epigraph from Antonio Porchia, and end with an image of the headless Scheherazade, while his accomplished poem, 'The Lover', is an adaptation from Propertius. One of Paterson's most explicit accounts of sexual pleasure is presented in a mock classical 'Letter to the Twins', with its doubling references to Romulus and Remus and to Russell and Jamie Paterson. In *Landing Light*, love is both sexual and paternal, as the sonnet on his newborn child makes clear, with father and son 'face-to-face like lovers', the father rediscovering a smile which has long since become a 'hard-pressed grin'. If Morgan has concluded that nothing is more real than love, for Paterson, nothing is more reviving. The poems on the birth of his children are poems of new experience and rediscovery, affirming creative directions and debts.

In Crawford's work, too, becoming a father has been similarly momentous, and his 1996 volume, *Masculinity*, is filled with thankful love poems about his own family. From the intimate moment in the Labour Ward, to the image of the poet buying cardigans for his post-natal wife, to that of the six-month-old baby sitting 'like a judge / On the High Chairage of Scotland', the startling discovery of new life and growth inspires poem after poem. The astonishment of birth brings memories of childhood and parents into new relief, while perennial insecurities are finally resolved. In a volume that questions conventional ideas of masculinity, the self-affirming fact of fatherhood is of the profoundest importance: ' "Hello, Mr Crawford?" That's me' (63).

Poets of the new Scottish Renaissance know that each creation is a rebirth, but from this crucial rediscovery comes renewed confidence in their own generation. The courage to write from intimate personal experience demonstrates a certain faith in the contemporary world, and an unqualified hope for the future. Poems about new life are inherently forward-looking, but the future is cradled by strong traditions, woven together from different pasts. Common to the younger generation of Scottish poets is an awareness of a collective unease in modern society, and much of their work is engaged with the combative struggle for alternatives. Admiration for children or for the natural beauty of Scotland is by no means a turning away from social and political realities, but rather a means to recover hope for the twenty-first century. As Jamie put it in 'Flight of Birds' in *The Tree House*,

> If *they* greet dawn
> by singing of a better place, can we complain?

The prospect may be dark, but in Scotland at least, it is not without the possibility of a better world.

NOTES

1 Edwin Morgan, 'Retrieving and Renewing: A Poem for ASLS', *Scottish Studies Review*, 7, 1 (Spring 2006).

2 *Ibid.*

3 Robert Crawford and Mick Imlah (eds.) *The New Penguin Book of Scottish Verse* (London: Penguin, 2000), p. 3.

4 Robert Crawford *Talkies* (London: Chatto and Windus, 1992), p. 9. Cf Crawford, *Identifying Poets: Self and Territory in Twentieth Century Poetry* (Edinburgh: Edinburgh University Press, 1993); 'Bakhtin and Scotlands', *Scotlands*, 1 (1994), 55–65.

5 'Ho ro the Poet', in Robyn Marsack and Hamish Whyte (eds.), *Unknown is Best: A Celebration of Edwin Morgan at Eighty* (Glasgow and Edinburgh: Mariscat and Scottish Poetry Library, 2000).

6 Liz Lochhead, *Dreaming Frankenstein and Collected Poems 1967–1984* (Edinburgh: Polygon, 1984), p. 14.

7 Liz Lochhead, *Bagpipe Muzak* (Harmondsworth: Penguin, 1991), p. 77.

8 Edwin Morgan, *Beowulf* (Manchester: Carcanet, 2002), Preface (1952), p. ix.

9 Robert Crawford (ed.), *Apollos of the North: Selected Poems of George Buchanan and Arthur Johnston* (Edinburgh: Polygon, 2006).

10 'Douglas Dunn in Conversation', *The Dark Horse* (Autumn 1999), 29.

11 Edwin Morgan, *Collected Translations* (Manchester: Carcanet, 1996), pp. 37–41; 105–55.

12 Kathleen Jamie, 'The Queen of Sheba' (1994), in *Mr and Mrs Scotland Are Dead: Poems 1980–1994* (Newcastle upon Tyne: Bloodaxe, 2002), pp. 112–13.

13 Kathleen Jamie, 'A dream of the Dalai Lama', in *ibid.*, p. 150.

14 Kathleen Jamie and Sean Mayne Smith, *The Autonomous Region: Poems and Photographs from Tibet* (Newcastle upon Tyne: Bloodaxe, 1993), pp. 6, 33, 49.

15 *Ibid.*, p. 67.

16 'Glasgow 5 March 1971', Edwin Morgan, *Collected Poems 1949–1987* (Manchester: Carcanet, 1990), p. 217.

17 Douglas Dunn, *Under the Influence: Douglas Dunn on Philip Larkin* (Edinburgh: Edinburgh University Library, 1987), p. 10; Morgan, 'Glasgow Green', in *Collected Poems*, p. 168.

Further reading

Crawford, Robert, *Devolving English Literature*, Oxford: Clarendon, 1992
    Identifying Poets: Self and Territory in Twentieth-Century Poetry, Edinburgh: Edinburgh University Press, 1993
Crawford, Robert, and Kinloch, David (eds.), *Reading Douglas Dunn*, Edinburgh: Edinburgh University Press, 1992
Crawford, Robert, and Whyte, Hamish (eds.), *About Edwin Morgan*, Edinburgh: Edinburgh University Press, 1990
Hendry, Joy (ed.), *Edwin Morgan: A Celebration*, special issue of *Chapman* 64 (1991).
Marsack, Robyn, and Whyte, Hamish, *Unknown is Best: A Celebration of Edwin Morgan at Eighty*, Glasgow and Edinburgh: Mariscat Press and Scottish Poetry Library, 2000
Nicholson, Colin, *Edwin Morgan: Inventions of Modernity*, Manchester: Manchester University Press, 2002
Skoblow, Jeffrey, *Dooble Tongue: Scots, Burns and Contradiction*, Newark and London: University of Delaware Press, 2001
Whyte, Christopher, *Modern Scottish Poetry*, Edinburgh: Edinburgh University Press, 2004

JOHN REDMOND

Lyric adaptations: James Fenton, Craig Raine, Christopher Reid, Simon Armitage, Carol Ann Duffy

In the 1970s British poetry was noticeably fatigued, a reflection of a national mood. The consensual approach to politics of the time was mirrored, in the literary world, by a combination of weariness and diminished expectations. This was perceptible, for example, in comments made by Jonathan Raban in his *The Society of the Poem*:

> one sometimes senses that there's an underlying conviction in the work of some of our younger writers to the effect that the routinization of modern urban and suburban life has created its own poetry. The imprints of the same mass images, the same commuting time-schemes, the same communal hopes and neuroses, have given our lives so many shared versions of order and metaphor that the poet's work is almost done for him.[1]

In the difficult economic circumstances of the 1970s, this consensus, 'the same communal hopes and neuroses', came under increasing strain, culminating, of course, in the election of Margaret Thatcher in 1979. In the wake of the Movement's unambitious poetics, British poetry had good reasons to doubt itself. Famously, A. Alvarez, in his provocative 1963 essay, 'Beyond the Gentility Principle', had called for a 'new seriousness'.[2] His negative comparisons of British poetry to its American cousin struck a nerve. It is noticeable how anthologies of this period frequently draw anxious comparisons between poetry from Britain and poetry from elsewhere, particularly America, Ireland and Eastern Europe. In his anthology *The Mid-Century: English Poetry 1940 to 1960*, David Wright, for example, made a typically worried assault on contemporary American poetry, dismissing it as 'an industry rather than an art'.[3] But judgements were as likely to be made to British poetry's disadvantage. Alan Brownjohn helpfully outlined the charges:

> The principal symptoms of the neurosis wished on us are: a general lack of scale and ambition; a timid refusal to whip up some experimental vigour; a failure to seize chances, tackle the big themes, and face up to brute realities.[4]

Partly as a reaction to this self-doubting period, a significant number of British poets in the late 1970s began to adopt a self-consciously energetic manner: 'Here we are at the bay / of intoxicating discoveries', a poem by one announces.[5] Certainly, in the 1980s and 1990s British poetry discovered intoxication. Against that background, this chapter looks at five poets – the so-called Martian school, Christopher Reid and Craig Raine; a poet sympathetic to them, James Fenton; and two poets of the 'New Generation', Carol Ann Duffy and Simon Armitage.

Although one would not want to press analogies with political developments too far, the artificial and uneasy energies released by Thatcherism and its offspring New Labour are roughly mirrored by the energies released by 'Martianism' and its offspring the 'New Generation'. Preoccupied with branding, all of these movements, political and literary, advertised a rhetoric of the 'new' while affecting a concern for traditional values. The 'New Generation' differed from 'Martianism' as New Labour differed from Thatcherism: by cultivating a man-of-the-people, 'class-free' accessibility which masked the very individualistic will-to-power it affected to correct in its predecessor.

As a movement in British poetry, Martianism was small but influential. Christened by James Fenton (who was not a member), the movement, which favoured unusual similes and exotic descriptions, was largely the creation of two poets, Craig Raine and Christopher Reid.[6] Its name derived from the title poem of Raine's second collection, *A Martian Sends A Postcard Home* (1979), in which the eponymous Martian memorably misreads our planet – interpreting caxtons as 'mechanical birds' and noting how 'Rain is when the earth is television'. With its overtones of science fiction, 'Martianism' was a misleading term, since the movement's emphasis was firmly on down-to-earth, domestic environments. The impulses behind Martianism may be more readily understood by reference to a quote from Saul Steinberg, chosen by Christopher Reid to appear on the back cover of his first collection, *Arcadia* (1979):

> We spend almost our whole lives reading boisterous, ready-made messages (the mail, the newspapers, traffic-lights). To decipher the other kind of messages requires an effort that renders life rich, gay and, so to speak, inexhaustible.

Here is the real Martian credo: an optimistic emphasis on the richness of life made possible by the inventive reading of signs. Against the doleful resignation, the narrowed horizons, that one found in Philip Larkin's work, and in much of post-Movement poetry, Martianism maintained what was an almost naive spirit of enthusiasm. But Martianism was also, in other respects, continuous with Larkin's work and this is where the term's associations with otherworldly visitors is so misleading. Martianism accepted the Movement's 'parochialism' (to adapt a favourite term of the Irish poet, Patrick Kavanagh) – the kind of parochialism which Larkin admired, and identified with, in the work of John Betjeman:

> In a time of global concepts, Betjeman insists on the little, the forgotten, the unprofitable, the obscure; the privately-printed book of poems, the chapel behind the Corn Exchange, the local water-colours in the museum (open 2 p.m. to 4 p.m.).[7]

Martianism accepted, in other words, what soap operas accept: the limits of the parish – the most visible and typical fixtures of the rural village or the suburb: railway station, corner shop, pub, kitchen, garden. While the outside world and its 'global concepts' were mistily obscured, the inside world, as in a sunshower, took on a corresponding, and slightly unreal, brightness.

Craig Raine's first book, *The Onion, Memory* (1978), opens with a volley of poems which establishes this parochial typicality: 'The Butcher', 'The Barber', 'The Gardener', 'The Grocer', 'The Ice Cream Man', 'The Tattoed Man', 'The Window Cleaner'. The poems settle on subjects which are semi-public, individuals 'we all know' whose relationship with us may drift from the professional into the personal. By virtue of their subject matter, the poems suggest the presence of a community, but only in the artificially heightened manner of a heritage centre. Raine's manner of presentation imparts to his chosen figures an illustrative, doll-like quality – when, for instance, 'The grocer's hair is parted like a feather / by two swift brushes and a dab of brilliantine'. A similar kind of typicality can be found in the work of James Fenton. Although Fenton's style is not Martian, many of its attitudes and strategies converge with those of Raine and Reid: an over-bright tone; self-conscious displays of learned wit; a programmatic playfulness; a persistent concern with class boundaries. In many of his poems, but especially in his later period, Fenton appeals to an imagined community spirit. This appeal is often humorous, and mediated by his self-conscious use of popular form, but it is characteristic of how, from the 1970s onwards, poets assert the presence of a community in a manner which makes that community seem unbelievable. 'The Skip' provides an early example, with the speaker throwing his life on a skip and finding that 'the whole community joins in'.[8]

To this supertypicality, the voice in Reid's *Arcadia* (1979) brings the cajoling, heightening tones of a ringmaster. 'Canapés and circuses, of course!', one poem, 'A Valve Against Fornication', announces, as if by way of explaining its fellows. The imagery, and the typically bold Martian similes, often augment the parade-like sensationalism of the voice:

> jockeys in art-deco caps and blouses
> caress their anxious horses,
> looking as smart as the jacks on playing-cards
> and as clever as circus monkeys.
> ('A Whole School of Bourgeois Primitives')

The circus is a useful metaphor for the world of *Arcadia*. The poems conjure up a perpetual present tense of communal experience (the voice characteristically says 'we are', 'we walk', 'we listen'); the creatures and acts on display seem related to each other only by virtue of their peculiar extravagance, sealed off from the world beyond the brightly patterned tent. When Reid presents us with a family history, in 'The Old Soap Opera', for example, it amounts to an assortment of highly caricatured, wildly anachronistic clowns. The atmosphere of the whole volume is curiously Edwardian. The emotions are simple, the logic is internal, the shapes entertainingly emphatic: 'Conical knockabout bollards', 'a cochlear sticky bun', 'a tetrahedron of cream' (compare these examples to the use of geometrical shapes in Raine's 'The Grocer'). The human beings are either grotesque or comic, like the pensioners in 'Low Life':

> obliged to haul about on stumps,
> yet strong enough to contend
> with mountainous piggybacks on their humps –

Parochial as the subject matter may be, its treatment is coloured by non-British influences. In interview, Reid has acknowledged how much the Martians owed to American poetry (while conceding that Americans might not notice this is so):

> we [Raine and Reid] were totally committed to American poetry: not just Stevens and Bishop ... but Lowell and Berryman were big for us at the time, and obviously before that there was Eliot and Pound. There's something about the capaciousness of the vocabulary, and I don't just mean the lexical vocabulary, but the vocabulary of rhetoric and reference of these Americans. It was a sharp reminder to us provincial English that things could still be spacious and adventurous, and that was the lesson we thought we were putting forward as we crashed the scene.[9]

So while the influences on Martianism were American, its obsessions were English. We can guess from this passage that Reid would have broadly accepted Alvarez's negative diagnosis of English poetry, even if Reid's proposed cure – Martianism – was hardly the one Alvarez had in mind. After all, as Reid describes it, Martianism was 'a parish matter'.[10]

In its vivid parochialism, Reid's first book nevertheless defines its period. In this respect, it bears comparison with another Larkin-influenced volume, Douglas Dunn's *Terry Street* (1969). Both first volumes are united by their insistence on a determined mode of seeing – in the case of *Terry Street* the neutral stare of the journalist, in the case of *Arcadia* the vibrant gaze of the dandy. *Terry Street* is of a piece with the reductiveness of Larkin's vision whereas *Arcadia* is a partial reaction to, and rejection of, it. *Terry Street* anticipates the dreariness of England in the 1970s, *Arcadia* anticipates the rough, consumerist pragmatism of the Thatcher era. So the ethic of *Arcadia* puts great rhetorical pressure on the need for individual initiative – how we read the world alters it: read it well enough and the world will be correspondingly rich. In Reid's second, transitional volume *Pea Soup* (1982) this optimism is mostly dissipated, as the poems become more dramatic and more personal. Though slightly inferior to its predecessor, this volume is recognisably Martian. Reid's third book, *Katerina Brac* (1985), however, is a complicated swerve away from the manner of his first two collections. It is perhaps the strongest book by any of the poets in this chapter. Its witty premise is that its poems were written by an Eastern European poet and then translated by Reid. In the book's opening poem, 'Pale-Blue Butterflies', Reid characteristically flirts with the awkwardness of translation and with the heavy 'subtlety' of Eastern European poetry, walking a tightrope, as in the various registers below, between sentimentally 'bad' writing about seasonal change and overt political statement:

> Once again, magically
> and without official notification,
> it was the time of the year
> for the pale-blue butterflies to arrive.

Reid's parochialism, however, does not completely disappear. Instead it undergoes an exile's transposition within Brac's personality. From her delicate, first-person narratives, a life story emerges – that of a country girl who leaves for the city, experiences an unhappy love affair and returns home. As the poems journey through different locations, Brac seems to carry the village around with her, projecting her displaced feelings of intimacy on the positive and negative aspects of the city. Remembering her estranged lover, for instance, she describes how the urban buzz was caught in 'the stairwell that waited beyond your apartment door // like the deepest, most superhumanly patient of ears' ('When the Bullfrogs are in Love'). But although this poetry is as parochial as his earlier work, the mist which stands at the edge of the parish takes on a more sinister aspect. On the individual level, it symbolises nothingness, the erasing void beyond existence (as it had in Larkin), while on the social level it symbolises the erasing historical amnesia characteristic not only of totalitarian societies but of Western democracies too. The pressure on the reader which *Arcadia* created, the pressure to read cheerfully, collapses into a subtly shifting exploration of subjectivity where the emphasis is on the individual's relative helplessness. The book is a sensitive exploration of the masks of personality in which Reid reveals a marked talent for playing roles. At times we perceive him as an Eastern European female poet, as her translator, and also, to use Umberto Eco's term, as 'model author', the voice directing how the poems should be read. Sometimes, as in the last exclamatory line of 'Like A Mirror', all these voices come together:

> can mirrors
> be said to have memories?
> Yes, there is always beneath the surface
> an inordinate heaviness.
>
> So these touches of tarnish
> are an attempt to express
> a little of what it remembers.
> How sad!

Even out of context, this deceptively light poem is delicate and moving, but read with the rest of the book, the idea of the mirror's memories resonates with the reflecting relationships of East and West, Reid and Brac. The phrase 'touches of tarnish' nicely sums up part of the volume's aesthetic – its deliberate brushes with awkwardness – and, in the declarative naivety of the final line, the book's ruefulness is caught by the kind of direct emotional statement an English poet would be unlikely to make.

Reid's role-playing continued in his next book, *In The Echoey Tunnel* (1991), especially in the long poem, 'Memres of Alfred Stoker', an old man's account of a childhood marked by poverty, lack of education and an evangelical father. Though not quite as sustained or various as *Katerina Brac*, the mask is convincing and original. Reid's sophisticated ventriloquism, in which he mimics the man's eccentric writing style, leaves the frivolity of *Arcadia* far behind. *In The Echoey Tunnel* also contains what is perhaps Reid's single most impressive poem, 'Survival: A Patchwork', an intimate account of marriage and his reaction to his wife's illness. While this long work, and 'Memres of Alfred Stoker', are superior to anything in *Arcadia*, the same cannot be said for the short poems, which are notably lightweight, suggesting a close correlation between the ambitiousness of Reid's poems and their value.

Certainly the poems of what might be called his 'later period' – represented by the collections *Expanded Universes* (1996) and *For and After*

(2002) – are relatively short and unambitious. The poems are occasional, having the air of slight fancies, afterthoughts, and the result is a prevailing flatness very unlike Reid's best work, as in 'Scenes from Kafka's Marriage', for instance, from the former book:

> A workman came to mend my cupboard door
> that would not shut. My wife had got his name
> out of the *Yellow Pages*. He did the job
> in next to no time, and then, glancing around,
> asked if there was anything else he could fix
> while he was at it.

Not every poem from Reid's late period is as inert as this, but compared with *Arcadia* and *Katerina Brac*, there is an easily perceived loss of tension. To some extent this slackness is contrived – certainly these books are conscious enough of their own deficiencies to anticipate them. So great play is made, in passing, of lightness, of obliquity, of small, unobtrusive forms – feathers, ice-cubes, bluebottles, tears – which are meant to be infinitely suggestive. The final poem in *Expanded Universes*, 'Cobweb', hails a structure which is a 'scaffolding or support / for any whimsical, jejune, inchoate or passing thought'.

Although sometimes perceived as a junior member in the Martian duo, Reid is a more various and fluid poet than Raine. It seems to me that the American influences which are most important to Reid are Stevens and Bishop: notably oblique and feline poets. For Raine, by contrast, the major American influence is Robert Lowell. Like Lowell, Raine has a fondness for set pieces, staged fragments of action, which serve as excuses for the kinds of grand statement and colourful detail about which the author really cares. His speakers have a mechanical presence, their purpose, as Edward Larrissy suggests, to gesture towards 'the poet's ingenuity and well-stocked mind'.[11] In 'City Gent' in *Rich* (1984), for example, the speaker completes a series of Ovidian transformations of an ordinary office environment. After comparing a taxi, distantly seen, to a moorhen, the speaker shifts the centre of his attention:

> I turn away, confront
> the cuckold hatstand
> at bay in the corner,
> and eavesdrop (bless you!)
> on a hay-fever of brakes.

Just as the transition, here, seems very forced, the title suggests an exercise, as though Raine had simply chosen a random target and aimed his Martian gun at it. The character of the speaker is unconvincing and serves little other purpose than to draw the various impressions together. This poem, like many others, breaks into descriptive sections which arrest the rhythm, giving an effect of highly wrought passages of descriptive prose which somehow have become lineated. Indeed one of Raine's best achievements, 'A Silver Plate', is an extended piece of prose description, the centrepiece of *Rich*. It clearly owes a debt to Lowell's fragment of autobiographical prose, '91 Revere Street'. More grandiose still is *History – The Home Movie* (1994) (one notes the touch of Lowell in the title). This book-length poem aspires to treat his family history with novelistic breadth but the typically provocative local details distract from his larger scheme.

Raine's characteristic poetic voice is that of a teacher who wants to be liked. In 'Misericords' in *The Onion, Memory*, for example, he treats his subject matter as the opportunity for a quick cultural lesson:

> It is a world without heroes,
> without abstractions, without combs –
> everyone has hair like bark ...
>
> Shiny as a coalman's sack,
> they are postcards from the continent
> of darkest dailiness, diaries
> by the English negro.

This poem has a suggestion of the end of Lowell's 'Beyond the Alps' ('Now Paris, our black classic, breaking up / like killer kings on an Etruscan cup'). The eponymous misericords are treated as an index of the speaker's cultural knowledge, an opportunity to display his educated wit and fluency. The tone of superiority is enhanced by his decisive judgements. By telling us that the depicted characters are 'ordinary as water', the speaker rather implies that he is not. The description of an 'English negro' coming so soon after references to 'continent' and 'darkest' is meant to be politically uncomfortable, although one feels that references of this sort have been included, as often in Raine's work, not to make a substantial point but to challenge the reader to make an objection. Such challenges may persuade us that the father's pugilistic example, characterised with such relish in 'A Silver Plate', has not been lost on the son.

James's Fenton ambitious early poems play with the late Modernist style of W. H. Auden. His major achievements, all written early in his career, include poems such as 'A Staffordshire Murderer' and 'A Vacant Possession', although these owe as much to Auden's 'Paid on Both Sides' and 'The Orators' as lighter, later poems like 'Gabriel' and 'I Know What I'm Missing' owe to Auden's 'As I walked Out One Evening' and 'Some Say

That Love's A Little Boy'. Fenton's later manner has strong parallels with that of Christopher Reid: arch in tone, old-fashioned in style, fond of gags, strict forms, and sharply inferior to his early work. His later manner is seen at its best in a poem like 'Out of Danger':

> Heart be kind and sign the release
> As the trees their loss approve.
> Learn as leaves must learn to fall
> Out of danger, out of love.

Like a good many of his poems, early and late, this is a brilliant piece of mimicry, its mood and diction squarely in the manner of 1930s Auden poems like 'A Summer Night' or 'May with Its Light Behaving'. And yet this is the title poem of a collection published in 1993, not 1933. From the point of view of style, 'Out of Danger' is simply out of date. Its carefully established lightness of manner has an unsettling double effect. It maintains some of the intended accessibility of Auden's earlier manner, while at the same time wielding it as a distancing weapon. The speaker invites us in (this is really me, it seems to say) while keeping us at arm's length (this is really Auden, it says *sotto voce*). Reading such lines, one has the feeling that Fenton has not got over Auden, and that this might even be said of English poetry as a whole. The speaker of the poem adopts a tone of frank intimacy, but in a style which is entirely copied. It is a kind of *professional* intimacy, a voice skilfully feigning concern. This insistence on closeness with an imagined audience is one that Fenton shares with the 'New Generation' poets. Like their versions of accessibility, his insistence makes the existence of a closely tuned-in audience seem more like an enabling myth than a fact.

Carol Ann Duffy's style aimed at accessibility from the start. Her poetry contains many characters, mostly brought to life using dramatic monologue. In 'You Jane', from her first full collection, *Standing Female Nude* (1985), Duffy caricatured a male speaker in a manner which was to persist in her later collections:

> At night I fart a guinness smell against the wife
> who snuggles up to me after I've given her one
> after the Dog and Fox. It's all muscle. You can punch
> my gut and wait forever till I flinch. Try it.
> Man of the house. Master in my own home. Solid.

Absurdly crude as this is, it illustrates many of the features of Duffy's style: a liking for dramatic monologue, short (often one-word) sentences, aggressive caricature, clichés (renewed or otherwise), provocative contrast and punchy colloquialisms. Characteristically, these monologues try to close the distance from their audience by imagining the reader to be immediately present (here, close enough to punch the speaker's stomach). Like many of her other works, it adopts an attacking stance, the effect of which is to establish a sense of collective superiority which is shared with the intended audience. Duffy's targets are the usual ones of Left-wing Britain in the 1980s and have much in common with those chosen by the 'alternative comedians' of that period. 'Ash Wednesday, 1984', for instance, hits out at the Catholicism of her upbringing: 'Miracles and shamrocks / and transubstantiation are all my ass. / For Christ's sake, do not send your kids to Mass.' Because her works do not require any special sources of knowledge to be understood, this sense of superiority is widely available and the invitation to share it is often taken up.

For Duffy, voice is an index of moral health. Characters tend to be diagnosed by the words they speak, as in 'Mouth, With Soap' in *Selling Manhattan* (1987):

> She didn't shit, she *soiled*, or *had a soil*
> and didn't piss, *passed water*. Saturday night,
> when the neighbours were fucking, she *submitted*
> to *intercourse* and, though she didn't shit cobs then,
> later she *perspired*. Jesus wept. Bloody Nora. *Language!*

Like Auden's 'Miss Gee', the nameless individual depicted in this poem is so severely repressed that she has contracted cancer. The poem deals with its caricature in a brisk, dismissive manner, veering back and forth between formal and informal levels of diction. The energy is not carried by the characterisation (which is barely two-dimensional), but by the speaker's impatient, almost accusatory attitude to the victim. What a reader responds to is the performance of that impatience. Duffy tends to be let down by her sense of humour – her satirical poems are especially laboured. Despite her widespread use of dramatic monologue, she never sounds convincingly like anyone but herself (a comparison with Robert Frost would be instructive). Instead of enlarging her poetic self, Duffy's invented characters dwindle into it. The salutary self-erasure achieved by Reid in *Katerina Brac* seems to be beyond her. For Duffy, translation is loss – as illustrated by her poem 'Translating the English, 1989' in *The Other Country* (1990). There she satirises British news coverage of foreign countries by imagining caricatured foreign reporters covering the news in Britain. While the poem is meant to point up the lazy racism of the British by means of a witty 'translation', it relies on caricature so much as to seem questionable.

Simon Armitage's poems also insist on a close relationship to their audience and the insistence affects the quality of the closeness. His early style owed a lot to Paul Muldoon: a combination of unreliable narrators, renewed clichés, off-rhymes, colloquial vagueness and black humour. Characteristic

Muldoonian turns of phrase like 'one or the other', 'which is which', 'out on a limb', 'this and that' reappear with relative frequency, as at the end of 'Poem' in his second book, *Kid* (1992):

> And for his mum he hired a private nurse.
> And every Sunday taxied her to church.
> And he blubbed when she went from bad to worse.
> And twice he lifted ten quid from her purse.
>
> Here's how he rated them when they looked back:
> Sometimes he did this, sometimes he did that.

Here, the enigmatic male subject is remembered in a deliberately arbitrary, ad hoc manner, a partial list of his actions followed by an enigmatic summary. The poem occupies the same supertypical landscape of the Martian poets, but the voice now has a cheery classlessness to which the Muldoonian last line adds extra linguistic spin. Just as the Martians domesticated exotic American influences, Armitage here domesticates an exotic Ulster influence.

Armitage's poems are surprisingly violent and often involve one form of bodily deformation or another. The impact of this violence, however, is relatively muted because the reader is given to understand that it is *violence within a comic mode*. Certainly, it is quite different in nature from the kind of violence which one finds in a Muldoon poem. One might think here of the central image of *Book of Matches* (1993), where the mild self-harm of the title poem is of explicitly brief duration – a life story linked to the prospect of (unnecessary) bodily pain. One characteristic example of Armitage's treatment of violence is 'The Serpent' in *Cloudcuckooland* (1997):

> Both kinds of – not necessarily in this order:
> the little matter of the twelve-stone fisherman
> inside the anaconda: the business of the adder
> in the spinal column, feeding on spinal marrow.

Armitage often suppresses main verbs, a conversational manoeuvre, which has the effect of drawing the reader in. Here, the framing provided by the deliberately brisk colloquial phrases ('the little matter of', 'the business of') is crucial – the first one makes a joke about size which we might read as cruel – but only if we linger on the point in a way that the poem's tone discourages. Both phrases are conversational understatements which hardly allow us to register any horror. We are more likely to feel that the poem is an amusing grotesque, as though (in Martian style) we are encountering a spectacle worthy of a seedy fairground tent.

As his poetry develops, the fascination with violence shades into a kind of self-loathing. This is noticeable, for example, in a poem like 'I Say I Say I Say' in *The Dead Sea Poems* (1995):

> Anyone here had a go at themselves
> for a laugh? Anyone opened their wrists
> with a blade in the bath? Those in the dark
> at the back, listen hard. Those at the front
> in the know, those of us who have, hands up,
> let's show that inch of lacerated skin
> between the forearm and the fist.

Here Armitage enters the territory of Sylvia Plath and it is instructive to see what changes. Unlike Plath, Armitage emphatically links his discussion of self-harm to the presence of a community, even if it is unclear what sort of a community is present. The relationship which the speaker draws between himself and his shadowy audience is one of hectoring authority ('hands up'). A dark private experience is given a communal treatment but in a manner which suggests that something is wrong with the framing. Why, for example, does the poem have a joke title and why is the tone humorously sarcastic? The poem teases us with its confessionalism but we are left to wonder if it is, in fact, a confession. If so, it is the kind of confession which can also be understood as a claim for public attention, a type of self-advertisement. Again Armitage asserts the presence of a community in a way that calls attention to its probable absence and as part of a process which ends in loneliness.

Armitage's voice is that of a professional *involver*. His use of 'we' is like that of a Friday-night disc jockey, hustling, hectoring, the voice of one who is paid to bring people together. Its sense of 'oneness' with its audience has a calculated, strategic quality. Armitage's poems, like Muldoon's, make no pronouncements on the meaning of life, of politics, or art – they don't try to leave the reader with a neat moral (in this respect, they compare favourably with Duffy's work). Rather than individual lines or phrases, what the reader responds to in Armitage is a successfully produced voice that reappears, intact, from one poem to another. And the claim that this voice has on our attention is closely connected with what it claims about our attention, what kind of 'we' we are (or think we are). The voice assumes that our attention is not especially prolonged or intense, that what we are looking for is a mixture of colour and sensation, and that our understanding of the larger mysteries of being is bound up with what one might call 'New Age patterns of significance'. *Cloudcuckooland*, for example, organises itself around astronomy, but it is an astronomy that shades into astrology – the stars as much magical powers as balls of gas. At the beginning of the same book the poems play with epiphanies drawn from shapes or objects which are readily associated with religious feeling (circles, angels) but which may also be easily secularised.

A similar pattern is detectable in the ambitious long poem, 'Five Eleven Ninety Nine'. This is a millennial set piece which revolves around another object with hazy communal resonance: a Hallowe'en bonfire. Like Elizabeth Bishop's 'The Monument', the shape of the (unlit) bonfire material has a mobile vagueness which allows it to suggest a range of other communal objects (it lies somewhere between *The Wicker Man* and *The Angel of the North*). These possible shapes include The Cross which a Christ-figure attempts to add to the bonfire material. This action is presented as undertaken on behalf of the watching community but the significance of the act is left unstated. The poem's trajectory suggests that the burning of the Cross (and of the rest of the material) is merely a dramatic cover for the emptiness of life, a kind of grand distraction. At key moments the poem veers into an uncomfortable vagueness which has echoes of Larkin poems like 'Church-Going', as in the following parody of the Bible:

> He falls a second time and then a third,
> but rounds the final corner on his knees
> and finds his feet when he sees the remains
>
> of the light and heat, and raises the cross
> to its full height, and hugs it like a bear.
> Upright, it seems to stand for something there.

The Larkinian vagueness of this is emblematic of the current state of English poetry. The accessible, 'audience-friendly' tone suspects its own emptiness and wavers. The pattern of expending energy simply for its own sake, begun with Martianism, collapses in on itself. The increasingly implausible relationship with an imagined audience (in this poem the watching community who might be saved) is abandoned and we are left back where we started, with the Larkinian anomie of the suburbs.

NOTES

1 Jonathan Raban, *The Society of the Poem* (London: Harrap, 1971), p. 70.
2 A. Alvarez (ed.), *The New Poetry*, revised edn (Harmondsworth: Penguin, 1966), pp. 28–9.
3 David Wright, 'Introduction' to *The Mid-Century: English Poetry 1940–1960* (Harmondsworth: Penguin, 1965), p. 17.

4 Alan Brownjohn, 'A View of English Poetry in the Early Seventies', in Michael Schmidt and Grevel Lindop (eds.), *British Poetry Since 1960* (Manchester: Carcanet, 1972), p. 240.

5 Christopher Reid, 'A Holiday from Strict Reality', *Arcadia* (Oxford: Oxford University Press, 1979), p. 13.

6 James Fenton 'Of the Martian School', *New Statesman* (20 Oct. 1978), p. 250.

7 Philip Larkin, 'It Could Only Happen in England: A Study of John Betjeman's Poems for American Readers', in *Required Writing: Miscellaneous Pieces, 1955–1982* (London: Faber and Faber, 1983), p. 208.

8 James Fenton, 'The Skip', *The Memory of War and Children in Exile, Poems 1968–1983* (Harmondsworth: Penguin, 1983), p. 55.

9 Elisabeth Frost, 'Found in Translation: An Interview with Christopher Reid', *Electronic Poetry Review* 6 (Spring 2003), www.epoetry.org/issues/issue6/text/prose/reid.htm

10 *Ibid.*

11 Edward Larrissy, *Reading Twentieth-Century Poetry: The Language of Gender and Objects* (Oxford: Blackwell, 1990), p. 161.

Further reading

Corcoran, Neil, *English Poetry Since 1940*, London: Longman, 1993

Crawford, Robert, *Devolving English Literature*, Oxford: Clarendon Press, 1992

Gregson, Ian, *Poetry and Postmodernism: Dialogue and Estrangement*, Basingstoke: Macmillan, 1996

Kennedy, David, *New Relations: The Refashioning of British Poetry 1980–1994*, Bridgend: Seren, 1996

Larissy, Edward, *Reading Twentieth-Century Poetry: The Language of Gender and Objects*, Oxford: Blackwell, 1990

Mole, John, *Passing Judgements: Poetry in the Eighties – Essays from Encounter*, Bristol: Bristol Classical Press, 1989

O'Brien, Sean, *The Deregulated Muse*, Newcastle upon Tyne: Bloodaxe, 1998

Raban, Jonathan, *The Society of the Poem*, London: Harrap, 1971

Rees-Jones, Deryn, *Carol Ann Duffy*, Devon: Northcote House, 1999; 2nd edn, 2001

Robinson, Alan, *Instabilities in Contemporary British Poetry*, Basingstoke: Macmillan, 1988

Trotter, David, *The Making of the Reader*, London: Macmillan, 1984

Waugh, Patricia, *The Harvest of the Sixties: English Literature and Its Background 1960–1990*, Oxford: Oxford University Press, 1995

INDEX

The Cambridge Companion to Literature

AUTHORS

TOPICS